SECRET KNOWLEDGE

EXPLORING THE BOUNDARIES
OF THE POSSIBLE

SECRET KNOWLEDGE

EXPLORING THE BOUNDARIES
OF THE POSSIBLE

edited by

J. DOUGLAS KENYON

FROM THE ATLANTIS RISING® MAGAZINE LIBRARY

Published in 2016 by Atlantis Rising®
Distributed to the trade by Red Wheel/Weiser, LLC
65 Parker St., Unit 7 • Newburyport, MA 01950-4600
www.redwheelweiser.com

ISBN: 978-0-9906904-4-3

Library of Congress Cataloging Data available on request

Cover and text design by Kathryn Sky-Peck
Photos and Illustrations © *Atlantis Rising Magazine*
Photos on pages 40, 176, 218 © Bigstock.com
Photo on page 204 © IStock/Getty Images

PRINTED IN THE UNITED STATES OF AMERICA
MG
10 9 8 7 6 5 4 3 2 1

CONTENTS

PART THREE:
EGYPTIAN MYSTERIES

PART FOUR:
TRACKS OF THE TEMPLARS

PART FIVE:
MARKS OF THE MASONS

LETTING GO OF REALITY

BY J. DOUGLAS KENYON

A recent *Wall Street Journal* headline proclaimed, "Most Science Studies Appear to be Tainted." The piece by columnist Robert Lee Hotz focused on the research of medical scholar John Ionnidis who, after extensive study, has concluded that more than half of peer-reviewed published scientific research these days is "false."

Ionnidis is a very influential epidemiologist who has studied research methods at academic institutions in Greece and the United States. The problem, he believes, is not so much fraud as bad analysis and erroneous conclusions. He cites the intense competition for research dollars and the eagerness to assert any possible newly discovered fact; but the sheer scale of the problem can hardly be taken as anything but grounds for rejection of the authority of modern science across its entire range of inquiry.

For those who have long advocated controversial notions, such as those advanced in this book, the conclusions of Ionnidis come as no surprise. For us, the holier-than-thou accusations of "junk" science from the establishment have always sounded more hollow than holy.

As has been previously written in our publication *Atlantis Rising Magazine*, "the scientific establishment, which, we are told, is committed to the pursuit of facts, without regard to consequences, draws its authority from a badly corrupted peer review system exposed by recent headlines (a major Korean genetic scientist is caught falsifying results, a Norwegian researcher manufactures 900 phony case studies for a cancer study, a Japanese archaeologist fakes the discovery of important artifacts, and so forth). Yet, simultaneously, important alternative research, often reported in these pages, is virtually excluded from the process."

The problem with today's secular scientific and historical research, we suspect, goes much deeper than its methodology. The type of corruption now so widely reported, seems to us to be but the inevitable result of a school of thought that denies the connectedness of things, consistently evading the deeper questions of life on Earth, failing to discern the underlying relationships that might reveal the "truth." Indeed, the mere possibility that real "truth" could be knowable is scoffed at by the academic authorities, even as they insist on the reliability of their own conclusions.

Compounding the corruption of truth is the current practice of assigning the ultimate authority for the resolution of most disputes in our society to an anointed scientific elite, making them the virtual high priests of our modern materialistic world—a situation not without great irony, since it is science that, a couple centuries ago, supposedly delivered us from the dark clutches of the corrupt priesthood of the Church.

In the meantime, highly specialized research, without any central star to guide it, wanders shortsightedly from one insignificant fact to another, lacking sufficient vision to see the forest for the trees. And, so we find ourselves learning more and more about less and less.

If science were more sincerely concerned with questions of real significance—who are we? where did we come from? where are we going?—than with the trivial (or, to borrow a phrase from John Anthony West, "with inventorying Tutankhamen's underwear"), maybe those of us in the alternative science camp would be less inclined to view their many self-important pronouncements as suspect.

In one early issue of *Atlantis Rising*, writer Jeane Manning focused on "Impossible Inventions that Work." From heavier-than-air flight to free energy, she cited many examples of technological achievement that have already proven, and will continue to prove, that conventional wisdom is often wrong. The point is: Just because some people say something is impossible doesn't make it so. Unfortunately, declarations of "impossibility" are nevertheless not without impact—effecting perhaps the very fabric of personal and collective reality. So, in mapping the parameters of personal potential, it is important to consider where the line is drawn between what is believed possible and what is considered impossible.

Some say, for instance, that life after death is "impossible" and others that it is not; some believe material reality is all there is, for others that is "impossible"; some say free energy exists, but to others that too is "impossible"—the list is long. And even in our supposedly enlightened and politically correct age, the frontier between what is believed possible and impossible remains potentially more explosive than ever. People might not be burned at the stake for rejecting the official dogma of the ruling Church, but that does not mean the stakes are not still very high. Indeed, since our very souls may be on the line, they could not be higher.

When we make up our mind that something is "impossible," we are committing to certain limitations on reality, and whether realizing it consciously or not, we are defining and limiting our own domain—our very being, if you will. Any data that might challenge such deeply held assumptions thus becomes personally threatening and must be defended against (consciously or otherwise). This may indeed be more than ordinary bullheadedness. Our human nature directs us to hold on dearly to "reality," and thus we allow the scientific status quo to continue to define that reality.

But there are others—those whose work appears in this book—who easily see the world of physical phenomena and recognize the self-inflicted imprisonment of individuals who, clinging to conventional wisdom, can not—*will not*—see it, and thus remain unconscious of its presence. The old saying comes to mind, "There are none so blind as those who will not see."

In this collection of 30 essays, we present the research and theories of those who *do* see, who have kept their eyes open and explored the boundaries of the often perplexing world of physical phenomena. Let their findings light the way to a new view of "reality." That new view is nothing less than crucial to understanding who we are and where we came from.

PART ONE

PREHISTORIC CLUES

"Fall of the Angels," by Gustav Doré

1

THE FATE OF THE WATCHERS

*Exploring Ancient Texts for Secrets of
the Beings "Who Fell" to Earth*

BY ANDREW COLLINS

The Genesis Secret by Thomas Knox (HarperCollins, 2009) is a novel centered around the discovery in southeast Turkey of the proto-Neolithic megalithic complex of Gobekli Tepe, constructed circa 10,000 BC by an unknown race of people at the end of the last Ice Age.

Thomas Knox is the *nom-de-plume* of British journalist Sean Thomas, who first contacted me back in 2007. He had become interested in Gobekli Tepe, which I'd written about extensively since visiting there and nearby Harran back in 2004. He wanted to know how to get to the megalithic complex, so Sue and I gave him the necessary instructions. A few months later, his article on the subject appeared in newspapers worldwide. It highlighted the fact that Dr. Klaus Schmidt, the German archaeologist in charge of excavations at the site, had unofficially admitted that the region was most probably the biblical Garden of Eden. This, of course, was the conclusion I made in *From the Ashes of Angels*, published in 1996, which provides ample evidence that Eden was located where the headwaters of the Tigris, Euphrates, and Greater Zab rivers converge, a region close to Lake Van in southeast Turkey (a brand new theory at that time). My book appeared four years before the first announcements regarding the discovery in 1994 of Gobekli Tepe, which is even now being uncovered by Schmidt and his team. What I stated also was that the heretical Jewish work known as the Book of Enoch spoke of Eden—known also as "Paradise" or "Heaven"—as being the home of the Watchers, a race of mythical beings often identified as human-like angels. They are credited with having revealed the forbidden arts and sciences of Heaven to mortal kind, causing mankind's fall from divine grace and his expulsion from the Garden of Eden.

THE STORY OF THE WATCHERS

In both the Book of Genesis and the Book of Enoch, the rebel Watchers are said also to have come upon the Daughters of Men, that is to say, mortal women, who afterward gave birth to giant offspring called Nephilim. For this transgression against the laws of Heaven, the renegades were incarcerated and punished by those Watchers who had remained loyal to Heaven. The rebel Watchers' offspring, the Nephilim (a word meaning "those who fell"), were either killed outright or were afterward destroyed in the flood of Noah. However, the Torah—the first five books of the Old Testament—makes it clear that some Nephilim survived and went on to become the ancestors of giant races named the Anakim, Gibborim, and Rapheim.

Watcher (drawn by Billie-Walker John, ©Andrew Collins)

I wrote that the story of the Watchers is in fact the memory of a priestly or shamanic elite, a group of highly intelligent, human individuals, who entered the Upper Euphrates region from another part of the ancient world sometime around the end of the last Ice Age, circa 11,000–10,000 BC. On their arrival in what became known as the land or kingdom of Eden (a term actually used in the Old Testament), they assumed control of the gradually emerging agrarian communities, who were tutored in a semi-rural life style centered around agriculture, metal working, and the rearing of animal livestock. More disconcertingly, these people were made to venerate their superiors; i.e. the Watchers, as living gods, or immortals.

The precise same region of the Near East, now thought to be the biblical Garden of Eden, has long been held to be the cradle of civilization. Here a number of "firsts" occurred at the beginning of the Neolithic revolution, which began circa 10,000–9000 BC. It was in southeast Turkey, northern Syria, and northern Iraq, for example, that the first domestication of wild grasses took place, the first fired pottery and baked statues were produced, the first copper and lead were smelted, the first stone buildings and standing stones were erected, the first beautification of the eyes took place among woman, the first drilled beads in ultra hard stone were produced, the first alcohol was brewed and distilled, etc., etc. In fact, many of the arts and sciences of Heaven that the Watchers are said to have revealed to mortal kind were all reported first in this region of the globe, known to archaeologists as Upper Mesopotamia, and to the indigenous peoples of the region as Kurdistan.

Sean Thomas acknowledges my help at the beginning of the The Genesis Secret, which follows exactly the same themes as From the Ashes of Angels (and my later book Gods of Eden, published in 1998), including the fact that the Watchers and founders of Eden were bird men; i.e., proto-Neolithic shamans who wore cloaks of feathers, and that local angel worshipping cults in Kurdistan, such as the Yezidi, Yaresan, and Alevi, even today preserve some semblance of knowledge regarding the former existence of the Watchers or angels as the bringers of civilization. Their deity, for instance, known as Melek Taus (or Melek Tawas), the "Peacock Angel," goes also by the name Azazel, one of the two leaders of the rebel Watchers (the other being Shemyaza) according to the Book of Enoch.

It is an honor for my work to be acknowledged in this manner by Sean Thomas, especially as The Genesis Secret has become a bestseller (as was From the Ashes of Angels in 1996). I won't spoil the plot so will not reveal Sean's conclusions, or indeed the climax of the book, although I must warn you that it is extremely gory in places!

A Clue in Albinism

I am sure people will ask me about some of Sean's assumptions in his book regarding the origins of the Watchers.

All I can say is that in my opinion, accounts of the Watchers from so-called Enochian texts, the earliest forms of which have been found among the Dead Sea Scrolls, tend to suggest that at least some of their number bore physiological traits resembling those of albinos. Repeatedly, the Watchers are described as extremely tall, like trees, with long, viper-like faces, penetrating eyes, long wiry, white hair and skin as white as snow but also as red as a rose. It is even suggested that the Watchers covered their skin with oils, perhaps in order to protect themselves against the UV radiation from direct sunlight, another familiar trait of albinos.

In medical science albinism is the result of a recessive gene that effects only one in every two or more generations of offspring. In other words, if the gene exists in previous generations of a family line, then a couple with no obvious albino traits themselves can produce albinos as offspring. Such recessive genes cannot, in theory, produce whole families of albinos, even though extremely fair features in Caucasians can be classed as a form of mild albinism, and these traits can be passed on from one generation to the next. This said, if in the past, albinism was seen as a special or mystical trait in humans, whereby (as was the case in parts of Africa in the past) albino children were set aside at birth, removed from their parents and trained as priests or shamans, then it is possible that elite groups of shamans could have contained a high proportion of individuals with similar such traits. Today, in various African cultures, albinos are still seen as having magical powers, a belief that has degenerated in some regions into a macabre trade in albino body parts, which are used in spell potions by witch doctors, since they are believed to bring about good luck. In Tanzania in particular, albinos live in fear of being abducted, maimed, and killed in this sick trade, something that has only recently been exposed by the international news media.

It is possible that groups of shamans, including individuals with distinctive albino features, were forced to migrate from one part of the ancient world to another at the end of the last Ice Age due, perhaps, to severe climatic upheavals (caused perhaps by a comet fragmentation, circa 11,000–10,000 BC, a matter I discuss in two books *Gateway to Atlantis,* 2000, and the new book *Beneath the Pyramids*). If so, then their entry into a foreign territory, such as Upper Mesopotamia where the Palaeolithic hunter-gatherers might have been, say, shorter with darker features and more rounded heads, could have led to this shamanistic group of individuals commanding instant recognition as social and/or religious leaders with virtual otherworldly qualities. An acceptance of their assigned rank among individual communities might have been compounded not simply by their strange appearance and apparent difference in height, but also by their existing knowledge of life skills, such as agriculture, metal working, beautification, and other forms of primitive technology, such as lapidary, ceramics, stone construction, and the manufacture of drugs and alcohol, beer in particular, from domesticated grasses such as emmer wheat. It is thus possible that the Watchers used this situation to their advantage, perpetuating the belief that they were quite literally divine beings, the same stance adopted by the first Europeans to encounter native peoples of the Americas. In this manner, the incoming Watchers, as they became known, were able to more easily control the emerging population of the Near East through a mixture of fear, respect, and total domination. In this manner, the memory of the Watchers has survived in ancient texts, such as the Book of Enoch, as the sudden appearance of a race of gods, angels or immortals that came out of nowhere and revealed to mortal kind the forbidden arts and science of Heaven.

It is remotely possible that the Watchers, as flesh and blood individuals with albino traits, represented the last strains of a former branch of humanity, perhaps an offshoot of the Neanderthals or even Homo Heidelbergensis, who were the precursors of Homo sapien sapiens. Yet such an idea must remain speculation until we find anatomical evidence for the former existence of the Watchers, whose descendents, I have long suspected, existed until the second millennium BC, when the last of their kind died out. This evidence will one day, hopefully, be located; yet until then, the origins of the Watchers must remain a mystery.

WATCHER ORIGINS ON THE NILE

So where did the Watchers as the bringers of civilization come from in the first place? I have always maintained that prior to their appearance in Upper Mesopotamia, the original Garden of Eden, sometime around the end of the last Ice Age, the ancestors of the Watchers thrived among the advanced Palaeolithic communities of Sudan and Upper Egypt. If so, then perhaps they were the social and religious motivators behind Palaeolithic groups such as the Isnan and Qadan, who thrived circa 13,500–10,500 BC, and possessed a superior form of microblade technology, unequalled anywhere else in either Europe or Western Asia. The Isnan and Qadan also lived in organized settlements, unlike anything else existing in the ancient world until the coming of the earliest Pre-Pottery Neolithic communities of Upper Mesopotamia, the builders of Gobekli Tepe, and would seem even to have developed a form of proto-agriculture, the first anywhere in the world. Did the ancestors of the Watchers leave the Upper Nile for new territories at the end of the last Ice Age, circa 10,500 BC, when the advanced life style of the Isnan and Qadan vanished virtually over night? Was such a move prompted by climatic upheavels, instigated perhaps by some kind of global cataclysm, such as the aforementioned comet fragmentation, a subject much debated among scientists today? Others have seen fit to explain the sudden appearance of the Watchers as the bringers of civilization in Upper Mesopotamia around the end of the last Ice Age in different ways.

For instance, anthropological writer and physician Stephen Oppenheimer in his essential book *East in the East* (1998) saw the original homeland of the long-faced founders of civilization as the drowned regions of Southeast Asia. Some have seen the Watchers as having come down from the cold wastes of Siberia, where albinism might have thrived in low temperatures, giving rise to legends of the frost giants (or Northmen) of Nefilheim. Still others see the Watchers as having come from outer space, after the sensationalist books of Zecharia Sitchin, a theory I find untenable.

THE WATCHMEN OF GOBEKLI TEPE

That the Watchers might have been behind the creation of Gobekli Tepe, now officially the "oldest temple in the world," and the oldest known megalithic (great stone) complex anywhere, is almost beyond question, as is their role in the genesis of civilization. As to where their advanced knowledge and wisdom might have come from, the answer is, I suspect,

otherworldly journeys using shamanic flight, something clearly indicated by the astral nature of the art found at these proto-Neolithic cult centers, which is predominantly avian in nature. Yet in addition to reliefs and carvings of birds, including the vulture and ostrich, many other examples of relief and sculpture have been found at Gobekli Tepe. These show felines, boars, spiders, ants, reptiles, and composite creatures. They also show abstract humans, which head excavator Dr. Klaus Schmidt from the DAI (German Archaeological Institute) sees in terms of the "watchman (sic) of

Archaeogical dig at Gobekli
(Photography © Andrew Collins)

the period," a term he uses for those responsible for the construction of these strange, dark monuments of stone. The word "watchman" is so close to "Watcher" that this cannot be coincidence.

That Gobekli Tepe was constructed a full 7,000 years before either the Great Pyramid or Stonehenge is mind numbing in its implications for the history of human capability. More disturbing still is that the descendents of those Watchmen, or Watchers, who built Gobekli Tepe went on to construct further megalithic complexes. As these went on, they became cruder and cruder, until the early Neolithic peoples of southeast Turkey were simply erecting uncut standing stones or slabs either in circles or in lines. Much of the finesse of Gobekli Tepe and its contemporaries (Karahan Tepe and Nevali Cori, for instance) was lost, tending to suggest that these people were losing the impetus to create more complex structures. Despite this, we can see here the foundation of the megalithic culture, which then spread, circa 7000–5000 BC, from Upper Mesopotamia carrying with it the technologies and sciences of the Neolithic age, including an understanding of plant domestication in order that the world could settle into a more sedentary lifestyle, away from its previous course of constant hunter-gathering. Yet it is clear that those who first emerged on the scene in southeast Turkey around 10,000 BC, and built Gobekli Tepe, were the ones who possessed the advanced capabilities that kick-started the Neolithic revolution. This is the story told in veiled form within the Book of Enoch, unravelled by me in From the Ashes of Angels and Gods of Eden, and novelized in *The Genesis Secret* by Sean Thomas, writing as Thom Knox.

This article first appeared in *Atlantis Rising* #81 (May/June 2010).

2

EASTER ISLAND'S MYSTERY SCRIPT

Is This the Fearful Story of a Planetary Catastrophe?

BY ROBERT M. SCHOCH, PH.D.

Easter Island (Rapa Nui; Isla de Pascua) is a tiny speck of land, a mere 64 square miles, in the South Pacific just below the Tropic of Capricorn, 2300 miles west of South America. The closest inhabited land, Pitcairn Island (where mutineers of the Bounty settled in 1790), is over 1200 miles to the west.

The moai, those giant heads and torsos of Easter Island, are emblematic of ancient mysteries and lost civilizations. Viewing them firsthand in all their magnificence during a recent geological reconnaissance trip to Easter Island, I could only be impressed. Carving, transporting, and erecting these inscrutable megalithic statues (some of which are over 30 feet tall and weigh tens of tons) was no mean feat. Surely they reflect a sophisticated society of which we are but dimly aware. Yet, conventional archaeologists have considered the big heads to be, well, big heads— the product of a Stone Age culture that spent its energy carving monotonously stereotypic megalithic monuments as part of some primitive religion, perhaps ancestor worship, or simply as busy work devised by the ruling elite to keep the populace in line on an island from which there was no escape.

The moai are fascinating, and by applying geological expertise to the problem of their chronology (as I did for the Great Sphinx in Egypt), new light might be shed on the island's enigmas. I hope to organize a full-fledged geological expedition to the island and pursue such research. But the moai, literally the biggest mystery in terms of their physical size (an unfinished moai still in the quarry is over 60 feet long), are not alone when it comes to the perplexities of Rapa Nui. Though tiny in physical comparison, inscribed wooden tablets have been the subject of curiosity and heated debate ever since they came to the attention of 19th century European missionaries.

Numerous wooden tablets covered with a strange hieroglyphic-like script were found in many of the natives' houses, according to Brother Joseph-Eugène Eyraud, reporting to his superiors in Paris. The writing became known as rongorongo ("lines of inscriptions for recitation"). Unfortunately between the missionaries' zeal, attempting to separate their new converts from old pagan ways, and internecine warfare, almost all of the rongorongo tablets were burnt or otherwise destroyed. Today just upward of two dozen remain. Furthermore, those natives literate in rongorongo were killed in fighting, succumbed to disease, or were carried off the island in slave raids. By the late 19th century, no one could genuinely read the rongorongo script, and to this day nobody has put forth a convincing decipherment.

Easter Island moai. (Photo: R. Schoch & C. Ulissey.)

I became fascinated by rongoronogo, immersing myself in the voluminous literature on the subject and pursuing firsthand analyses of the script. There is no agreement among researchers concerning even the fundamentals of rongorongo. How far back in time it may go is a subject of debate. Some scholars assert it was invented on Easter Island during the late 18th century, in imitation of European writing the natives had observed. Others believe that rongorongo traces its ancestry back thousands of years, though the surviving wooden tablets are at most a couple of hundred years old. Indeed, the known tablets could simply be copies of copies of copies . . . Perhaps the scribes, for many centuries, were not able to truly read the script but piously copied and recopied something they knew was important and held in reverence. Brother Eyraud wrote in 1864, "But the little they [the Easter Islanders] make of these tablets persuades me to think that these characters, probably a script in origin, are for them now just simply a custom they preserve without attempting to account for it" (quoted by S. R. Fischer, *Rongorongo*, 1997, p. 12).

Far from being an indigenous creation of the Easter Islanders, some researchers suggest that the rongorongo script originated in parts of

Rongorongo tablet (Photo: W. J. Thomson)

Polynesia well west of Easter Island, or perhaps even in China. Others look to South America for its origins. Still others have seen similarities between rongorongo characters and the enigmatic ancient scripts of the Indus Valley civilization of modern Pakistan and neighboring regions. One researcher seriously suggested that rongorongo might be related to ancient Egyptian hieroglyphics. I have long advocated that there is good evidence supporting cultural contact across both the Pacific and Atlantic Oceans in remote ancient times (see my book Voyages of the Pyramid Builders), so I do not automatically revile diffusionist ideas as many conventional archaeologists and historians do. But looking carefully at such rongorongo analyses, I do not find them particularly convincing. A stylized fish, human figure, Sun, or vulva could conceivably look similar across unconnected cultures. Or, might ancient Chinese scripts, Indus Valley scripts, Egyptian hieroglyphics, and rongorongo all stem from a common source or inspiration?

Perhaps simply treating rongorongo as a script, as a form of writing comparable to a European alphabetical language, or even as a script based on pictographs, ideographs, or hieroglyphics, is either the wrong approach, or an incomplete approach. Here I offer a different interpretation of rongorongo, an idea initially suggested to me by my wife, Catherine Ulissey.

Just back from Easter Island (January 2010), steeped in the conundrums of its history and culture, I could not get my mind off of rongorongo (as well as other enigmas of the island). One evening, needing some relaxation, Katie insisted that we re-watch the video *Symbols of an Alien Sky*, Episode One (MIKAMAR Publishing, 2009), written and narrated by David Talbott. Katie had the hunch it might pertain to the questions we were grappling with concerning Easter Island. In the video Talbott, author of the 1980 book *The Saturn Myth*, discusses his conclusion, based on mythologies collected around the world, that the sky was very different in ancient times, and Earth and the solar system underwent major upheavals. For those familiar with the writings of Immanuel Velikovsky, it should come as no surprise that Talbott was influenced and inspired by the research of that great heretical scholar.

In the *Symbols* video, Talbott discusses the work of Los Alamos National Laboratory physicist Dr. Anthony L. Peratt, a specialist in plasma physics. Plasma, sometimes referred to as the fourth state of matter (in addition to solids, liquids, and gases), consists of ions (electrically charged atoms or particles) and is perhaps most familiar in such forms as lightning, fire, or the glowing material in a neon tube. Auroras, the northern and southern polar lights, are also the result of plasma phenomena, caused by inter-actions between the solar wind (plasma emitted by the Sun) and Earth's magnetic field and magnetosphere.

Powerful plasma phenomena form various diagnostic configurations. Some look like intertwining snakes or pieces of rope, others like stacks of circles. In fact, plasma columns can expand in places and form donut shapes and cup shapes and become narrow at other points (due to what are known as "pinch instabilities"). In profile these plasma columns may look remarkably like human stick figures, with an upper cup shape (head) that has the appearance of a bird in profile. Peratt, when he first studied ancient petroglyphs (carvings on rocks), was struck that many appear to mimic plasma configurations.

For a number of years, Peratt and his team of researchers have been documenting the occurrence of ancient petroglyphs around the world that appear to represent plasma configurations (their work can be found in the *Institute of Electrical and Electronic Engineers Transactions on Plasma Science*, December 2003 and August 2007). But how do they explain these plasma configurations apparently recorded by ancient peoples in the form of petroglyphs? Today the auroras are typically seen only at very high lati-tudes and apparently with none of the strength resulting in the diagnostic

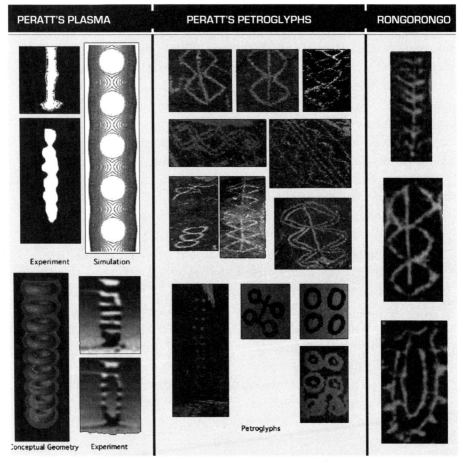

PERATT'S PLASMA	PERATT'S PETROGLYPHS	RONGORONGO

Experiment   Simulation

Conceptual Geometry   Experiment

Petroglyphs

Plasma configurations, petroglyphs, and rongorongo glyphs. (Plasma and petroglyph illustrations courtesy of Dr. Anthony L. Peratt, reprinted with permission from *IEEE Transactions on Plasma Science*, December 2003, vol. 31, page 1200.)

configurations recorded in ancient times. Peratt suggests that there was a major solar plasma outburst thousands of years ago. Earth may have been subject to solar plasma winds up to hundreds of times stronger than current solar winds!

Peratt's work is incredibly exciting in its own right, but I think there is more. The figures of the rongorongo script are curiously similar to many petroglyphs found repeatedly around the world—from Australia to Arabia, to North and South America, to Mongolia, and everywhere in between. Even on Easter Island petroglyphs are found abundantly. As we watched the Symbols video, Katie turned to me and suggested that the rongorongo script, just like many of the petroglyphs, may have been inspired by the observation of plasma configurations in the ancient skies.

The more I thought about it, the more compelling I found the suggestion that rongorongo records observations—very important and unusual observations—in the skies of long ago. Indeed, I felt confident enough that this was a hypothesis worthy of serious consideration to announce the idea during my presentation at the International Conference on Ancient Studies in Dubai on 13 February 2010. Supporting this interpretation are native terms and legends from Easter Island. Francis Mazière records an indigenous name for the island as "Matakiterani," or "eyes gazing at the sky" (*Mysteries of Easter Island*, 1968). He also records a legend of the sky falling:

"In the days of Rokoroko He Tau the sky fell. Fell from above on to the earth. The people cried out, 'The sky has fallen in the days of King Rokoroko He Tau.' He took hold: he waited a given time. The sky returned; it went away and it stayed up there." (p. 57)

This legend could refer to strange plasma configurations, perhaps even manifested in part as tremendous bolts of lightning, seen in the sky and making contact with the land. Subsequently the plasma "went away" and the sky returned to normal. Also, and perhaps it is only a coincidence, the legendary king's name bears a striking similarity to "rongorongo" and "Tau" is similar to "ta'u," a category of inscriptions commemorating a series of deeds or events (Fischer, 1997). When a staff covered with rongorongo texts was collected in 1870 by Chilean naval officers, the commander Don Anacleto Goñi reported that the natives could not decipher them but "we, in asking explanations of the natives about said staff, were shown the sky and the hieroglyphs that [the staff] contained with such respect that I was inclined to believe that these hieroglyphs recalled something sacred" (quoted by Fischer, 1997, p. 26).

Peratt posits that the plasma configurations recorded worldwide on petroglyphs may date, very roughly, to the Neolithic or Early Bronze Age (that is somewhere around 12,000 to 5,000 years ago, beginning at the end of the last ice age). Peratt and his team have established, based on the distributions and orientations of petroglyphs, that the ancient auroras and plasma configurations resulted from a plasma flow directed predominantly toward Earth's south pole. Concerning Easter Island in particular, they determined that the main petroglyph sites have a southern field of view from which such a plasma flow would be best observed.

The rongorongo script appears to share elements in common with the petroglyphs of Easter Island, such as the image of a birdman. Remarkably, according to Peratt's work, the birdman motif may have been inspired by the characteristics of a plasma column, and the concept of a post, staff, or human-like body surmounted by a bird for a head is found around the globe. In my assessment, rongorongo is not just a portable form of petroglyph equivalents inscribed on wood. Petroglyphs, for the most part, are found either isolated or in small groups and are often seemingly randomly scratched or carved over rock surfaces. I suspect rongorongo is something of a book, a scientific text that records, at least in part, plasma configurations observed in the ancient skies from Easter Island. On these tablets the glyphs are carved in neat linear lines, perhaps recording plasma configurations as seen sequentially, possibly with some "commentary" on, or "punctuation" between events. They may be a record of exactly what was happening in the skies, in what order, and perhaps even for how long.

If this hypothesis has merit, what might have caused the plasma events recorded by the Easter Islanders? Several thoughts come to mind. Peratt, as noted above, suggests that intense solar discharges, possibly on the order of hundreds of times stronger than any such phenomena observed in historical times, could be the culprit. Solar outbursts may have rained down lightning-like discharges. Intense heat associated with such electrical

Birdman Petroglyphs (Photo: R. Schoch & C. Ulissey)

discharges may have reached Earth's surface in places, causing the melting and vitrification of rock (literally turning it to glass), the evaporation of bodies of water, and the incineration of all organic material (including any humans!) hit by the onslaught. In some cases, I speculate, the damage was very narrowly focused, analogous to the damage of a tornado. The way to save oneself may have been to retreat underground into natural or artificial caves or carve protective shelters in the sides of rock cliffs. Perhaps on their small volcanic island containing many natural caves, surrounded by ocean, the Easter Islanders were afforded some degree of natural protection.

Solar outbursts from our Sun are not the only possibility. An electrically charged comet or other extraterrestrial object, either in close fly-by or collision with Earth, might generate major plasma discharges. Or, if our Sun has a binary companion, as Walter Cruttenden (*Lost Star of Myth and Time*) suggests, perhaps interactions between our Sun and its companion, or interactions between both with another celestial object, could generate intense plasma discharges. Possibly, periodic plasma discharges may emanate from the galactic center or from an occasional nearby exploding star or other object. We may not know the cause, but I believe the ancients may have been trying to warn us of the consequences!

If the plasma hypothesis is correct, the rongorongo tablets were not merely a record of pretty lights in the skies that occurred thousands of years ago. They did not simply record something beautiful to behold, aesthetically pleasing and inspiring, but of little importance otherwise. No, there was more to the displays in the skies and the ancients knew it. These displays, caused by strong electrical and magnetic interactions, would have affected human health and mental consciousness (perhaps supplementing, or diminishing, intelligence and mental paranormal abilities). Plasma discharges may even have completely obliterated the evidence of many very ancient cultures. When I first re-dated the Great Sphinx of Egypt to an extreme antiquity, one of the questions I was asked by mainstream historians and archaeologists was where is the other evidence? It might have been incinerated!

Perhaps we should take ancient knowledge to heart. The displays of plasma configurations seen ages ago in the skies, meticulously recorded in rongorongo script, may be a record of our past and the key to predicting future cataclysmic Earth changes.

This article first appeared in *Atlantis Rising* #82 (July/August 2010).

3

THE REMARKABLE INCAN CALENDAR

*What Was the Ancient Andean Civilization Telling Us
about Human Beginnings and Endings?*

BY FRANK JOSEPH

Although the Maya calendar is receiving attention these days because of its come-and-gone end-date of 2012, far less well known is the Incan calendar. While its Mesoamerican counterpart was far more complex, the two systems nonetheless shared some fundamental similarities, suggesting both may have derived from a common, outside source; archaeologists believe little or no direct communication existed between the peoples of pre-Columbian Middle and South America.

In any case, both calendars were divided into astrological and historical halves: the former for the prediction of coming developments, the latter for the commemoration of past event-horizons. Fourteenth century Aztecs inherited the Mesoamerican system from their Maya precursors, and graphically enshrined it in the famous calendar stone, a 12-foot tall, 24-ton, circular basalt slab sculpted with mathematical and mythological symbols. At its center, the god of time, Tonatiuh, is surrounded by four squares, each one representing a former age, or "Sun."

The first, located top-left of Tonatiuh, represents 4-Ocelotl, when wild animals threatened mankind. This early challenge overcome, 4-Ehecatl signaled the organization of society, which was eventually ravaged by a "Windstorm." Men and women rebuilt their world and prospered until 4-Quihuitl climaxed with a "Fire from Heaven" that incinerated civilization. Once again, its survivors initiated reconstruction, this time creating the most splendid empire ever seen, only to have it engulfed by a great flood at the close of 4-Atl. Since then, mankind has flourished in 4-Olin, or "Earthquake," slated to end on the morning of December 21, 2012. The Andean version defined five, not four previous ages, but likewise identified them as "Suns," and provided each with its own time-frame.

The Aztec calendar stone offers no chronologies for its various "ages." Immediately after the Spanish conquest, conquistadors and friars got to work dismembering the Incan Empire, plundering all its gold and purging its traditional belief system with monotheistic Christianity.

Fortunately, at least the historical half of the Peruvian calendar was saved by a native convert to Catholicism, Felipe Guaman Poma de Ayala. Born in Huamanga, in the central Andes mountains, his father had been a provincial nobleman serving as emissary of the Inca Guascar to Francisco Pizarro when the conquering Spaniard was headquartering at Cajamarca. After receiving intense ecclesiastical indoctrination from local priests, de Ayala enthusiastically demonstrated his religious fervor by combating any perceived form of "idolatry." To assist him in doing God's work, he collected everything the natives told him about pre-Christian spirituality, all the better to extirpate it.

The mysterious Incan city Machu Pichu.

Between 1583 and 1613, de Ayala amassed an enormous collection of myths, folklore, and religious ideas in a 1,200-page manuscript entitled *Nueva corónica y buen gobierno* or "New Chronicle and Good Government." His chief intention was not to preserve the Indians' cultural legacy, but to familiarize himself with it in his campaign against the faith of their fathers. In so doing, however, de Ayala saved a great deal of the Incas' oral tradition from certain oblivion, including their calendar.

Remarkably, the calendar reflects not only current Andean archaeology, but coincides with a global catastrophe that may have destroyed the motherland of civilization and dispersed its survivors throughout the world. The historical calendar comprises five ages, or "Suns," each roughly separated by one thousand years. The first belonged to the Wari Wiraocha Runa. Their name signifies "cross-breed"—referencing the camellid, offspring of a llama with an alpaca—because the Wari Wiraocha Runa were themselves the result of unions between native South Americans and the Viracochas. These were the followers of "Sea Foam," the creator who traveled from his kingdom in the far west across the Pacific Ocean, and made landfall in coastal Peru during the ancient past.

Viracocha

Because they were remembered as bearded, red-haired, fair-complected "giants," all modern Europeans were similarly referred to as "Viracochas" by the Incas. The Wari Wiraocha Runa were primitives who knew only a rudimentary culture. According to de Ayala's native sources, they emerged as a people around 2800 BC. This date matches the onset of an archaeological period known as the pre-ceramic phase, when various Andean tribes began to coalesce into the fundamentals of organized society. De Ayala compared the Wari Wiraocha Runa to the pre-Flood people in Genesis, because their era ended with a natural catastrophe reminiscent of the deluge Noah from escaped with his family.

The Wari Wiraocha Runa were followed by the Wari Runa around 1800 BC, when these more advanced Peruvians, likewise described as "Viracochas," introduced the benefits of agriculture. Two hundred years later, their era came to a sudden close, when it, too, was terminated by a catastrophic deluge. Here, as well, de Ayala's chronology matches some important event horizons. 1800 BC sparked the so-called initial period, a vital transition from pre-ceramic primitivism to pottery manufacture and the rise of village life. The global flood cited by the Inca calendar circa 1600 BC coincides with the eruption of Thera, a volcanic explosion that devastated the eastern Mediterranean in 1628 BC.

The black cloud above Thera, known today as Santorini, 60 miles north of Crete, was filled with sixty thousand miles of ash, rising 23 miles into the sky. It was the result of 7 cubic miles of rhyodacite magma ejected from a 30-cubic-mile hole, its crater nearly 50 square miles in area. Multi-ton boulders were ejected into the stratosphere, and some have been found as far as the Black Sea, 700 miles from the blast-center. More than 70 miles to the east, over a foot of ash fell on the islands of Kos, Rhodes, and Cyprus. Phaistos, Minoan Crete's second city, as though struck by the shockwave of a hydrogen bomb, was carbonized in a flash.

This truly cataclysmic event was not limited to the Aegean Sea, but part of a global disaster. Geophysicists, volcanologists, oceanographers, and scholars in related fields of study suspect this may have been triggered by meteoric debris colliding with seismically sensitive areas of our planet. At an international convocation of professional researchers at Fitzwilliam College in Cambridge, England, during 1997, a determination was made that the near miss of a comet in the early 17th century BC set off a chain reaction of seismicity and volcanism expressed in monstrous tsunamis and unprecedented rainfall around the world.

While Thera erupted with the force of 200- to 500-megaton atomic bombs, New Zealand's Taupo Valley volcano simultaneously exploded, generating 200-foot-high walls of water that traveled several hundred miles per hour as far as the Arctic Circle. Additional tsunamis were sent careening back toward the southwest by the contemporaneous eruption of Akiachak volcano in Alaska. Islands standing in their way were over-whelmed and swept clean of every obstruction. Whole archipelagoes vanished or were utterly depopulated.

The Klamath Indians of south-central Oregon and northern California believe that Kmukamtch, a shining demon from the sky, endeavored to destroy the earth with his celestial flame, followed by a worldwide deluge. This self-evident reference to the comet associated with the Lemurian catastrophe is underscored by the appearance of the lost Mother-land's name in "Kmukamtch." To another California tribe, the Modoc, Kmukamtch means literally the "ancient old man from Mu," the creator of mankind. According to New Mexico's Ute Indians, "the sun was shattered into a thousand fragments, which fell to earth causing a general conflagration." Their name for this heavenly explosion was Ta-wats, who ravaged the world "until at last, swollen with heart, the eyes of the god burst, and the tears gushed forth in a flood which spread over the earth and extinguished the fire."

It was this 1628 BC catastrophe that may have been responsible for the final destruction of Lemuria, a high culture spread over the same island chains spanning the south-central Pacific Ocean. Also known as Mu, Kahiki, Hiva, Horai, Marae Renga, and many other names, it is memorialized in the oral traditions of numerous peoples throughout the Pacific realm, where the enigmatic ruins of Nan Madol, Kuai, Guam, Easter Island, and many other archaeological zones testify to its former existence. The Lemurians were consistently portrayed as the possessors of an extraordinarily sophisticated civilization, who passed on its greatness to other peoples after calamitous events of the early 17th century BC. The Lemurian story seems reflected in the Incas' historical calendar, which cites a contemporaneous flood that closed the age of the Wari Runa.

They were followed by the Purun Runa, or "Wild Men," who applied the deluge-survivors advanced technology. Mining for precious metals—particularly gold and silver—was undertaken, and jewelry manufacture became an art. But these luxuries engendered greed that soon led to strife and even warfare. The Purun Runa's "Sun" was supposed to have dawned around 800 BC, a critical moment in Andean archaeology, when the initial period turned into the early horizon. This phase is most important for the founding of Chavín de Huantar. Located 155 miles north of Lima, the site is the first stone city of its kind in Peru, and came to typify the entire epoch. De Ayala does not tell us how the age of the Purun Runa came to its close, suggesting perhaps that transition to the next epoch was peaceful. In any case, the Auca Runa who followed in AD 200 instituted a decimal system; built mud-brick fortifications called pucaras, and worshipped guaca bilcas, translated by de Ayala as "supernaturals." They also invented the ayllus. These were social, religious, and ritual organizations that exerted political power through a combination of kinship and territorial ties. Once again, the Incan calendar accurately reflects crucial archaeological transition when, during the early intermediate period, the Moche civilizers began building cities along Peru's northern coast around AD 200.

The Moche, like the Auca Runa, operated the first ayllus, erected pucaras, employed a decimal system as the basis of their construction projects and astronomical calculations and, instead of confining their worship to variations of Viracocha, venerated a pantheon of "supernaturals."

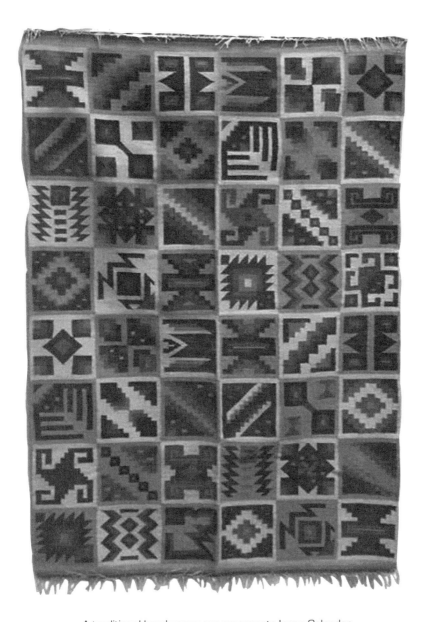

A traditional hand-woven rug represents Incan Calendar.

Although their day ended around AD 700, the peoples who came after them—such as the Huari, Chimor, Llacuaz, Chachapoyas—all at least fundamentally upheld and carried forward the cultural principles created by the Moche. Once again, de Ayala does not explain how or why the Auca Runa vanished, although the extensive warfare he implies through the construction of pucaras did typify those centuries leading up to the rise of the Incas.

The last "Sun" arose in AD 1200, when the first Sapa Inca, or emperor, founded the Kingdom of Cusco, the imperial capital. This last age did not end with the execution of Atahualpa, the last Sapa Inca, in August 1533. The Spanish conquest only terminated an initial phase of an epoch that includes our own time. It is scheduled to climax in the next 192 years, around the turn of the 23rd century. If the Incas made any prediction for the conclusion of the fifth Sun, de Ayala did not include it in his *Nueva corónica y buen gobierno.*

More certainly, the Andean calendar demonstrates that the Incas understood their history with at least a fundamental accuracy that went back some 40 centuries before their own time. This record-keeping feat is made all the more remarkable when we realize that the Incas kept no written documents; the only aids to memory they relied upon were devices such as quipu, knotted cords signifying numerical units. No less impressive, each of their five "Suns" closely correspond to the major event horizons of Andean archaeology, including an early 17th century BC global catastrophe that appears to have destroyed the Pacific Ocean Motherland of civilization. It was, in fact, from a Lemurian kind of island kingdom that Viracocha and his followers were said to have escaped by sailing to Peru from the west.

The Incan calendar is testimony to the power of oral tradition, which is able to preserve the historic legacy of a people with a surprising degree of accuracy over the course of millennia. As such, it is proof that enduring myths are neither mere fables nor unreliable legends, but, on the contrary, important truths enshrined in the national memory of a folk that may no longer exist.

This article first appeared in *Atlantis Rising* #72 (November/December 2008).

SECRET KNOWLEDGE

4

CODE OF THE ROCKS

What Were the Ancient Indigenous People Trying to Say About Life in This World and the Next?

BY FRANK JOSEPH

Travelers to the American Southwest are often intrigued and perplexed by the profusion of Native American rock art spread throughout the desert regions of Utah or New Mexico. Known as petroglyphs—from the Greek *petros* for "stone" and *glyphein*, "to engrave"—these Native American images are actually found around the globe in places as far afield as China, Polynesia, Scandinavia, and South Africa. In fact, petroglyphs represent the most numerous art form on Earth. In Utah alone, there are more than 7,500 of them. Within a four-state area (Arizona, New Mexico, Colorado, and Utah), some 30,000 petroglyphs have been identified. Only a few thousand are protected by state parks, however; for the rest, only their anonymity can save them from vandalism.

Visitors to Jeffers' Petroglyph State Park, near the southwestern corner of Minnesota, will find one of the world's greatest collections of Native American rock art, with specimens numbering in the hundreds. We know how they are made— removing part of a rock surface by incising, pecking, carving, and abrading it to create a specific image. Not exactly a written language, petroglyphs may be more properly understood as ideograms— graphic symbols representing objects or ideas without expressing, as in a phonetic system, the sounds supposed to identify them. Petroglyphs are not pictographs, or images drawn and sometimes painted on a rock face, though many petroglyphs have been chalked in or even painted during modern times for purposes of clearer delineation.

How old are petroglyphs? Who made them? What do they mean? These are questions that have bedeviled professional archaeologists and curious tourists for generations. As long ago as 1853, Ronald Morris, a leading archaeologist of the time, summarized no less than 104 theories then current to explain Scotland's rock art alone. While answers may be debatable, we do know what the petrolgyphs are not: They are not graffiti, doodles, or hieroglyphs. Petroglyphs may not be "read" in the same sense we understand Egyptian or Mayan hieroglyphs as signifying words or sounds in a language. Instead, petroglyphs may be symbolic representations of whole scenes or concepts.

Determining their age is far less certain, because they are only rarely found in the company of contemporary material, such as organic substances that may be submitted to carbon-dating processes. Even so, investigators believe the oldest known petroglyphs were created by Neolithic Europeans around the Upper Paleolithic Boundary, at the close of the last Ice Age, between 12,000 and 10,000 years ago. Sometimes, petroglyphs give away their own age. Images of horses or human figures wielding rifles were obviously engraved after the arrival of modern Europeans, beginning in the 16th century. A few petroglyphs at the Jeffers' site have been confidently dated to circa 3,000 BC, making them some of the oldest specimens on the North American continent, because they represent men wielding *atl-atls*, a kind of spear-thrower archaeologists know was introduced to the Minnesota region about 5,000 years ago. These images may commemorate a particularly successful hunt, as suggested by their close proximity to images of bison or buffalo, a double line extending from their open mouths to their hearts.

Anasazi drawings on red rock canyon wall in American Southwest several thousand years old.

In an effort to make sense of such a great variety of so many petroglyphs, archaeologists have systematized them into five, separate categories: the Archaic Style, the Anasazi Style, the Hohokam Style, the Fremont Style, and the Rio Grande Style.

The Archaic Style groups the oldest known specimens, all of them in the American Southwest, from approximately 5000 BC to 1200 BC Many of them are serpentine or circular and at least a few surprisingly resemble

Chinese letters known as kanji. Before visiting Japan in 1996, I had the chance to copy a particularly Asian-looking glyph on the side of a canyon wall in New Mexico. While in Japan, I showed my faithful rendering of the New Mexico character to Professor Nobuhiro Yoshida, President of The Japan Petroglyph Society, in Kyushu. He recognized it immediately: "That is kanji for 'king'." Other investigators have found similarly close resemblances between Chinese characters and Archaic petroglyphs in North America, suggesting early visitors came from across the Pacific Ocean during the remote past.

A later group is known as the Anasazi Style, ranging from AD 300 to AD 1300, and largely confined to the Four Corners Region (where Arizona, New Mexico, Colorado, and Utah meet). Anasazi petroglyphs are commonly identified by intercon-necting spirals and palm prints. Their contemporary is the Hohokam Style of squares and swastikas; the later—both leftward- and rightward-oriented—signify solar and lunar movement, respectively, and/or ancestral migrations into central and southern Arizona, according to Hopi tradition.

A wall of ancient petroglyphs on a rock face in the remote Dominguez Canyon Wilderness Study Area, Colorado.

Beginning some 200 years after the Ana-sazi and Hohokam, the Fremont Style was typified by anthropomorphic figures attired in ceremonial dress and holding shields. These continued to appear until shortly before the arrival of modern Europeans in central and southeastern Utah, where they were most often pecked into cliff faces fol-lowing the Green River, or caves near the Colorado River. Their warlike appearance coincides with the mass-murder that engulfed the entire Southwest and put an end to civilization there begin-ning in the late 13th century.

The most recent of the "classical" petroglyphs, as embodied in the Rio Grande Style, feature warlike themes accompanied by avian motifs, mostly found in central and northern New Mexico, beginning around AD 1300, and continuing into the present.

But why were all these petroglyphs made? Anthropologists believe their artists intended seven different functions: historical, astronomical, spiritual, narrative, visionary, directional, or economic.

Historic petroglyphs are often obvious enough when they portray men on horseback or warriors carrying weapons.

Astronomical examples are composed of starbursts, crescent moons, or rayed circles.

Spiritual petroglyphs feature horned figures with outstretched arms, or musicians, most famously, the shamanistic Kokopelli flute player of the Hopi. A large, if precisely unknown percentage of this genre were created by shamans themselves; so-called "medicine men," who entered a deep trance to bring back guidance and healing for their people from the Otherworld.

For his June 2000 *Fate* article, "16,000-Year-Old Visions" (vol. 53, No. 6, issue 603), Dr. V. Fred Rayser found that the prehistoric artists at Little Petroglyph Canyon in the Cocos Mountains of California's Mojave Desert were Shoshone and Paiute shamans. He described them as "tribal elders and wise men, who were believed to have powers to heal, make rain, control animals, and predict the future. They carved their visions in stone immediately after emerging from the trance, because these mind pictures, like dreams, tend to be easily forgotten."

Their images were often expressed in repetitive geometric designs recognized by modern medical practitioners as "form constants." These are the same patterns produced by drugs, severe headaches (such as "migraine auras"), and similar stimuli. Shamans routinely used mind-bending hallucinogens to achieve profoundly altered states of consciousness. The medicine man's favored spiritual inducement was *Datura stramonium*, more commonly known in North America as jimson weed, devil's snare, or loco weed.

Datura stramonium contains tropane alkaloids, among the few substances which cause true hallucinations indistinguishable from reality. The active ingredients are atropine, hyoscyamine, and scopolamine, all classified as deliriants, or anticholinergics, that generate visionary experiences. The user is entirely awake during their effects, but believes he is in a living dream on the flip side of reality. Accounts of mental telepathy, conversing with ghosts, bilocation, seeing gods and demons, reading auras and particularly tele-transportation into realms of the dead or the gods—the famous "flight of the shaman"—are common. Ingesting *Datura stramonium* is extremely hazardous, however, and its so-called "recreational use" often ends in death. A Navajo folk tradition admonishes anyone taking loco weed: "Eat a little, and go to sleep. Eat some more, and have a dream. Eat too much, and don't wake up."

Shamanistic encounters with *Datura stramonium* are often expressed in the swirling or geometric designs that typify abstract rock art. Sometimes, the mind-altering flower itself is depicted as a trumpet-shaped figure. Other petroglyphs are an oval, its outline covered with spikes, the interior split into four spaces, each containing a few images resembling kidneys. These illustrations portray the *Datura stramonium's* egg-shaped, prickle-covered fruit. The size of a walnut, it is divided into four chambers where the hallucinogenic seeds are found.

Spiral petroglyph chipped into rock at Dinosaur National Monument, Utah, U.S.A.

Good examples of drug-induced shamanism may be seen at an archaeological site known as Painted Cave, north of Santa Barbara, on the Pacific coast. Until 400 years ago, the Chumash Indians brilliantly adorned its walls and ceiling with spirals, sunbursts, serpentine figures, rainbows, and similarly expressionistic designs accompanied by representations of flowers and fruits of the *Datura stramonium*.

Petroglyphs such as those at Painted Cave indicate that the shaman encountered his visions there—Mother Earth's womb and tomb, where his soul flew beyond this life to the Otherworld, but returned with guidance for his tribe; hence his "flight" and its hallucinogenic imagery depicted inside the underground sanctorum. As an indication of his fundamentally human experience, some of the same symbols inside California's Painted Cave occur at Hal Saflieni's hypogeum, a subsurface temple on the island of Malta dating to the Mediterranean Neolithic, circa 2800 BC, more than three millennia before Chumash shamans decorated their cave with identical illustrations.

Narrative petroglyphs tell stories by illustrating characters or events, and may have been used as mnemonic devices to assist the storyteller. A well-known example shows a waterfowl using its long beak to grasp a frog. Other petroglyphs symbolically narrate seminal myths for preliterate peoples who must otherwise rely entirely upon oral tradition for the preservation of their folk memories. As a representative example, we return once more to Minnesota's Jeffers' Petroglyphs, where visitors may notice three, strange figures: a man wearing a horned helmet between a circle and a turtle. Combined, the trio signifies the Flood familiar to every Native American tribe. The circle represents an ancestral "lodge" far to the East, where the forefathers of all Indians were created by the Great Spirit, with whom they lived in harmony for many generations.

Over time, however, these early humans became arrogant, and grew to believe they could dispense with the Great Spirit altogether. Angered by their ingratitude, he pushed the lodge under the Sunrise Sea, drowning most of them. Only a few, virtuous persons escaped the deluge, and these the Great Spirit saved by scooping them up in his arms. There were too many of them to carry, however, so he conjured a giant turtle from the ocean bottom. As soon as remaining survivors climbed on the animal's back, the turtle began swimming westward with the Great Spirit wading behind through the water. At length, they arrived at an unfamiliar shore, where the people made a new home for themselves. Henceforward, they called it "Turtle Island," the name by which tribal Indians still refer to North America. Visionary petroglyphs most commonly depict persons changing into animals, or surrounded by so-called "energy lines."

A little known sacred site at the very tip of southern Illinois not far from the Ohio River, near the little town of Gorham, features a sequence of petroglyphs incised on the sandstone wall of a rock shelter at the base of a high bluff.

It was not by accident that the Gorham Bluff was chosen for the permanent display of the sacred petroglyphs. The gargantuan earth-energies that pushed it in a molten, semi-solid condition out of the planet's bowels are so potent that they radiate from the massive formation. For persons in tune with these signals, the bluff is irresistible. Its theatrical milieu, complete with a natural stage setting, as though crafted by some divine agency, was the *mise en scene* for wonderful spiritual dramas, shamanistic initiations.

Here the tribal adepts gathered to inspire the vision quests of manhood, to conjure and cure, and to deliberately alter the consciousness of men and women seeking personal contact with the Great Spirit. The petroglyphs are well-preserved and easily read from left to right, from north (the Spirit direction for most Native American tribes) to south (the traditional

"Direction of Becoming"). They begin at stage-left, as it were, with a cross inside a circle beside a crescent moon and star. This is an archetype, a universal human symbol found around the world, signifying the "sacred center." The moon in relation to a "star" (probably the planet Venus) marks the time for the beginning of the ritual.

Human figures incised into the rock face walk toward the main body of the petroglyphs. The images of birds in flight merge with palm prints—some child-sized—implying human striving to attain the divine. In front of them lies a boulder decorated with circle-cross and a figure kneeling before a half-man, half-bird creature. This is the Rock of the Shaman, the bird-man symbol of spiritual transformation, and before whom reverence is shown at his place of power. Back at the cliff wall, the largest circle-cross is faced on either side by a pair of deer, one white, the other black. They define the sacred center mysteries practiced here as a power directing and harmonizing the resident energies, a psychic fulcrum positioned midpoint between day and night,

"Misshepezhieu, canoe and serpents." Agawa Rock Pictographs. Lake Superior Provincial Park, Ontario. Canada.

the Sacred Balance, the Special Duality. Deer are additionally symbolic of transformation, because of their ability to stealthily appear and vanish in the woodlands, and of regeneration by way of their rejuvenating antlers.

A single palm print appears beside a bird-man, implying the initiate's growing identification with the shaman spirit. In order for him to properly see the ultimate glyphs, he had to climb to the top of another boulder before the cliff face. There he would behold the mingling of human and bird shapes pictured among the stars, as though the elevated soul were being lifted into the higher realms of consciousness. Back down on ground level, the crescent moon reappears, but the Venus-star is further to the right, indicating the passage of time and the end of the ceremony. Sure enough, the final images belong to a bird flying away from the sacred-center cross, symbolizing the transubstantiation of human mortality into the soul's immortality.

Just beyond the theater of petroglyphs, to the right (south), is a small, circular mound with a depression in the center. It is identical to ancient burial mounds found throughout Wisconsin. In the depression of this donut-like structure, the initiate experienced or completed his or her vision quest. The confines of Gorham's sacred precinct suggest only a few individuals at a time were shepherded through their initiation by the shaman. To better appreciate the life-changing effect of their spiritual adventure, it is important to realize that all the participants were part of a culture in which nature-mysticism was accepted as a common fact of their existence. They therefore entered into their psychic exercises already deeply convinced of the efficacy of what they were about to do. Preparatory to their initiation, they fasted in silence and alone at some remote spot. Their consciousness was further altered by mild narcotics administered by the shaman to achieve the desired receptivity. They doubtless never saw the petroglyphs before the moment of their prepared viewing. As indicated by the drawings themselves, empowerment ceremonies took place at night. Hence, the high drama of the scenes—staged under torch light to the otherworldly music of pipes and drums, together with a ferociously attired shaman chanting in a spirit-voice—must have been impressive, to say the least.

For those who long ago experienced such initiation, they undoubtedly felt that they had touched the face of the Great Spirit. A directional genre is evident in Norwegian petroglyphs during the Early Bronze Age (circa 2100 BC), when they defined territorial boundaries between tribes or families in the Bergen and Trondheim areas. Other petroglyphs are self-evident maps indicating rivers, lakes, mountains, and forests. Economic petroglyphs depict hunting scenes, especially quadrupeds stuck with arrows. Identifying petroglyph types and their interpretation are often problematical, because they are not universally recognizable signs, but symbols that arose from and were meant to be understood by a specific people and culture removed from our own.

Nonetheless, some human common denominators may be found throughout rock art everywhere. These more discernible images are happily among the most interesting, because they transcend the relatively mundane meanings of territorial delineation, directions to water holes, memorializing a hunt, celebrating a military victory, or tribal identification. For example, the depiction of a macaw or parrot from Mexico was associated in the American Southwest with ceremonial life, and a zig-zag line terminating with a horned head was synonymous with the presence of water, while a trio of bows and arrows signified the New Mexico region myth of Monster Slayer.

But the best way to understand the petroglyphs is by approaching them with respect and a sense of awe. Like all mysteries, if greeted with an open heart, they will speak to you in time—perhaps not in words, but more probably in dreams and in the imagery of your own spiritual life.

This article first appeared in *Atlantis Rising* #73 (January/February 2009).

PART TWO

SECRET HISTORY

Bernini's angel at Pont St. Angelo

5

SECRETS OF *ANGELS & DEMONS*

Exploring Bernini's Rome.
How Much Did the Movie Get Right?

BY PHILIP COPPENS

Whereas the inspiration for Dan Brown's *The Da Vinci Code* (2009) can be clearly tracked down—so much so that the likes of Baigent and Leigh felt they should sue the author—Brown's *Angels & Demons* (2006) is far more original, both in theme and execution.

At the time of publication, Leonardo da Vinci, the Priory of Sion, and Opus Dei had been almost done to death both in fiction and non-fiction; however, no one had ever used the Italian genius Bernini as a source of esoteric intrigue . . . perhaps because, if anything, Bernini appeared to be a devout Christian and hence difficult to massage into controversy. Brown, however, transformed this architect into a secret alchemist, who left clues of his hidden alliance imprinted on the streets of Rome. But is this fiction, or not?

Brown commentator and author Simon Cox in *Illuminating Angels & Demons* writes that "Brown's inclusion of the so-called 'Father of the Baroque', Gian Lorenzo Bernini, in *Angels & Demons* was an inspired decision. This remarkable sculptor, painter, and architect has left an indelible mark on the face of modern-day Rome. Bernini is everywhere: his spirit is ever-present, and his legacy within the fabric of Roman society remains all-pervasive." Cox is nevertheless skeptical that Bernini was a member of a secret society.

Bernini (1598–1680) trained as a sculptor, and later became an architect. He was world-famous in both disciplines within his own lifetime. It is said that when he finally visited Paris, he found its streets crowded with admirers— something that few artists have ever achieved while living, but Bernini did.

Bernini's presence is visible in many locations across Rome. With a bit of artistic license, one might argue that Rome as we know it, *is* Bernini.

Critical to Brown's plot are four statues—"Altars of Science"—which represent the four elements: earth, air, fire, and water, which are, of course, more alchemical than scientific in origin. Water is represented by the Fountain of Four Rivers on the Piazza Navona. Fire is the Ecstasy of St. Teresa, a sculpture inside the church of Santa Maria della Vittoria. Air is West Ponente at Saint Peter's Square, while Earth is Habakkuk and the Angel in the Chigi Chapel of Santa Maria del Popolo.

The four locations are identified as the "Path of Illumination," a series of clues which an Illuminatus is able to follow and which will guide him to the secret meeting place of the Illuminati, whereupon he will gain admission into the Order. Brown's leading man Robert Langdon (played by Tom Hanks in the movie), however, is not out for membership, but hopes to uncover evidence that will answer the pressing enigma he needs to resolve. At each of the four locations, Langdon is confronted with a murder, the means of which is linked with the location's element. The first murder, a cardinal is buried and has soil lodged in his throat—Earth; the second murder, the victim's lungs are pierced—Air; the third victim is engulfed in flames—Fire; the fourth victim is drowned in a fountain—Water.

One key site is therefore the Chigi Chapel, which is inside Santa Maria del Popolo. The church was erected in 1099 over the burial place of the Roman Emperor Nero, in order to sanctify what was believed to be an evil place—the emperor's ghost had apparently appeared there numerous times. The Chigi Chapel itself was designed by Raphael for Afostino Chigi, a wealthy Italian banker; but two of the sculptures, of Daniel and Habakkuk, are by Bernini. The chapel was to house the tombs of Afostino and his brother Sigismondo. Their tombs are a pyramidal structure and it is likely that this design was copied from earlier Roman tombs. Each tomb has one sculpture on the side. Habakkuk is an angel, appearing in an apocryphal text, linked with Daniel's imprisonment in the lion's den.

This provides us with an angel, but, in fact, Bernini seems not to have been that interested in angels, or demons— a fact also shown in the novel. In fact, the all-important question is this: was Bernini a devout Christian, as the standard line has it, or did he side with scientists? Could he, indeed, have sided with those favoring Egypt as the font of all knowledge?

Visit the Pantheon and you will see next to it, in the Piazza della Minerva, another Bernini statue: that of an elephant with an obelisk on its back. The design is not original to Bernini and is, in fact, found in the Hypnertomachia Poliphili. This extremely enigmatic book is linked with much occult lore; and seeing that Bernini made a drawing from it into a statue begs the question: whether this is further evidence of a secret allegiance of Bernini to some occult tradition. Remarkably, however, the statue does not feature in Brown's book.

Equally, "official history" has gone out of its way to explain this statue, calling it "Bernini's Chick." Some interpret the statue as a reference to Pope Alexander VII's reign and claim that it illustrates that strength—the elephant—should support wisdom—the obelisk. Others will highlight that the statue, created in 1667, was done by one

Bernini's Elephant bearing an Egyptian Obelisk in the Piazza della Minerva (all Rome photos by Phillip Coppens).

of Bernini's students, Ercole Ferrata. They will talk about its smile and how one needs to move toward the rear end of the animal to see that its tail is shifted to the left, as if it is defecating, and how the animal's rear points at the office of Father Domenico Paglia, a Dominican friar, who was one of the main antagonists of Bernini and his artisan friends—a final salute and last word.

Though the elephant goes unmentioned in *Angels & Demons*, the Pantheon nearby, does get a mention. Inside, Langdon notices a Christian tomb which is out of line with the orientation of the building and he starts a lecture on how Christianity borrowed from the Egyptian religion, particularly on the topic of the sun. Langdon sees the Pantheon as the "first altar of science" and the tomb of Santi, also known as Raphael. Though a Catholic Church, the Pantheon, at first, was a temple to honor Roman gods. Originally built in 27 BC by Marcus Agrippa, it burned down in AD 110, and Hadrian completed the present structure in AD 125. It was consecrated a Roman church and dedicated as Santa Maria ai Mariti in allusion to bones found there in AD 609.

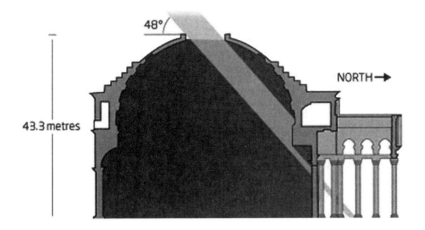

48°

NORTH→

43.3 metres

Bernini's Pantheon

The rotunda's interior is a perfect sphere, with a diameter of 43.4 meters, equal to its height. The walls are 6.1 meters thick and support the dome. The oculus in the center of the ceiling is the only location of lighting. Recent research has shown that the Pantheon is in fact a sundial. When Robert Hannah of the University of Otago visited the Pantheon in 2005, he realized that during the six months of winter, the light of the noon sun traces a path across the inside of the domed roof. During summer, with the sun higher in the sky, the shaft shines onto the lower walls and floor. At the two equinoxes, the sunlight coming in through the hole strikes the junction between the roof and wall, above the Pantheon's grand northern doorway. A grill above the door allows a sliver of light through to the front courtyard—the only moment in the year that it sees sunlight, if its main doors are closed. Hannah thinks that by marking the equinoxes, the Pantheon was intended to elevate emperors who worshipped there into the realm of the gods. The equinoxes, of course, have always been very important for sun worshippers, like the ancient Egyptians. And the obelisk on the back of the elephant next to the Pantheon is, of course, a pure Egyptian symbol and specifically linked with the sun cult.

Rome is the religious center of the Catholic world. But remarkably for a town that claims to be Christian, its piazzas are crowned by Egyptian obelisks. The four rivers of the fountain in the Piazza Navona are the Danube, Ganges, Nile, and the Rio de la Plata, each one representing its continent. From the base, there is also a red granite obelisk, 15.8 meters high, topped with a statue of a dove. The obelisk was quarried in Aswan for Emperor Domitian, probably to mark his ascension in AD 81. It was originally placed in Rome between the temples of Isis and Serapis, then moved to Circus de Massenzio, and then moved here.

Another Egyptian obelisk stands outside the Santa Maria De Popolo. It came from Heliopolis and was erected by Seti I and Ramses II. It rises 23.8 meters high and weighs no less than 235 tons. It was moved to Rome in 100 BC and was placed on the Circus Maximus in Rome, where it later toppled, and whereupon it was then moved to its present location by Pope Sixtus V in 1589.

The obelisk outside of Maria della Vittoria is thought to have been created by Emperor Hadrian, while the obelisk of the Piazza della Rotunda is part of a pair, erected at the temple of the sun god Ra in Heliopolis by Ramses II. It was brought to Rome and stood at the temple of Isis, was then moved to the Capitoline Hill in the 14th century, and then moved again in 1711 by Pope Clement XI.

But it gets better: Bernini is also responsible for creating St Peter's Square, which is not square at all, but which is, instead, an elliptical plaza in front of St Peter's—the "stadium" where the Catholic community gathers for the Christian festivals and other important events, such as papal elections and funerals. Three hundred thousand people can easily fit inside. St Peter's Square was built between 1656 and 1667. It has 284 Doric columns, each 18.3 meters tall. In the middle rise two fountains, one by Bernini himself, the other by Carlo Maderno.

The obelisk in the Fountain of Four Rivers in Piazza Navona.

Bernini chose the ellipse apparently to symbolize Copernicus' discovery that our solar system was based on ellipses—the planetary orbits around the sun. No wonder that Brown therefore worked him into his plot and saw him as a "closet scientist." But a more interesting possibility arises: great emphasis should be placed on the fact that the middle of the square—marking the position of the sun—is occupied by an Egyptian obelisk, which originates from the city of Heliopolis, the city of the Sun. Such symbolism—despite the addition of a cross on top—is not Christian. And as Robert Bauval has pointed out: the hieroglyph for Heliopolis was actually an obelisk with a cross on top, begging the question whether it is a coincidence or design that this obelisk has a cross on top. Furthermore, the entire layout was constructed at a time when the Vatican itself was still very uneasy about its relationship with science. And it does appear that Brown is correct and that Bernini had chosen sides . . . though perhaps not as obvious as Brown works it out in his novel.

So, indeed, there is even an obelisk in the very heart of St Peter's Square, a grandiose 25 meters high and 320 ton in weight. This one is not covered with hieroglyphs and, as such, its origins are officially unknown, though there are two theories: one, that it dates from the reign of Amenenhat II, and came from Heliopolis; or that it was more modern, and came from Alexandria. Pliny, a contemporary of Caligula, said that it had been made for one Nuncoreus, the son of Sesotris. If so, Sesostris I ruled from 1971 till 1926 BC and he is known to have carried out extensive work in Heliopolis. It is thought that the obelisk was then transferred to Alexandria by Emperor Augustus Caesar and raised there in the Julian Forum. In this scenario, two competing theories have become compatible. From there, it was moved to Rome by Caligula in AD 37 and raised in Caligula Circus, where St Peter was believed to have been martyred in AD 64, the site of modern St Peter's Square.

Interestingly, the hieroglyph for Heliopolis is not only the obelisk with cross, but also a circle or ellipse, divided into eight, the symbol of the city. It is a rather remarkable coincidence that Bernini's design for St Peter's "Square" has the eight divisions there. Coincidence? Or design? It surely must be the latter, and if so, though a devout Christian he might have been, he was definitely fascinated with ancient Egypt.

Since making an appearance in Brown's *Angels & Demons*, Bernini has

The twisted columns in St. Peter's Bernini said were designed by Solomon.

also played a small role in Kathleen McGowan's *The Book of Love*. McGowan underlines that Pope Urban VIII commissioned Bernini to create a marble tomb for Matilda of Canossa, the main character of her book, when in 1635 her body was moved from the Monastery of San Benedetto Po. She also notes that inside St Peter's, the *baldachino*, the bronze centerpiece beneath the dome, is supported by twisted columns that Bernini claimed came from a design drawn by Solomon himself for the first Temple. Finally, she claims that Bernini inherited the design for St. Peter's from Michelangelo. Thus, from hardly a mention, within a decade, Bernini has become part and parcel of various esoteric traditions that might have made Rome into what it is today.

There is, however, one potential mystery about Bernini that none of the novelists have touched upon so far. We know that in 1656, the French painter Nicolas Poussin—who resided in Rome—apparently confided something to Louis Fouquet, who wrote about this matter in a letter to his brother Nicolas Fouquet, the right hand of the French King Louis

XIV. Some time later, Fouquet fell out of favor with the king—for reasons still not totally explained. The king personally went through Fouquet's documents, and when a jury found Fouquet not guilty, the king single-handedly changed that verdict and imprisoned Fouquet for the rest of his life, also making sure Fouquet would never receive any visitors. But that is not all. The king had also organized a campaign to lure Poussin to France. In the end, Poussin had to indulge his head of state but as soon as he could, he left France once again for Rome. Noting that in 1665, in the aftermath of Fouquet's arrest, Bernini was invited by Louis XIV to design the new façade of the Louvre, one can wonder whether the French king was inviting key architects and artists for other reasons than those given. The fact that Bernini's design was never used might hint that the king was not so much interested in Bernini the architect, as Bernini the man.

If so, it means there is further mystery to a man who, thanks to novels such as *Angels & Demons*, is slowly beginning to be recognized for his out-standing contributions in decorating Rome and as a man who may have more hidden depths to him than have so far been identified.

This article first appeared in *Atlantis Rising* #77 (September/October 2009).

6

THE LOST MIND

Plumbing Dan Brown's Latest Book for
Even More Secrets

BY PHILIP COPPENS

With an initial print run of five million copies, *The Lost Symbol* (2012) instantly became the biggest-selling adult hardcover of all time. Most attention at the release of the book went to the Masonic themes woven into the story line, as these themes were seen as controversial. However, there is a far more interesting and bigger storyline that forms the veritable backbone of the story: the fact that advances in modern science have been made that reveal deep insights into the afterlife, the nature of reality, and God.

In Brown's now typical style, he points out at the beginning of the book that the Institute of Noetic Sciences is a real organization. The Institute was the brainchild of astronaut Ed Mitchell, who founded "IONS" after having a deep spiritual revelation while in space. After walking on the moon, Mitchell realized that the next frontier to explore was the mind and human consciousness, and hence, in 1973, the Institute was founded. The word "noetic" itself is derived from the Greek *nous*—the very word the Greeks used for the type of knowing that came through a personal revelation, normally acquired by initiation into a mystery tradition.

Since 1973, the Institute has been involved in pioneering research, trying to bring the study of consciousness firmly within the bailiwick of "normal science," which is largely hands-off when it comes to tackling these topics. In *The Lost Symbol,* Brown gives one fictional example of how a person's soul is weighed when leaving the body of the deceased. The fact is, truth is far more interesting than this example, and Brown knows it and points this out, though he does not truly highlight it.

Early on in the book, Brown mentions Lynne McTaggart's 2007 book *The Intention Experiment*, a book that is subtitled "Use Your Thoughts to Change the World." That is indeed the central message that Brown imparts

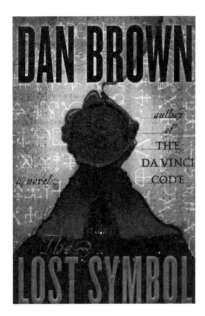

Lost Symbol cover

to his readers. Throughout the book, he argues that human thought, if properly focused, has the ability to affect and change physical mass. It is, in fact, the basic tenet of quantum physics, which argues that human consciousness—thought—determines the outcome of what happens in our reality. To paraphrase Brown: If we can have focused thought, "we are the masters of our own universe." Living consciousness, somehow, is the influence that turns the *possibility* of something into something *real*.

Lynne McTaggart's first book, *The Field* (2001), focused on the so-called Zero Point Field, which is that "all matter in the universe is connected on the subatomic level through a constant dance of quantum energy exchange." In the 1970s, physicist Hal Puthoff discovered that the constant energy exchange of all subatomic matter with the Zero Point Field accounts for the stability of the hydrogen atom and the stability of all matter. Remove "the field," and all matter would collapse in on itself. The universe would simply cease to exist.

McTaggart defined consciousness as "a substance outside the confines of our bodies—a highly ordered energy with the capacity to change physical matter. Directing thoughts at a target seemed capable of altering machines, cells, and, indeed, entire multi-celled organisms like human beings." She thus highlighted that far from being a by-product of evolution, consciousness is central to the universe: we think, therefore we create reality.

Indeed, the greatest scientific revolution of the 21st century will likely come from scientific experiments in the area of quantum physics and exploring consciousness, which brings science closer toward the concept of religion, addressing the very topics Brown has singled out: death, God, and so forth. And this revolution is closer at hand than we think, and closer than traditional scientists and most religious leaders would like to believe.

Brown points this out, and others, like McTaggart, have given an overview of the research on this subject to date. Much of the original research occurred either behind the closed doors of CIA affiliates or in little known research facilities, like the Institute of Noetic Sciences and the Esalen Institute—though Brown does not refer to the latter in his book. Indeed, it is now an established fact that the CIA, throughout its history, experimented with the mind, sometimes for less than noble ends. It was these "mind control" experiments, the most notorious of which was Project MK-ULTRA, which were brought to public attention in 1975 by the US Congress in the aftermath of the Watergate scandal. But as early as 1973, then CIA Director Richard Helms had ordered all project files destroyed, which means that the true extent of decades-long covert, scientific experimentation on US citizens was virtually impossible to reconstruct.

From the available evidence, the late Senator Ted Kennedy summarized how "the Deputy Director of the CIA revealed that over thirty universities and institutions were involved in an 'extensive testing and experimentation' program which included covert drug tests on unwitting citizens 'at all social levels, high and low, native Americans and foreign.' Several of these tests involved the administration of LSD to 'unwitting subjects in social situations.' At least one death, that of Dr. Olson, resulted. The Agency itself acknowledged that these tests made little scientific sense. The agents doing the monitoring were not qualified scientific observers."

Although the CIA insisted that MK-ULTRA-type experiments had been abandoned by the early 1970s, CIA veteran Victor Marchetti stated as late as 1977 that this was not the case.

Dan Brown does not touch upon these mind control experiments in *The Lost Symbol*, but does highlight another CIA project that ran in the 1970s and which focused on the mind: remote viewing. This project addressed the question of whether or not the mind could retrieve information that was not available by technical means. The project was outsourced to SRI—Stanford Research International—and was lead by Hal Puthoff and Russell Targ, two qualified scientific observers. In subsequent years, the Defense Intelligence Agency took over the project and continued to run it as a highly classified project. When the existence of the project was declassified in 1995, the release was accompanied by much—carefully created—public ridicule, so that the implications of the central findings of the project would hopefully be overlooked. Those were that the mind was indeed able to "see" things no satellite or other instrument could, including locations of nuclear submarines, and much more.

Indeed, upon declassification, it was agreed that remote viewing had worked; the "problem" was that the CIA claimed that the study was also meant to find out "how" it worked, and that "problem" had not been solved in more than 20 years of research. Hence, they argued, it was best to stop the project. The subject of remote viewing was later fancifully made into the 2009 film *Men Who Stare at Goats*.

But just like there is controversy over whether or not the mind control projects were terminated when the CIA said they were, questions remain as to whether the CIA or other factions of the American intelligence community truly have stopped their remote viewing unit(s). After all, they themselves agreed that they had specific intelligence gathering benefits, so why should they be stopped?

Finally, though Brown takes a snap at so-called "spoon bending"—a clear reference to Uri Geller—it was actually Uri Geller who was brought from Israel, with the full agreement of the Israeli intelligence agency Mossad

Uri Geller

and the CIA, to the United States and SRI to be tested as part of these remote viewing projects. When Geller left the project, he soon became notorious for his spoon bending and now considers himself to be part and parcel of the entertainment industry. But the now declassified scientific experiments at SRI show that during the experiments, Geller was able to influence computers—some of which were in charge of military applications—as well as demonstrate the power of the mind on numerous other occasions, including driving while blindfolded. Such displays convinced the participating physicists at SRI and other laboratories, time and again, that the mind was indeed the master of reality—thus proving the basic tenet of quantum physics.

Of course, the CIA was not the only one to study the mind. Very intriguing conclusions were reached by Fritz-Albert Popp, who was the first to discover that all living things emit a tiny current of light. Indeed, Popp himself identified how tiny frequencies were mainly stored and emitted from the DNA of cells, which was a conclusion also reached by anthropologist Jeremy Narby, when he studied DNA and the manner in which shamans seemed to be able to access information not accessible to the "ordinary" senses . . . a finding therefore on par with the CIA remote viewing experiments.

Gary Schwartz and Kathy Creath followed in the same vein and were the first to show that light emanated from a living thing: a geranium leaf. Others have since been able to show how streams of light flow from a healer's hands. As such, McTaggart argues that "if thoughts are generated as frequencies, then healing intention is well-ordered light."

Taking it one step further is the work of British inventor Harry Oldfield, who has created photon cameras. These instruments are able to photograph photons, particles of light that are everywhere but not visible to the naked eye. His research has shown how the crown chakra of a drug addict is indeed totally open, "leaking" energy, and how energy can be seen to become more organized during meditation, especially group meditations, affecting specifically those people in the group that were indeed consciously meditating, rather than just "being there." Other research has shown that the concentrated thinking of a group has an exponential effect: it is far more influential than if the members of the group were concentrating on an individual basis.

All of this confirms what McTaggart and many others have identified: in order to have the most powerful effect, a healer or sender needs to become "ordered"—he needs to be attentive, believe, be motivated, and compassionate. McTaggart also refers to the Love Study, conducted by Elizabeth Targ and Marilyn Schlitz, the latter of the Institute of Noetic Sciences, and specifically one of its resident researchers, Dean Radin. The conclusion was that "intention is the perfect manifestation of love. Two bodies become one." This finding has enormous implications for the concept now known as "soul mates": how at the dawn of time, one soul—one consciousness—beating as one, decided to split and incarnate in two bodies—something already highlighted in the writings of the Greek philosopher Aristotle. Though Brown does not highlight the concept of soul mates, he does argue that intention is a learned skill and forms the missing link between modern science and ancient mysticism, of which Aristotle is a prime example.

In short, today scientists accept—some reluctantly—that physical matter isn't solid and stable. At a quantum level, reality resembles unset jelly. Living consciousness somehow is the influence that turns the possibility of something into something real. How this works is secondary; it works. Full stop. It is the central message that Brown tries to impart in this book, a message we should learn as soon as possible and which is hopefully spread through *The Lost Symbol*.

Indeed, to quote McTaggart once again: "The universe is democratic and participatory." We create reality, which is the role of Free Will in the universe: the Divine Plan is the potential, and we manifest it. "Every movement we make appears to be felt by the people around us."

Brown does not use the work of Puthoff, Schwartz, or Poff but instead uses historical examples, such as a statement by Albert Einstein: "Behind the secrets of nature remains something subtle, intangible, and inexplicable. Veneration for this force beyond anything that we can comprehend is my religion."

Brown argues that each individual has the potential to create miracles: "The question was not whether God had imbued man with great powers… but rather how we liberate those powers." He quotes from Jesus Christ, "The kingdom of God is within you," but also from other religions, such as "Know Thyself" (Pythagoras) or "Know ye not that ye are gods" (Hermes Trismegistus).

But however controversial and trendsetting Brown is, his entire oeuvre has never been original. As such, Brown is not the first to play with "intent" in his novels. Another best-selling author, Kathleen McGowan, has taken the notion of the mind and intent much further, specifically in her 2009 book *The Book of Love*. McGowan draws attention to the *hieros gamos*, in which two soul mates unite in a "sacred marriage," whereby, with intent, a specific soul is willed to be born in the body that is being created by its two parents in the sexual act. Though this might sound extreme, there are numerous examples, both from mythology (Isis and Osiris creating Horus), as well as history (as described by Archie Roy in *The Eager Dead*) that this is a primary mystical tradition, practiced at least from ancient Egyptian times to this very day. It underlines that ancient mystical traditions—to which Brown frequently refers in his book—were perfectly aware of the power of intent and applied it to everything that they felt was sacred, whether the creation of divine offspring, or the numerous religious monuments we see, whether they are Egyptian temples or Gothic cathedrals like Chartres.

As mentioned in the book, Brown tackles how faith and intention are also pivotal in creating miracles. This theme too is explored by McGowan, in *The Source of Miracles*, in which she argues that for a very long time, she believed—like so many others—that miracles, the way in which they were described in the Bible, were allegories . . . until a veritable miracle happened and she realized that there were real miracles within the reach of every human being. And what does it take to create miracles? Focused thought and "applied thinking," to unlock the divine potential that is resident within each one of us.

As such, *The Lost Symbol* is part of a wave of books, whether they are scientific, novels or self-help, that are beginning to highlight how, almost a century after quantum physics posited that conscious thought was central to our reality, we are indeed masters of our own universe. The question of *The Lost Symbol* is whether readers will pick up this central message, which Brown has largely coded—rather than ostentatiously revealed—into this novel.

This article first appeared in *Atlantis Rising* #79 (January/February 2010).

7

THE LOST LIBRARY OF IVAN THE GREAT

Beneath Modern Moscow a Centuries-Old Search Continues

BY STEVEN SORA

S tudents of history, religion, science, and sociology can never forgive the destruction of some of the world's most important libraries. The ancient library at Alexandria once held 500,000 volumes before it was destroyed by Julius Caesar, and the 200,000 volume library at Carthage met the same fate after war with Rome. The Chinese Emperor Shi Hwang-ti had all his kingdom's books burned in 214 BC, and Mao revived this tradition in 1966. From ancient Pergamus to modern Germany, books and libraries have regularly come under attack. One of the greatest libraries, however, was saved at the last minute from destruction, only to be lost. Literally.

In the middle of the 15th century, the Ottoman Empire was spreading west, conquering everything in its path. It was only a matter of time before Constantinople itself would be invaded by the Asian hordes. Constantinople was nearly two thousand years old when the Turks threatened it. Founded by a Greek, Byzas, in 667 BC, the city had survived an earlier catastrophe in AD 1204 when the Christian crusaders decided on looting the city as a dress rehearsal for conquering Jerusalem. The lesson, having been learned the hard way, was not forgotten.

The greatest treasures of the city were to be protected at all costs. Sultan Mahomet II with an army of 150,000 men was on his way. Constantine XI had a force only one tenth the size of his enemy, and this included his Genoese mercenaries. Defeat was just a matter of time.

The niece of the emperor Constantine, Sophia Palaiologina, was hastily married to the young Ivan III who would soon become the ruler of Russia—the purpose of the marriage to stave off the coming onslaught. Her entourage left the city and made it to Moscow via Rome. Her baggage included the treasures of the Byzantine library as well as the treasures of Constantinople's library.

Amassed, this was no ordinary library, and it may have been the greatest library outside the Vatican at that time. Chronicles preserved in Moscow state one hundred carts of rare books traveled overland. Books from Asia, Africa, and Europe written in Hebrew, Arabic, Greek, Latin, and Egyptian were part of the library. Early editions of Pindar, Polybius, Tacitus, and Cicero were also part of the library, as were the poems of Kalvos,

Ancient books—lost forever?

the works of Virgil, and the "Lives of the Twelve Caesars" by Suetonius. They were written by hand and considered one-of-a-kind. Seven hundred books were editions hand-bound for the emperors themselves, and encrusted in jewels. The value of the library was then and now incalculable.

Sophia (also known as Zoe) and her treasures made it to the safety of Moscow and her new husband via Rome. She also collected a handful of Italian artists and architects who would participate in the modernization of the Kremlin. One hope, that of uniting the Orthodox Church of Constantinople, the last vestige of the Roman Empire, with the Orthodox church of Russia, was never achieved. There would be no theological union, and it would quickly be known there was no hope of a military union. And the fate of Constantinople was sealed.

The troops of the Ottoman sultan overwhelmed the city's walls with cannon and sheer numbers. The Ottoman navy surrounded the port. When chains were put across the harbor, Mahomet had his ships put on rollers, pulled overland, and relaunched at a point past the blockade. When the ships reached the inner harbor, cannons brought down the walls, and the massive military contingent entered the city on May 29, 1453. The culmination of a seven-week siege had the Ottoman leader hailed as Fatih (the Conqueror) as he rode on horseback into the Hagia Sophia, the greatest Church in the World.

Massacre and pillage followed as Constantinople was "converted" into Istanbul, the capital of the Turkish Empire. The greatest church, 180 feet tall, became a mosque and others were quickly constructed. The Eastern Roman Empire was no more. Moscow now became the head of the Orthodox Christian Church. A Russian Orthodox monk, Philotheos, declared Moscow "the Third Rome."

A New Home for Constantinople's Treasures

One of Ivan III's most lasting achievements was to begin the building of the Moscow Kremlin into what it is today. In his time, it was a 300-year-old encampment built of wood. Standing tall. it had turned back numerous assaults. The old-Russian word for "citadel," *kreml*, served as the base of the modern word, kremlin. He took the 130-acre fortress and replaced wood with brick and stone. Much of the brick work that has survived until modern times is the original.

There was a reason for the upgrade from oak to stone: Sophia requested of her husband that the books she had brought from Constantinople be safe from the fires that regularly plagued the fortress. Cathedrals of wood, and barracks and homes, regularly burned and were vulnerable to Tartar attacks, and the library needed to be safe from that threat. Another threat, voiced by her uncle, was his belief that the library was coveted by Rome and the Vatican. They had offered to buy the complete collection, and the emperor had turned the offer down. Would Rome use force? For this reason Moscow was chosen.

Ivan went a step further and built the vaults of the "Liberia" as the library came to be known, underground. The Italian architect Ridolfo (Aristotle) di Fioravanti had the job of constructing the vault deep under the Kremlin. There were once believed to be 300 hundred underground tributaries of the Muscovy River. The architect closed off such waterways, then lined the walls with brick. No one knows just how many rooms and tunnels exist in the labyrinth under the Kremlin.

Meet the New Boss

When Ivan III (who, as ruler, became Ivan the Great) died, the rule of Russia passed to Ivan IV, known to history as Ivan the Terrible. The word "terrible" actually once meant "awesome," but Ivan was a terrible person even though his ability to rule was "awesome." He detested the aristocracy of Russia called the *boyars*. For them, he extended his underground city further. The labyrinth under the Kremlin now included prisons and torture chambers designed to break the power of these elite families.

At first he targeted specific families that had "neglected" him. However, his cruelty went beyond the practical, and evil, growth of power. He even threw cats and dogs out of Kremlin windows. His secret police, the Oprichniks, grew more violent as their "Czar" became more unbalanced. Ivan IV was the first to take that title, which is derived from *Caesar*. After stripping the boyars of their wealth, he began attacking his own population. The Massacre of Novgorad saw over thirty thousand Russians killed and the city nearly depopulated. He beat his daughter-in-law until she miscarried and then killed his son who had tried to stop him.

Ivan the Terrible

Ivan's reign of terror did not end until his death. In his last three years, he suffered from a horrific disease that bloated his features and caused him to emit ghastly odors. Most likely it was the result of poisoning, and the last person to see him alive was his adversary in chess, Boris Godenov, who was suspected of finishing him off with more poison. While Ivan was losing his mind and finally his life, Russia was losing the knowledge of the library's location. More important issues allowed the library to be nearly forgotten. Moscow itself would fall from importance when Peter the Great, czar and emperor, modernized his country (1682–1721). Peter might have moved the library, if he found it (by now it had been hidden almost 300 years), but despite a massive search of the maze under the Kremlin defied even the Romanov emperor.

THE SEARCH FOR THE LOST LIBRARY

Fast forward past the days of the czars to the time of the dictators and the library was still missing. Joseph Stalin (1878–1953) wished to create one of the world's greatest subway systems. The massive tunneling, which is today still evident in the endless escalators that seem to descend to the earth's core, was done with care in the hopes that one of the secret rooms of the library would be uncovered. Over one hundred subway stations, many decorated with artworks, are connected by miles of track stretching throughout the city. But none penetrated the "Liberia" of Ivan III, as the library became known. Even a secret subway designed to protect the rulers and generals never uncovered the treasures of the Byzantines.

As Moscow improved its infrastructure, numerous underground levels were built. While no one knows for sure, in some places it is believed there are as many as 12 levels underground. Subways, water tunnels, a sewage system, and the passageways that are long forgotten have never been mapped.

Nikita Khruschev, in the 1960s, brought about even more development under the Kremlin. He further extended the subway system and may have merged the secret subway with the public metro, although not all of it. The Arbatskaya station is just under the ministry of Defense and secret doors are always under active guard. While many stations are beautifully designed and appointed with artwork, no photographs are allowed. Tourists are sternly warned to not even *think* of sneaking a photo or two. Khruschev, too, wished to uncover the famed library. He instructed the project managers to take all steps necessary to locate and preserve with care the library of Ivan. But despite his instructions, all the dictator's men could not uncover what had been covered so long ago.

In the 1990s, the mayor of Moscow, Yuri Luzhkov, renewed the hunt for the library. One of the hopes of the search was possibly to open the

underground for tourism. Visitors to the Kremlin are often rudely awakened to the city's endless ability to charge admission to just about every building of interest. So the lost underground might prove another

Subway station on the Moscow Metro (Photo by Pete Verdon).

rich revenue source. Unfortunately for the mayor, the only new discovery was a tunnel filled with skeletons— the victims of Ivan IV's secret police.

Underground tourism so far has been confined to the underground shopping malls that contain Moscow's most posh shops.

In modern Russian media, stories of the secret subway have made their way into the tabloids and it is claimed that thousands are employed in both the secret transportation system and a secret city to which it connects six miles away. While the tabloid media is seldom reliable, a portion of the subway that connects the Kremlin to Moscow's airport is no longer a secret. It is, however, open only to government officials.

The Russian people cynically regard this secret subway as "Metro 2," although officials of the FSB (the successor to the KGB) are not amused. Journalists who have openly mentioned it have been subject to interrogation.

MOSCOW'S DIGGERS

Modern urban explorers, though, are braving the threat of government and are illegally transversing their city underground. They call themselves the "Diggers" and despite the military actively patrolling some of the complex tunnel system, they bravely risk arrest and subsequent consequences. Sewers, subway stations, and even the newly constructed underground shopping malls provide access to the subterranean world of catacombs, tunnels, bomb shelters, and secret vaults.

While the city has granted access to the tunnels to a handful of tour operators, the military is equally concerned with a terrorist group penetrating beneath the Kremlin. In 1988, near the Spasskiye Gate of the Kremlin, a construction project found a treasure hoard dating from the late Viking period. The works of both Scandinavian and Russian jewelers included items never found before in Russia, and most likely hidden during the Mongol invasions, were part of the discovery.

Must the world wait for another construction incident for the library to someday be unearthed? The founder of the Moscow Diggers, Vadim Mikhailov, told the *Ottawa Citizen* that he firmly believes the treasure will someday be found. He claims to have more information than anyone alive. His greatest source is a 90-year-old nearly-blind man nicknamed Appolos who claims to have found it. His poor treatment at the hands of the government is his reason for depriving the government of the location of this literary treasure.

Vadim and his group have broken through an underground brick wall directly into the Kremlin's Palace basement, now moldy from the flowing waters. They have found skulls, weapons, deserted passageways, and dry water courses. They even found radioactive material lying beneath the Moscow State University and alerted the government. They have also been threatened on occasion by the darker side of modern Russia: Gypsies, drug addicts, alcoholics, homeless families, and ex-convicts. On one occasion, the group aided police in recapturing three escaped murderers. On another, they instructed Moscow's elite Alpha unit on how to navigate the sewage tunnels to end a hostage crisis in the Dubrovka Theatre.

Will Vadim and the Diggers someday uncover the secret vault of Ivan's library, or will a future construction project uncover the priceless collection? What is fervently belived, at least by those who have investigated this treasure, is that it still exists, far below the Kremlin.

This article first appeared in *Atlantis Rising* #66 (November/December 2007).

8

NAZIS AND THE OCCULT

Just How Deep Did the Evil of the Third Reich Run?

BY MARK STAVISH

"It has been ordained by the Karma of the Germanic world that he (Hitler) should wage war against the East and save the Germanic peoples—a figure of the greatest brilliance has become incarnate in his person...whom men would regard in centuries to come with the same reverence that they had accorded to Christ."—Heinrich Himmler

Ordained, Karma, Incarnate, Christ. Words of a priest who would pretend to be a prophet. These are the words of Heinrich Himmler describing his Messiah, the dark soul of Adolph Hitler. This is not poetic license, or sentimental prose, but words of devotion, ideology, an apostle's creed, of the hidden, better-be-forgotten, occult mythology behind the Nazi movement.

ARIOSOPHISTRY AND THE RISE OF HITLER

The German Worker's Party (Deutche Arbeiterpartei, DAP) was founded at Munich in January, 1919, by Anton Drexler. Drexler was employed at the nearby locomotive factory and an associate of Baron Rudolph von Sebottendorf. The purpose of the Party was to promote German militarism, anti-semitism, and the doctrine of racial superiority, known as Ariosophistry.

It is because of Drexler's association with Sebottendorf that it is believed that the German Worker's Party served as the outer political wing of the Thule Society (Thule Gesellschaft), founded by Sebottendorf.

The Thule Society was a secret society operating in Germany that mixed right wing politics, occultism, and Teutonic paganism into a single belief system. Sebottendorf was a self-styled aristocrat who added "von" to his name to hide his more average origins as the son of a railway worker. Sebottendorf traveled extensively by working on a steamship and while visiting Egypt became interested in occultism, and may have been initiated into Islamic mystical practices while in Turkey. It was in Turkey that he began studying astrology, alchemy, and Rosicrucianism. In 1901, he was initiated into a Masonic lodge connected to the Grand Orient of France, a common feature among Masonic lodges in the Middle East. Nine years later, Sebottendorf formed his own society in Istanbul, combining his previous studies with right-wing politics and anti-semitism.

In 1916, after returning to Germany, he contacted the Order of Germans (Germanenorden) which by the end of the first world war had moved to Munich and changed its name to the Thule Gesellschaft, or Thule Society. The Germanenorden was formed to oppose the perceived Jewish-Masonic conspiracy to dominate the world, a favorite theme in nationalist circles of the period.

Thule was believed to be the prehistoric homeland of the German people, a kind of Nordic Atlantis. The newly named society continued to promote its brand of esotericism, including the return of the Hapsburg monarchy. By 1918, it had over 250 members in Munich, and almost 1,500 across Bavaria, with its headquarters consisting of several floors in the swank hotel Vierjahres-zeiten.

As its symbol, the Society chose a swastika (an ancient eastern religious symbol dating back to 2nd century BC) with a dagger enclosed in laurel leaves.

Thule members included the rich and the powerful from all areas of business, political, and military life, all predominantly upper and middle class. Franz Gurtner, Bavarian Minister of Justice before and during the Nazi period, was a member as was the Munich police commissioner, and Wilhelm Frick, assistant police chief, future Minister of the Interior for Hitler.

Dietrich Eckart (1868–1923), a publisher of anti-semetic materials, sponsored séances for prominent society members and published the Thule Society's newspaper, the "Volkischer Beobachter" or the "People's Observer." The VB was quickly absorbed and became the official organ of the Nazi Party. It was Eckart who introduced Hitler to the rich and powerful and taught him the etiquette needed for high society.

Unfortunately for Sebottendorf, his period of influence was over before Hitler's had even begun. By the time Hitler had obtained control of the German Worker's Party, Sebottendorf had resigned as head of the Thule Society. He attempted to revive the society in 1933, and quickly fell into disfavor with Nazi authorities for claiming to be the forerunner of National Socialism. After hearing of the German surrender, Rudolph von Sebottendorf, self-made aristocrat, would-be Grand Master of German occultism, and father of National Socialism, committed suicide in Turkey.

PROTOCOLS OF ZION, THE MASTER RACE AND GERMAN TEMPLARS

While Hitler and Hess were in prison for the failed *putsch*, Alfred Rosenberg, the official Party Philosopher, led the NSDAP from 1922–1924. Rosenberg, along with Eckart, were part of a plan to bring copies of *The Protocols of the Elders of Zion* into Germany to stir up anti-Jewish, Freemasonic, and Communist feelings.

Rosenberg believed that the Aryan race was the former priesthood of the antideluvian continent of Atlantis and had fled prior to its destruction, eventually settling in the Middle East, Mongolia, India, and Tibet. Rosenberg held to the earlier 19th century theosophical belief that the reason for Atlantis's destruction was that the gods were angry at the Atlanteans, who were mating women with animals and creating half-breeds to use as slaves. Many of these half-breeds survived in the existing "sub-human races" of the Jews, blacks, slavs, and others. Like other Nazi and right-wing Indiophiles, he saw the Hindu caste system as a shadow of the original racial divisions of prehistorical times.

Rosenberg flirted with the idea of pre-Christian Germanic paganism, asserting that Christianity was not strong enough for the German yolk. In an attempt to sway those Germans who might be turned off by the elimination of Christian churches by the Nazis, plans were made for the establishment of a National Reich Church, and Jesus was aryianized by making him blond. Rosenberg's book, *Mythus of the Twentieth Century,* which outlined his esoteric, neo-pagan, racist, and anti-Christian ideologoy, as well as its relationship to National Socialism, was the second best-selling book in the Third Reich next to *Mein Kampf.*

However, by 1940, Rosenberg had fallen out of influence, as he simply was not brutal enough to survive in Hitler's inner circle. While given several high-sounding titles, he had little power. Only his Einsatzstab Rosenberg (Special Section) managed to exercise any practical impact. Through his minions, Rosenberg looted the archives of dozens of occult, fraternal, and esoteric societies and orders across occupied Europe. The stolen goods were then shipped back to Germany for inclusion in a special

"Hohe Schule" (high school), which was to be the main intellectual center of National Socialism. Among those most seriously affected in these round-ups were the Freemasons, various Rosicrucian groups, Martinists, members of the Theosophical Society, Anthroposophists, and any group, organization, or printing house thought to have occult connections that could be used against the Nazis.

Karl Haushofer, Professor of "Geopolitics" at the University of Munich, advocated expansion into Asia in order to reclaim the original homelands of the Aryan people. It was in these lost lands that the Master Race of Aryans would reestablish their rightful place of power in the world. While a student in Munich, Rudolph Hess, future Deputy Füher, met Haushofer and became his assistant. How much influence Haushofer had on Hess's occult development is unknown.

However, Hess, like Himmler and Rosenberg, was one of the few leading Nazis who we know had a deep and lasting interest in the occult, wherever it may have come from. While Hess would fly to Scotland on an ill-fated and still unknown mission, and Rosenberg would fade into obscurity, left to loot the esoteric lodges and libraries of Europe, Himmler would remain true to his beliefs and retain power until the end.

Heinrich Himmler despised Christianity and renounced his Catholicism in 1936 to set an example for the SS rank and file. Like Hitler, Himmler believed that after the war, they could eliminate the churches altogether. However, he admired the church's organizational structure and began to model the SS after the Jesuit Order.

Himmler, Hitler & Hess

SECRET KNOWLEDGE

Incorporating ideas of Freemasonry, the Knights Templar, Teutonic Knights, the mythos of the Holy Grail and Round Table, Himmler began to create a secret society out of the SS. This society was to form the "elect" (auserwahit) who would serve the Fuhrer in his mission. This "elect" would consist of only those who believed in a supreme being, called "*der Uralte* or *Altvater*," and "...in the Führer Adolf Hitler whom He sent to us."

Himmler believed that he was the reincarnation of Heinrich der Lowe, Duke of Saxony and Bavaria (1129–1195), and enjoyed being referred to as "King Henry." He read, and esteemed highly, Buddhist, Hindu, and Zoroastrian holy scriptures along with the Vedas, and astrological writings.

Every King must have his castle and Himmler was no different. Complete with Round Table, monastic cells, and coats-of-arms for his chosen Grüppenführer, who were the spiritual elect of the elect, the castle at Wewelsburg, near Paderborn, was to be the capital of a future SS state.

In the North Tower they were to meet at planned ritualistic intervals, and in the tower crypt an eternal flame burned. Renovated by slave labor from a nearby concentration camp, esoteric symbolism was used throughout the structure. The entire town was to be rebuilt so that it radiated out in concentric circles, with the main road forming the shaft of a spear, and the triangular castle its point. Himmler believed that the castle lay on a mystical power grid, known as ley lines by dowsers, and was the "center of the world" (Mittlepunkt der Welt), a theme in Nordic mythology.

This ideology of revived romantic Germanic paganism was not limited to the leadership alone, although they were seen as its best and most capable. For the officers of the SS, special training schools were established known as Ordensburgen. These Ordensburgen were under Himmler's direct supervision, and as such, even higher than the previous Junkerschulen led by Reichleiter Ley, and the later "SS-Verfungungstruppen." Here, ideological training was given prime importance (and the reason for higher than average SS casualties early in the war), and equinox and solstice ceremonies were celebrated along with Hitler's birthday. SS weddings were pre-Christian in design, with the married couple being instructed to sire their offspring near the tombs of fallen Nordic heroes so that those heroes might reincarnate into the newborn. To facilitate couples in their duty, listings of preferred cemeteries appeared in SS newspapers.

Actual membership in the SS was an important ceremony in which the ring and dagger were bestowed upon the candidate. The magical ring and ceremonial dagger are two of the most important magical items in occultism, and suggest strongly the notion and symbolism of the SS as a secret society. The ring was given to those who had great devotion to the organization and its mission, the dagger as a symbol of the candidate's mission, and the sword, the highest symbol of all, was bestowed only on those who were members of the innermost circle.

While many of the SS leaders saw their task as political and military, and tolerated Himmler's idiosyncrasies, it was clear to Himmler and Hitler, as it had been to Hess, and the still hopeful Rosenberg, that National Socialism was a religious, albeit quasi-mystical, movement drawing on the inherent mythological desires of the German people.

American William Shirer, an early 20th century war journalist, writes, "He [Hitler] is restoring pageantry and color and mysticism to the drab lives of twentieth-century Germans." In his description of the seven-day-long Nuremberg rallies, Shirer states that the Nazi's were successful because they offered not only a political ideology but a philosophical one, complete with cosmology, as well.

Blood became the rallying point of the movement. "Blood and Honor" was engraved upon the daggers and minds of the Hitler Youth. "Sieg Heil" and "Heil Hitler" were the mantras and prayers of a nation. They were sacred rituals allowing the German people to touch the supernatural. Even the Mayor of Hamburg proclaimed, "We need no priests. We can communicate direct with God through Adolph Hitler."

The most sacred relic of the movement, however, was the Blood Flag, carried during the ill-fated putsch in Munich. Exhibited only twice a year after 1933, it was elevated to icon status, and with its unveiling, was read the roll call of martyrs. Those initiated into the fold were done so using the *blutfahne* (blood flag), and each banner passing in succession was brought into contact with it. Like a perverse form of apostolic succession, or esoteric initiation, contact with the relic, this blood talisman, was the means of linking each member and each banner with the great stream of National Socialism.

Although used by other groups, and rooted deep in western and eastern symbolism, the swastika was picked by the Thule Society because it represented the solar myths of pre-Christian Europe. Hitler adopted it as the symbol of the Nazi Party, and a leading member of both organizations, Dr. Fredrick Kohn, presented the final version of the flag to Hitler. While sticking to the original design, Hitler turned the swastika counter-clockwise, in turn, making it the traditional symbol of death.

Even those who did not believe in the metaphysical rationale given as the force behind National Socialism, men such as Bormann, and even rank and file Party and SS men, confessed to believing in a superior being, or "Gottglaubig." This "belief in God" was required for admittance into the SS, even if its more bizarre beliefs were not adhered to, with atheism being a worse offense than receiving Christian sacraments, and cause for denial of membership or dismissal.

Hitler (Art by Randy Haragan)

THE CRACKDOWNS

For those who belonged to esoteric organizations, fraternal orders with esoteric overtones, such as Freemasonry, even if the teachings were absent, or simply practiced astrology, psychicism, or parapsychology on their own, life inside the Third Reich was even harsher than usual.

If Hitler was god incarnate, Himmler his priest, Hess his scribe, and the SS its disciples, then there could be no alternatives.

The first crackdowns against what were officially viewed as competing forces began in Germany itself. In 1933, the Fraternity of Saturn, a 300-year-old occult order, was shut down. In 1934, official actions against Freemasons began, and the enforcing of the so-called "witchcraft laws" against "occult manifestations" (stopped by Rudolph Hess) followed by the banning of the Anthroposophical Society in 1935, and its sister sect, the Christian League in 1941. In 1937 several of the leading occult and mystical organizations in Germany were closed down, including many smaller ones who had even helped the Nazis in their seizure of power.

One month after Hess's flight to Great Britain, in June 1940, "Aktion Hess" was undertaken across all of occupied Europe. The action was so named as it was thought that somehow occultists had influenced or tricked Hess into flying to Great Britain, resulting in his subsequent capture. Thousands of affiliated and independent occultists, publishers, and astrologers were arrested and interrogated. Special, poorly worded questions were even sent from Berlin to assist in the questioning. Many of those arrested were even forced to participate in Nazi-sponsored parapsychology experiments, although morale was poor, and results negligible.

Not to be outdone by their German occupiers, Vichy French authorities were among the first to independently crack down on secret societies, particularly in Southern France, a historical center of occult activity. Here, even the Catholic Church joined in the bloodletting, supporting the elimination of what it has always considered heretics and undesirables.

Prior to the war, particularly in France, and for decades after it, much has been written and said about the occult influences behind the Nazi movement. Most of it is sensationalized fiction passed as second- and third-hand research and not worth reading.

However, occult ideas did shape the formation of the National Socialist ideology, that is clear. Fortunately, they did little else, and what activity was carried out during the war—Himmler's castle, Rosenberg's Hohe Schule, and so forth—was to be of use "after a successful conclusion of hostilities." Within the Nazi movement the emphasis on ideology slid increasingly into the background, limited to research centers such as the SS-Ahnenerbe, or the persecution of non-Nazi esoteric societies, through Gestapo Section IV-B, as the war dragged on.

The failure to stop or even prevent National Socialism prior to the military conflict was a result of the inability to understand its deeper roots. National Socialism, by the admission of its creators, and denied by its prosecutors and historians alike, was never simply a political movement. It was, and continues to be, primarily a metaphysical one, with deep roots in the human psyche. Yearnings for a "Golden Age," messiahs, and saviors who free us from responsibility, promises of becoming one of the chosen, the elect who rule, and commune with the ancestral spirits and forces of the race, and the need to control and be controlled—all are what lead us down the path of doom, of which National Socialism is the leading example.

This article first appeared in *Atlantis Rising* #59 (September/October 2006).

9

UNEASY STONE

The Ancient British "Stone of Destiny" Has Had a Checkered—if Not Magical—History

BY PHILIP COPPENS

The "Stone of Destiny," the stone placed inside the coronation chair upon which British monarchs are crowned, could be as recent as five decades old, seven centuries, or even three, if not more, millennia. Known as the Stone of Destiny—or Stone of Scone, after the Scottish castle where the Scottish kings were formerly crowned—it used to sit under the coronation chair in London's Westminster Abbey, until Thursday, November 14, 1996. On St. Andrew's Day, November 30, 1996, the stone went on display in Edinburgh Castle, with the intention to shuttle the stone back to Westminster Abbey for future coronations of the British monarch.

Edinburgh Castle in Scotland was one of several candidates for displaying the stone, and it was chosen for tourist, rather than a historical, reasons. The stone used to sit in Scone, now a suburb of Perth, on the Moot Hill, next to Scone Palace. The Hill was created by sand, brought in the boots of those lords who had sworn allegiance to the Scottish king. Here, Scottish kings were crowned, coinciding with regal processions.

The relationship between Scotland and England has never been straightforward. In 1296, Edward I of England annexed Scotland—remember the film *Braveheart?*—and took the Stone of Scone, which functioned as a talisman to the Scots, south of the border. The stone weighed 990 kilos, and Edward I had iron rings fixed to each side for its journey south. It would remain in England until 1996 . . . or rather, 1951. For it was in 1950 that the Stone was stolen from Westminster, on Christmas morning. Though often perceived as a student prank, one of the protagonists, Ian Hamilton, has always tried to make clear that he did it with political motivations. When the police believed the Stone was making its way back to Scotland, the border between Scotland and England was closed, for the first time in 400 years. But despite these efforts, the stone did make it into

Scotland, where it was "left to be found" shortly afterward, after which it was taken back to Westminster.

The culprits were never charged, as the Crown Prosecution could apparently never make the argument that the Crown actually owned the Stone. Possession, it seems, is often nine-tenths of the law even when it comes to the Crown itself. But amidst all of this legalese, modern legends were created—if not fabricated—to underline the pain of the Scots over "their Stone" being in England.

Hence, some believe that the real Stone was substituted with a copy in 1951. Amateur historian Archie McKerracher states that Bertie Gray not only made a copy of the stone in 1928, but that he also made one in 1950. He thinks that the 1950 copy is the one that was returned to Westminster Abbey. "The 1928 copy which wasn't quite as accurate is in the church in Dundee, and the Westminster Stone is at a secret location in the Arbroath area . . . it is produced on certain occasions and taken through the streets of Arbroath. I don't think the Westminster people, having got a stone back, were going to quibble."

If the real stone was substituted with a copy in 1950, then this would make the stone on display in Edinburgh Castle in 1996—a fake. But even if that were the case, there are those who doubt that the stone taken by Edward I in 1296 was the real one. Author Pat Gerber believes a fake stone was given to him, with the real stone secreted somewhere nearby. It may explain why Edward I sent a raiding party of knights back to Scone on August 17, 1298. They ripped the Abbey apart in a desperate search. But for what? The real Stone? Whatever they were looking for, it is known that they returned empty-handed. Furthermore, Gerber and others point out that the Treaty of Northampton in 1328 included the offer of return of the Stone. But the Scots did not ask for the insertion of that clause. Edward III offered it again in 1329, even suggesting the Queen Mother could take it to Berwick. Offered a final time in 1363, again, the Scots did not seem to want their talisman back. Did they know the "real one" being offered was false?

So, is the "official" Stone of Destiny the real deal? Cambray, in his *Monuments Celtiques,* claims to have seen the stone when it bore the inscription: "Ni fallat fatum, Scoti quocumque locatum Invenient lapidiem, regnasse tenetur ibidem": "If the Destiny proves true, then the Scots are known to have been Kings wherever men find this stone." There is no such inscription on the current official Stone.

In 1968, Wendy Wood wrote that she went to Westminster Abbey "and slipped a piece of cardboard under the complicated iron railings, on which was printed, 'This is not the original Stone of Destiny. The real Stone is of black basalt marked with hieroglyphics and is inside a hill in Scotland.'" She was referring to Dunsinnan Hill, a hill to the east of Scone, and a story that has been popular for many decades.

In the late 19th century, Seton Gordon stated that the Earl of Mansfield, whose family has owned the lands of Scone for more than 300 years, had told him of a tradition that had been handed down through several generations. It stated that somewhere around the dates 1795–1820, a farm lad had been wandering with a friend on Dunsinnan Hill after a violent storm. The torrential rain had caused a landslide, and as a result of this, a fissure, which seemed to penetrate deep into the hillside, was visible. "The two men procured some form of light and explored the fissure. They came at last to the broken wall of a subterranean chamber. In one corner of the chamber was a stair which was blocked with debris, and in the center of the chamber they saw a slab of stone covered with markings and supported by four stone 'legs.' As there was no other evidence of 'treasure' in the subterranean apartment, the two men did not realize the importance of their 'find' and did not talk of what they had seen. Some years later, one

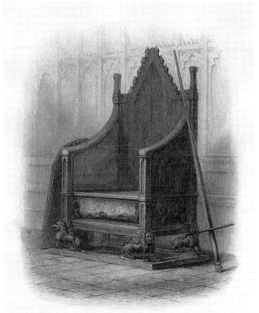

19th century depiction of the coronation chair in Westminster Abbey with the Stone of Destiny beneath.

of the men first heard the local tradition, that on the approach of King Edward I, the monks of Scone hurriedly removed the Stone of Destiny to a place of safe concealment and took from the Annety Burn a stone of similar size and shape, which the English King carried off in triumph. When he heard this legend, the man hurried back to Dunsinnan Hill, but whether his memory was at fault regarding the site of the landslide, or whether the passage of time, or a fresh slide of earth had obliterated the cavity, the fact remains that he was unable to locate the opening in the hillside. It may be asked why the monks of Scone, after the English king had returned to England, did not bring back to the abbey the original Stone of Destiny; but the tradition accounts for this, explaining that it was not considered safe at the time to allow the English to know that they had been tricked, and that when the days of possible retribution were past, the monks who had known the secret were dead. This tradition, it is held, explains why the Coronation Stone in Westminster Abbey resembles geologically the sandstone commonly found in the neighborhood of Scone."

It does appear that the stone in Westminster Abbey/Edinburgh Castle is sandstone, and is thus perhaps local to Scone. And if so, it may be the official "Stone of Scone," but not the real one. For according to legend, the Stone of Scone did not come from Scotland, but from Ireland, and before that Spain, and before that Egypt, and before that . . . the Holy Land.

But before retracing this voyage, amidst this myriad of possibilities, let us note what is known. It is known that at least by AD 906, Scone was a royal city and that kings were crowned on the royal stone chair. According to an old chronicler, "no king was ever wont to reign in Scotland unless he had first, on receiving the royal name, sat upon this stone at Scone, which by the kings of old had been appointed to the capital of Alba."

Though "typically Scottish," its origins do not seem to be Scottish at all. Around the time the Stone was taken to England, Robert of Gloucester (1240–1300) wrote that the first Irish immigrants brought the stone with them into Scotland, stating it was a "whyte marble ston." So rather than sandstone, or black basalt, the stone is then said to be white marble. As Robert of Gloucester wrote at a time when an official stone was still in residence in Scone, his account of the nature of the stone carries much weight—and would indeed indicate that the official Stone is a fake.

But the history goes further back in time than Ireland. Hector Boece wrote in the *Scotorum Historiae* in 1537, that Gaythelus, a Greek, the son either of the Athenian Cecrops or the Argive Neolus, went to Egypt at the time of the Exodus, where he married Scota, the daughter of the Pharaoh, and after the destruction of the Egyptian army in the Red Sea, fled with her by the Mediterranean until he arrived in Portingall, where he landed, and founded a kingdom at Brigantium, now Santiago de Compostella. Here he reigned in the marble chair, which was the "lapis fatalis cathedrae instar," or "fatal stone like chair," and wherever it was located, portended kingdom to the Scots—those who had followed Scotia in exile.

Simon Breck, a descendant of Gaythelus, brought the chair from Spain to Ireland, and was crowned in it as King of Ireland. Later, Fergus, son of Ferchard, was first King of the Scots in Scotland, and brought the chair from Ireland to Argyll, and was crowned in it. He built a town in Argyll called Beregonium, in which he placed the Stone. The 12th king, Evenus, built a town near Beregonium, called after his name Evonium, now called Dunstaffnage, to which the stone was moved. Dunstaffnage is near Oban, on the west coast of Scotland, and the same legend states that Fergus MacErc built a church on the island of Iona, and commanded it to be the sepulchre of the future kings. It should no longer come as a surprise that some argue that the "real stone" never came to Scone, but instead remained "somewhere" in or near Dunstaffnage.

Iona was indeed a sacred island, "in the West," of pagan religious importance, for it became one of the key objectives of early Christianity to have it as a power base. As funerals of kings and coronation ceremonies go hand in hand, the stone's location in Dunstaffnage would make great sense, because of its proximity to Iona.

There are several ancient accounts that speak of the foreign origins of this stone, though not all accounts are identical—they do largely overlap. The "Scalacronica," compiled in AD 1355, states that Simon Brec, the youngest son of the King of Spain, brought the stone from Spain, where it was used for coronations. Brec "placed it in the most sovereign beautiful place in Ireland, called to this day the Royal Place (Tara), and Fergus, son of Ferchar, brought the royal stone before received, and placed it where is now the Abbey of Scone." In this account, there is no stop-over in Dunstaffnage, but the story does identify the Stone of Scone with the "Lia Fail," "the speaking stone," which named the king who would be chosen. Its residence was the coronation place of Ireland, Tara, near modern Dublin.

A similar account can be found in the *Scotichronicon*, compiled in 1386, which repeats that Gaythelus married Scota and led those that survived the disaster to Spain. Simon Brec then went to Ireland, setting up the stone in Tara, before Fergus took it to Scotland.

Legend, or a memory of a real odyssey? Historians are quick to condemn, but perhaps we should not be so quick. Herodotus stated that the enigmatic Etruscans that lived near Rome originally migrated to Italy from the Near East, an "opinion" archaeologists have largely disregarded and denigrated. Herodotus stated they emigrated from Lydia, a region on the eastern coast of ancient Turkey. After an 18-year-long famine in Lydia, Herodotus reports, the king dispatched half of the population to look for a better life elsewhere. The emigrating Lydians built ships, loaded all the things they needed, and sailed from Smyrna (Izmir) until they reached Umbria, in Italy. For millennia, that is where the debate rested. But recently, geneticists have shown that the Etruscans—and their cattle—did migrate to Italy from the Near East, vindicating Herodotus. And as there is a logical reason why these Egyptians would have fled their country, dismissing the possibility of the legend of the Stone of Destiny as a factual account, may come to haunt those who do so too vociferously.

In case you wonder whether in an Egyptian context the stone might have been "white marble," the answer is possibly—if not probably—yes. Though some have argued that Jacob's stone (his famous "pillow" described in the Bible) may have been a meteorite and that its iron content may have instigated his vision, sacred stones made in marble are known in ancient Greece: the so-called *omphalos* stones, not only markers of the "center of the world," but also linked with oracles (sacred visions, such as Jacob's) and centers of "divine kingship," such as that of the Scottish monarchs. For the link between such stones and visions is definitely known to be extremely old, such as in the Egyptian coronation and Heb Sed festivals, in which the ceremony involved a ritual in which the Pharaoh was asked not merely to unite "the land," but also the land with "the Afterworld."

In Scone, the land was symbolized by the combined earth, carried in the boots of the vassals, making the Moot Hill into a primordial hill. But if this Stone was of Egyptian origin, it may indeed have been the desire of this Egyptian princess, Scota, to take the coronation stone with her, so that it would not fall into the hands of the invaders. And if—*if*—the Stone in Edinburgh Castle is indeed the original Stone, then it may—*may*—be that Scottish and British kings have been crowned according to a tradition of sacred kingship. The British Queen or King is, of course, even without the Stone, one of the few remaining heads of State that is also the Head of the Church. And thus, the Stone, whether real or merely symbolic, continues to play a key role in a tradition of sacred kingship, which in the 21st century has become extremely rare.

This article first appeared in *Atlantis Rising* #73 (January/February 2009).

10

THE RETURN OF THE
KING OF THE WORLD

*Why Myths and Legends from Many Cultures
Share This Common Theme*

BY MARK AMARU PINKHAM

The legends and scriptures of the Near and Far East are full of references to an ancient "King of the World" who supposedly ruled the earth thousands or even millions of years ago and is destined to make his reappearance on the world stage as we inch toward a new age.

The Tibetans maintain the King of the World resides in Shambhala, the fabled Land of the Immortals, and has been patiently waiting for hundreds and thousands of years for an opportunity to lead his army out of his kingdom to destroy the darkness and "evil" that covers the planet during its latter days. The Buddhist Lamas in Mongolia echo this Tibetan belief, although they differ from their Asian neighbors by asserting that the home of the world's monarch is Agharti, a subterranean kingdom underlying much of continental Asia. But in tandem with their Tibetan neighbors the Mongolians similarly assert, "The King of the World will appear before all people when the time shall have arrived for him to lead all good people of the world against the bad." (from *Beasts, Men and Gods*, p. 317).

Perplexed by these exotic prophecies regarding the King of the World, Westerners have long debated over their merits and whether they should be interpreted literally and/or figuratively. Is the King of the World an actual human entity, or is he an energy or spirit that will in some way transform and cleanse the world when it re-emerges? What could be proof of the monarch's physical existence, however, may have come to light over the past two hundred years through the expeditions of such Western explorers as Nicholas Roerich and Ferdinand Ossendowski. These Russian explorers crossed the deserts and mountains of eastern Asia during the 1920s and returned from their travels with documented testimonies from those who claimed to have seen the King of the World during his appearances in India, Mongolia, Tibet, and Thailand.

In the book of his travels, *Beasts, Men and Gods* (1945), Ossendowski even claims that during his visit to the Mongolian monastery in Narabanchi he was shown a chair the planetary ruler is alleged to have sat upon in 1891 while making prophecies to the resident monks regarding the ensuing fifty-year period. Following this revelation his Buddhist guides told Ossendowski that the ancient name of the King of the World was "Om," and that he was "the first Guru" and "the first man to know God." Because of his saintly character, they stated, "God gave him power over all forces ruling the visible world." But once Ossendowski left Mongolia, a fascist regime descended upon the country and the Russian's sources regarding the King of the World quickly dried up. The same must be said for Roerich, whose information related to the world's monarch was derived principally from Tibetan Lamas who greeted him as he visited their monasteries with ecstatic cries of "It is the time of Shambhala!" meaning the world's king was soon to emerge from his land of Shambhala and initiate a new age. But Tibet's king and the golden age he was heralding never materialized, and soon after Roerich left the mountainous Asia country; soon after it was ravaged by Chinese Communists and its monks slaughtered. But because of this twist of fate, should the West now turn a deaf ear to prophecies regarding the King of the World?

"King of Shambhala" (Nicholas Roerich, Zanabazar Art Museum, Ulaan Baatar, Mongolia).

What if the "monarch's" re-entrance onto the world stage was delayed or miscalculated? And what if his reappearance was always destined to occur in a different location? There is, in fact, another location in Asia's southern extremity which for hundreds and thousands of years has also been referred to as a home of the King of the World and the place he will reemerge from. This is the tiny island nation of Sri Lanka, where within the small temple city of Kataragama the adherents of three major religions currently join together to worship this deity who has been called "King of the World." In the traditions of the Moslem Sufis, who refer to him as Al-Khadir, it is believed that this semi-mythical deity makes a public appearance at Kataragama every 500 years. The world has currently reached the end of another 500-year cycle, which is why many Sufis are making annual visits to Sri Lanka in hopes of catching a glimpse of their deity. According to their prophecies, the current reappearance of the world monarch will be very special because it will mark the beginning of a golden age.

There is certainly a case that can be made for the "monarch" having chosen Sri Lanka as his headquarters in the ancient past. For example, Moslems throughout the world claim that the island is the site of the original Garden of Eden, and as proof of this they refer a seeker of the truth to the top of the island's second highest mountain, Adam's Peak, where set into stone is a five-foot long footprint they claim was made by Adam when God set the first man in the Garden of Eden. If the Moslems are right about Sri Lanka being the birthplace of human civilization it would follow that it could also have become home to the world's first ruler. In support of the Moslems' assertions regarding the island many mythologists, geologists, adherents of continental drift theory, and proponents of esoteric history have argued that Sri Lanka should be considered the Garden of Eden because it was once part of a larger Pacific continent that they regard as the "Cradle of Civilization." Also known as Lemuria, Mu, and Kumari Nadu, the "Land of the Sons of God," as well as Hiva, "the Motherland," and Havaii-ti-Havaii, "the place where life began and developed," the various names of this ancient land support its claim of being at least a Garden of Eden. Its claim to being the first civilization has most recently been researched by Stephen Oppenheimer, author of *Eden in the East* (1998), who lived in southeast Asia for many years while compiling reams of information claiming that many of the world's customs, legends, and languages were derived from "Sundaland," which is a name for the western extreme of Lemuria that is currently underwater. This sunken land mass, located in the Malaysia Archipelago, was above water as recently as 11,000 years ago when it served as the "Garden of Eden" and cradle of civilization for much of the language and culture that eventually covered Asia and Europe.

When the early Theosophists made Adyar, India, their world headquarters in the 19th century, their researchers found evidence that Lemuria was not only the Garden of Eden but also home to an ancient "King of the World." In some south Indian scriptures they discovered maps showing Sri Lanka and India joined to Lemuria as late as 30,000 BC, and later while poring over ancient Hindu and Tibetan scriptures they found references to Lemuria as being the place where the Sons of God, or Kumaras (their Sanskrit name), first taught humanity the path of spiritual transformation that leads to communion with God. It was their leader, Sanat Kumara, who is said to have become both the world's first Guru as well as its first monarch, thus elevating him to the throne of a planetary theocracy with himself as its priest king. The Theosophists also discovered that when Sanat Kumara became the first King of the World he merged his spirit with that of the earth's to become our planet's virtual will and mind, or as they called it, the Planetary Logos. After this merger was complete, it was said, the will of Sanat Kumara manifested as the actions of all creatures that lived and walked upon the earth, which had become his physical body. As far as humanity was concerned, Sanat Kumara became our collective mind, our collective consciousness. We were him and he was us. So when humans developed an ego and "fell," so did the world monarch, which is why the King of the World eventually became associated with the egotistical Lucifer during the Christian era. But before any Luciferian associations were ascribed to the King of the World he had been worshipped during the Neolithic Age as the Green Man, with his physical body being associated with the earth's prodigious vegetation. At that time, when the world's principal deity was the Goddess, it was said that the King of the World was the Son of the Goddess who was born annually from the body of his mother, the solid earth, in the spring and then died each autumn. Eventually the first resurrection legend emerged which stated that the Son of the Goddess lived and died each year and then was reborn the following spring.

The name discovered in the ancient texts for the King of the World, Sanat Kumara, is also a name he is known by within the temple city of Kataragama, Sri Lanka, where Buddhists, Moslems, and Hindus currently join together for his worship. Here the monarch's scepter is a golden spear, his symbol is the Tamil Om, and his sacred animal is the ferocious lion, king of the jungle. Sanat Kumara's sacred bird and mount is the peacock, an animal that has become throughout India, Tibet, China, and Sri Lanka a symbol for the primal guru and a head of state. Hindu legend claims that the king was given the throne of the world by his parents, Shiva and Shakti, and a replica of his Peacock Throne can be found at his temple city in Palni, India.

Besides Sanat Kumara, the monarch's Hindu epithets include: Murugan, Skanda, and Karttikeya, the Commander of the Celestial Army. The Moslems at Kataragama know him as Al-Khadir, the "Green Man," and also venerate him as the "Initiator" who discovered the fountain of youth. Outside of Sri Lanka and India he is known by similar names and regal associations. For many ages the Greeks and Egyptians have known him as their legendary monarchs Dionysus and Osiris. According to history, when the Greeks arrived in Sri Lanka under the command of Alexander the Great they visited Kataragama and instantly recognized Sanat Kumara, exclaiming, "We know him, he is our Dionysus!" Tibetan Buddhists no doubt have a similar experience when visiting Kataragama. Similar to Sanat Kumara, the spirit of their King of the World in Shambhala, Amitibha, rides upon a peacock, and the flag of the fabled land is the Peacock Banner. Within the Jewish tradition Sanat Kumara has been associated with King Melchizedek, and in Sumerian legends he has been linked to Ea or Enki, whose names denote "Lord of Wisdom" and "Lord of the World."

A popular depiction of the "King of Agharti."

In my book *The Truth Behind the Christ Myth: The Redemption of the Peacock Angel* I trace the movement of Sanat Kumara's myth as it traveled westward from Lemuria and across Asia during which time the monarch was adopted by the Persians as their King of the World, Mithra, while also becoming Melek or Malak Taus, the "Peacock King" or "Peacock Angel," the legendary world monarch of the Yezidi people of northern Iraq. It was through their interactions with the Yezidi and the Sufis during the 12th and 13th centuries that the Knights Templar became familiar with the King of the World and nominated him their patron, St. George, which means the man of *geo*, the Earth Man or Green Man. When the Templars returned to Europe and authored the original Holy Grail manuscripts, they wove the King of the World into their story as the Fisher King, the original Guardian of the Holy Grail and preserver of the secrets of immortality. In Knight Wolfram von Eschenbach's Parzival, the Fisher King reveals his heritage by wearing a hat made of peacock feathers.

Thus, Sri Lanka's claim to being the Garden of Eden and home of the first world monarch can be supported by both history and science. But the question still remains, will this semi-mythical King of the World manifest in a physical human form on the island? Certain Sufi leaders, such as Sheikh Nazim Adil Al-Haqqani, world leader of the ancient and prestigious Naqsh-bandhia Order of Sufis, are convinced that he will and they are currently making annual visits to Kataragama to catch a glimpse of him when he does. They believe their Al-Khadir is an immortal master who will herald the onset of a golden age. They claim that he anciently discovered the water of immortality near Kataragama, in a place where the Menik Ganga, the "River of Gems," merges with the underground Current of Grace, thus both making him immortal and giving him the ability to assist others in achieving that hallowed goal. He has been known to appear physically to those Sufis who have been destined to achieve physical or spiritual immortality. This is why Al-Khadir is also known as the Sufi "Initiator."

The physical appearance of Al-Khadir or Sanat Kumara has certainly not been an anomaly to the natives living in the area in and around Kataragama. In fact, they claim that he has been appearing to them for ages. They speak of a tree near Kataragama where Sanat Kumara has appeared in order to claim the fruits, flowers, and other offerings set out for him. And they also report that he has appeared to the natives in times of stress or crisis in the form of a young boy or even as an old man or woman. Within the temple compound of Kataragama Sanat Kumara has, for hundreds and thousands of years, also appeared physically to many yogis who come there to undergo intense meditation and austerities. This includes the famous two-thousand-year-old yogi named Babaji, who after performing intense spiritual disciplines for 48 days learned the secrets of immortality from Sanat Kumara when the world guru blessed him with his appearance.

But while his physical appearance is prophesied, some alternative thinkers believe that at this time in history it is more important that the ancient priest king manifest in another of his forms, that of a force or power to alchemically transform the planet. One of those is that of the transformative Kundalini, a power that humans desperately need now in order to keep pace with the earth's evolution to ascend to a higher frequency.

This article first appeared in *Atlantis Rising* #64 (July/August 2007).

PART THREE

EGYPTIAN MYSTERIES

Art by Ron O. Cook

11

ATLANTIS & THE GREAT PYRAMID

Is There Any Connection?

BY FRANK JOSEPH

The foreign tourists aboard our bus were worried because one of its headlights was out and the other flickered uncertainly. Combined with our driver's kamikaze-like recklessness in maneuvering through the densely packed nighttime streets over-crowded with cars, mules, carts, pedestrians, and other careening buses, some catastrophic mishap seemed inevitable. But we were unaware that the free-for-all traffic patterns of modern Cairo represented standard driving practices in the United Arab Republic.

All of us wanted to see the Great Pyramid after dark, under the moon and stars of Egypt. It would be my first time. There was going to be a "sound and light show," in which the Great Sphinx and its pyramidal companions were bathed in various colored spotlights, while a taped, dramatic narrative, alternating in French, German, and English language versions, related the site's history. I felt fully prepared. I knew what I was going to see. It was the fulfillment of a dream nurtured in childhood and all the years since. How many books I read about this place I could not recall. I was familiar with all the theories about the colossal enigma on the Giza Plateau, from no-nonsense archaeologists, who dismissed the structure as an over-sized tomb for some megalomaniacal pharaoh, to religious fanatics, who claimed it foretold the Second Coming. Theories that included any kind of "pyramid power" were the only explanations I refused to even consider at the time. Serious enthusiasts parading in public wearing copper-tube pyramids as headgear were not convincing. But then, neither was anybody else. No one really seemed to know anything with certainty about the Great Pyramid. Perhaps after seeing it in person, one or a combination of these numerous speculations might make sense.

Our bus jostled through the deepening night, as we pulled out of the big, ugly city. We still had a way to go before reaching our goal. Suddenly, someone shouted, "Look, there it is!" I turned around to face the open window behind me. A dramatic cymbal crash would have been appropriate just then. Quite unexpectedly, I beheld a huge apparition, hardly more than a triangular shadow looming against Cairo's artificial glare, and caught my breath. Without thinking (my mind seemed paralyzed at the sight), I sensed, in a flash, that the Great Pyramid was, strange to tell, broadcasting on some incredibly powerful frequency. In view of what I since learned, that first impression may have been more insightful than I realized at the time.

From grammar school days, probably a month did not pass when I did not wonder about the Great Pyramid: How was it built, when, by whom and for what purpose? These are questions people have been asking for thousands of years. And I seemed no closer to the answers when I began organizing my research papers about an apparently unrelated subject. In spring, 1995, I was trying to systematize several thick volumes of handwritten notes collected over the previous 15 years and tens of thousands of travel miles on behalf of investigating the credibility of Atlantis, the lost civilization described by Plato. In the midst of simply cataloging my profuse information, unsummoned and almost of their own accord, all the data I had been storing for a decade and a half suddenly began tumbling out into my everyday thoughts and arranging themselves into patterns and themes previously unconsidered.

Almost at once, every piece fell into place, and some of the hitherto insoluble enigmas of Atlantis and the Great Pyramid stood fully revealed, like twin Athenas sprung mature and in full armor from the forehead of Zeus. I simultaneously saw both mysteries as through a lens that allowed me, for the first time, to behold them in a clear, inter-validating relationship. It was not a question of endeavoring to prove one unknown by another. After all, the Great Pyramid still stands on Egypt's Giza Plateau, and Atlantis was described by the greatest mind in the Classical World. Who built the Great Pyramid, when, how, and, most importantly, why seemed now self-evident. Determining its true purpose led directly to the identity of its architects and the actual date for its construction.

At first, Atlantis and the Great Pyramid appeared unrelated. Both belonged to the Ancient World—one a "myth" the other a "tomb"—but that seemed the end of it. One single piece of information, however, began to unlock a vast stock-pile of evidence that confirms and elucidates their otherwise unsuspected association: The citadel of Atlantis, where the holy-of-holies was enshrined, as defined by Plato, was the same diameter (758 feet) as the base side of the Great Pyramid. This revelation becomes clear only after the dimensions of the citadel, as given in Greek stadia for Plato's account, are transposed into an original Egyptian unit of measurement, known as the *aroura*.

While such a parallel between Atlantis and the Great Pyramid might be coincidental in and of itself, an abundance of related information underscores its validity a thousand times over. If, as many archaeologists suspect, the Pyramid originally sat in the middle of a moat connected by causeways or canals, its physical resemblance to the innermost island, the sacred hub of Atlantis, becomes yet more clear. It would appear that the Great Pyramid was intended to simulate or memorialize the lost holy of holies. The identical dimensions of the Atlantean citadel and the base of the Great Pyramid comprise the first step in a grand staircase leading inevitably to mankind's most profound historical mystery. But the story of their relationship must, of course, begin in Egypt, where the foremost building on earth reveals itself in ten inescapable conclusions:

1) Geodetic information implicit in the Great Pyramid's construction demonstrates that its builders knew the size, shape, and position of all the continents in such detail that they accurately determined the precise center of the earth's land-mass.

2) They understood and applied the fundamental nature of telluric or natural "earth-energy" forces.

3) The pyramid builders possessed a technology sufficient to design and build a piezo-electric transducer to harness those forces.

4) Their geologic sciences and construction arts were at least the equal to, and in some respects superior to, our own.

5) They somehow foresaw some inevitable celestial catastrophe with a potential for extraordinary destructiveness. As the object's orbit began to noticeably decay, ground-observers concluded that an impact with our planet was unavoidable, and began to prepare for the event by constructing a device that would bolster earth's ionosphere, thereby deflecting the course of the falling object.

Atlantis Rising artwork

6) The pyramid builders erected their geotransducer because they understood that the earth was periodically endangered by recurring cycles of celestial bombardments. The Great Pyramid was built to guard against future collisions from outer space.

In his dialogue *The Timaeus*, Plato spoke of "a declination of the bodies moving around the earth and in the heavens, and a great conflagration of things upon the earth recurring at long intervals of time." In the late 1980s, the noted astronomers Victor Clube and William Napier showed that the earth passes within general proximity, sometimes much nearer and infrequently through a "cloud" or "swarm" of meteoric debris every early November, still the best time for viewing shooting stars in the northern hemisphere (*Cosmic Winter*, 1988). They determined that this meteoric cloud is today only a pale remnant of what was formerly a larger, densely packed aggregation of material which periodically threatened our planet with one or more collisions of cataclysmic proportions.

7) No monument, regardless how sacred or politically valuable, would have been important enough to command what amounted to the entire national labor force of a high civilization to build. Even the last of the powerful pharaohs at the end of the New Kingdom, Ramses III (20th Dynasty, circa 1187 BC), was scarcely able to complete his huge "Victory Temple" (Medinet Habu) in Lower Egypt—even though it would hardly amount to a forecourt at the Great Pyramid—because of disruptive strikes by his workers.

Only a national emergency of extraordinary general concern could have summoned what had to have been the participation of virtually every man, woman and child in the construction of a refuge from some apparent, impending catastrophe that threatened all levels of society, if not the whole world. A parallel historical example may be found in the construction of Holland's emergency dikes, which required the labor of every Dutch citizen to complete in order to save their country from its own great flood.

Moreover, the Great Pyramid does not satisfy descriptions of a tomb, temple, time-capsule, or observatory. In spite of its gigantic size; what it does resemble, more than anything else, is a relatively simple piezo-electric transducer, an identity demonstrated by static electricity displays still observed at the structure.

8) Through its deliberate, strategic placement at the center of the world's land-mass, the Great Pyramid identifies itself as an apparatus to collect and direct the earth's internal powers, and to outwardly transmute those potentially destructive forces into an electrical energy discharge. It achieves this in the same manner; accumulating seismic pressures are discharged in a phenomenon known as "earthquake lights" or the "Andes Glow." The Great Pyramid does, in fact, vibrate in harmony with the fundamental frequency of our planet, and therefore "responds to vibrations from within the earth," according to the renowned Christopher Dunn, whose *The Giza Power-Plant* (1995) is perhaps the single most revealing book ever written about the Pyramid.

9) The Great Pyramid was, in effect, "deactivated," when its chief component part was stolen during a period of social dislocation in Egyptian history contemporary with the biblical Exodus. That "component part" soon after became the central cult-object, eventually lost, of what was to become a world religion.

10) The Great Pyramid is a device modern technology has not yet invented, namely, an instrument capable of dissipating seismic energies harmful to mankind, and using those same energies to create a reinforced ionospheric shield for our planet against extraterrestrial falls of catastrophic potential.

Other investigators have independently arrived at fundamentally the same conclusion—that the Great Pyramid was an electrical device—but each had his own interpretation of its ultimate purpose. To physicist Joseph Farrell, the Great Pyramid was a weapon. Theoretically, it could have served military purposes, if only on the most limited scale, although controlling its immense, erratic energy output would have been highly impractical in terms of real application. His nonetheless brilliantly insightful book, *The*

Giza Death-Star (2003), does not convincingly demonstrate just how such a "phase conjugate howitzer" might have been "tuned" to hit targets, as the author claimed, from India to Mars. No, the closest match between the Great Pyramid's design and function lies in its identity as a geotransducer to serve early Egyptian society's most pressing need, namely, protection from cataclysmic natural forces from under the earth (seismic violence) and in the sky (meteoric material from menacing comets).

• • •

These determinations cascaded all at once into my mind like the abrupt realization of an enigma that had nagged me all my life. It was as though everything I ever studied and wondered about the Great Pyramid for the previous forty years, even after repeatedly visiting the Giza Plateau, suddenly ordered itself into a recognizable mosaic. Among the patterns which began to stand out in bold relief were new themes never before suspected. For example, true "pyramid power" appeared in the guise of spiritual transformation rooted in the internal energies of the earth itself. The motif of a world cataclysm threaded together apparently disparate peoples from southern Iraq and the Nile Valley to the Atlantic Ocean and the Americas. Most surprising of all, a nature-oriented technology developed by some lost race before the accepted beginning of civilization reached out across the millennia to play a potentially pivotal role in our time.

These and other revelations are not mere speculations, but bolstered by evidence for Atlantean influences in Egypt, Mesopotamia, and North Africa, as presented in my four published books on the subject. A straightforward examination of the evidence shows that the Atlanteans created a material culture in some respects superior to and in most aspects entirely different from our own. But their strange technology, however powerful, could not save them from the sudden oblivion that consigned Atlantis to the realm of legend. All this began prior to but also accompanied the official rise of high cultures, some 5,000 years ago. The fate of this lost race and the ultimate purpose of their Great Pyramid are interwoven motifs laying bare the roots of our civilization. Those roots are not hidden in the sands of Egypt, but under the dark fathoms of the ocean that derived its name from the lost homeland of mankind.

This article first appeared in *Atlantis Rising* #58 (July/August 2006).

12

THE LOST WORLD OF EGYPT'S ABU GHUROB

This Little-Known Site Offers Startling Clues to Ancient High Technology

BY WILLIAM HENRY

About 20 minutes drive from the Great Pyramid, and visible from the Giza Plateau on a clear day, is one of Egypt's greatest treasures from antiquity, and one of the most extraordinary places on our planet.

Abu Ghurob is a closed-to-the-public archaeological site in the pyramid fields that run alongside the Nile south of Cairo. Egyptologists quaintly refer to it as a "sun temple," a "burial center" or "funerary complex" for a new cult of Ra (they usually use these terms when the actual function of a place is unclear), dating to around 2400 BC.

Egypt is indigenously known as "Khemet." Egyptian tradition teaches that the site of Abu Ghurob is one of the oldest ceremonial centers on the planet and is a place where the ancients connected with divine energies.

According to Stephen Mehler's account in *Land of Osiris*, Abu Ghurob has a remarkable past. Oral tradition, relayed by Abd'El Hakim Awyan, the acclaimed teacher and wayshower of the sacred mysteries of ancient Khemet, claims this site dates deep into prehistory and is one of the oldest ceremonial sites on the entire planet. Moreover, he says the site was designed to create heightened spiritual awareness through the use of vibrations transmitted through the alabaster platform and other materials. This expanded awareness enabled one to connect with the sacred energies of the universe, known as Neters.

Mehler notes that Hakim's indigenous tradition teaches that the Neters themselves, in some sort of physical form, once "landed" and appeared in person at Abu Ghurob. It is for this reason that this site has been considered sacred for thousands upon thousands of years.

The massive alabaster (Egyptian crystal) platform at Abu Ghurob. It is a mandala depicting the four directions. [Photos by William Henry]

I could hardly wait to get up over the crest of a hill in front of me and cross the barrier to Abu Ghurob—this was in March/April 2006 when I visited the place during my stay in Cairo. I was particularly interested in the large square structure or platform made of alabaster ("Egyptian crystal") that sits in front of the mound where an obelisk once stood. Hakim proposes this platform created a harmonic resonance through sound vibrations to increase heightened awareness and to further open the senses to "communicate" and be one with the Neters.

Of course, Hakim is describing what is today called a "portal" or "stargate." I found some eye-opening connections to stargates at Abu Ghurob. Additionally, I found connections to both Atlantis and to the Anunnaki gods of Sumeria, which will be shared here.

Entering the site at Abu Ghurob felt like entering a Hollywood movie set for a movie titled *Forbidden World*, or something like that. The dunes of the great desert appeared lunar. The three pyramids (*per neters* or "houses of energy") of Abu Sir, about a mile away, seemed surreal—like three elder fires burning for eternity. Strangely, when I stepped into Abu Ghurob, I have never felt more at home in a place in my life.

The site itself appeared as if it had sat undisturbed for millennia. The vacuum-like silence accentuated that perception.

The red granite casing stones that once covered the pyramid at Abu Ghurob were scattered like Lego blocks. An obelisk ("sun stick") once stood atop this mound. Pieces of this original sun stick, or *ben ben*, are scattered all over the place. In fact, the entire site is one giant debris field, with pieces of limestone scattered everywhere that appear to have come from structures that once existed here. The whole place looked as if a massive hand had swatted it like a sand castle.

Climbing atop the mound, the alabaster platform revealed itself before me. It's a mandala—a sacred design—in the shape of the Khemetian symbol Hotep, translated by Egyptologists as "peace."

On close inspection this platform displays evidence of advanced machining that even challenges today's technology.

FORMLESS LIGHT BEINGS

I am highly intrigued by the recollections and rememberings concerning the Neter and Abu Ghurob in the Khemetian tradition, particularly since it is reminiscent of the Ancient American oral tradition from Tennessee, where I live. Cherokee wisdom keeper Dhyani Yahoo, in her book *Voices of Our Ancestors,* also describes formless "thought beings," called TLA beings, who rode a sound wave from the Pleiades star cluster through a hole in space in East Tennessee and created the Cherokee. All humans are dream children of these angels or elemental forces of Nature (the Egyptian Neter) who came from the stars. This legend obviously resonates with Khemetian belief concerning Abu Ghurob. The correspondence got me thinking: what, exactly, took place at this site?

In addition, there's the work of Dr. Eve Reymond, a scholar who had explored the ancient Egyptian building texts from Edfu, Egypt, in her book *The Mythical Origin of the Egyptian Temple.* Her interpretations of these texts also tell of formless beings who came from the stars and created an island civilization in Egypt. These sages, as they were called, constructed an original mound where the creation of humankind took place. This island was called the Island of the Egg and was surrounded by the primeval water.

The Edfu tale matches the Atlantis story, as told by Plato, of a civilization founded by the gods who created a hybrid race of humans. I believe the Edfu Building Texts are the source material for Plato's story of Atlantis, which he originally learned from Egypt. I further believe that shards of this tale are found in numerous indigenous traditions, and that it may even relate to Abu Ghurob. One connection is found in the stones.

The precision cut and polished red granite facing stones of the pyramid at Abu Guhrob is a trademark of Atlantean construction.

Alternative researchers uphold the use of megalithic red granite blocks as a trademark of "Atlantean" temple building. At Abu Ghurob, one sees colossal red granite blocks weighing several tons that were precision cut, polished, and mounted in place as facing stones on the pyramid. Whoever laid these in place had an accuracy that was extraordinary.

In its original state, the Abu Ghurob pyramid may have been a giant machine, specifically a water processing plant or power plant (like the other *per neters* of Egypt). Water, we are told, was channeled in from the Ur Nile to Abu Sir. We have to imagine water everywhere at Abu Ghurob as well, in pools in front of the pyramid, running underneath it, and perhaps even flowing down from the top of the red granite faced pyramid like a fountain. The "energy water" produced by the piezoelectric effect of the quartz crystal-laden red granite may have been one of the products of this power plant.

Lined up near the entrance to Abu Ghurob are giant square alabaster "dishes" or "basins" with strange gear-like designs on top. These dishes were apparently placed there at some point while enroute to another location. Significantly, a few more are still in situ. (Stephen Mehler told me in a conversation that the basins may originally have been arranged in a circular pattern around the pyramid.)

Egyptologists guess that these massive basins were used to hold sacrificial animal blood, which ran through perfectly round channels cut into the paving. There is not a single drop of DNA or other residual evidence to support this misconception. Interestingly, the inner surface of the basins are smooth to the touch and show signs of circular tool marks, suggesting that whoever crafted them did so with a technology we would admire today (and make fortunes marketing, too).

On my second trek to Abu Ghurob I was destined to wade even deeper into the mystery of this amazing place.

THRESHOLD TO THE LOST REALM

Videographer Ted St. Rain has an astounding grasp of the ancient mysteries. His list of visits to sacred sites alone could fill an entire tour guide's book, complemented with a who's who of alternative researchers. I'm not sure when the first domino began to fall in Ted's mind. However, after only a short time at Abu Ghurob with me, Ted proclaimed that he had the answer to the question of the purpose of this temple site.

Beautifully round holes in the basins. What are they for? How were they drilled?

"The *Lost Realms* by Zecharia Sitchin will help explain what we are seeing here," he said.

In his *Earth Chronicles* series of books, Sitchin claims that a race of extraterrestrials called Anunnaki came to earth over 450,000 years ago in search of gold. In addition to surface mining, the Anunnaki used sophisticated water mining techniques to filter or process the gold from the waters of earth. Abu Ghurob, it seems, matches the description of their processing plants.

The *Lost Realms* is about the massive pyramids built by South American and Meso-American cultures, and their interactions with gods who set up pyramid/workshops there.

Sitchin cites the Mexican pyramids of Teotihuacán to support his theory. There are two pyramids—the Pyramid of the Sun and the Pyramid of the Moon—with the Avenue of the Dead running between them. Some scholars believe the Teotihuacán complex was begun 6,000 years ago and was known as the Place of the Gods.

The Pyramid of the Moon is an earthen mound. Some 2,000 feet to the south, the path of the Avenue of the Dead reaches the Pyramid of the Sun. These pyramids are virtually identical to the Giza pyramids. Sitchin believes that there is no doubt that the designer of this complex had detailed understanding of the Giza pyramids. The most remarkable correspondence noted by Sitchin is the existence of a lower passageway running underneath the Pyramid of the Sun.

As Sitchin records, in 1971 a complex underground chamber system was discovered directly underneath the Pyramid of the Sun. A tunnel, seven feet high and extending for almost 200 feet, was also discovered. The floor of this tunnel was divided into segments with drainage pipes (possibly connecting to an underground water source?). The tunnel led to a strange hollowed-out area shaped like a cloverleaf and supported by adobe columns and basalt slabs.

The enigma posed by this mysterious subterranean facility was amplified for Sitchin when he observed a path of six segments running along the Avenue of the Dead. These segments, or compartments, were formed by the erection of a series of double walls perpendicular to the avenue, each fitted with sluices at their floor level. Sitchin proposes that the whole complex served to channel water that flowed down the avenue; it was, in fact, an enormous waterworks, employing water for a technological purpose.

This ceremonial center, notes Sitchin, has artificial water channels running through that diverted water from the nearby San Juan river. The water is channeled into the Ciudadela, a quadrangle that contains at its eastern side a third pyramid, called the Quetzalcoatl Pyramid.

As Ted continued his brainstorm at Abu Ghurob, he noted a key discovery at Teotihuacán. Underneath the Pyramid of the Sun, archaeologists discovered mica, a dielectric mineral composed of delicate crystal that is a semiconductor. Its presence has perplexed ancient mystery writers Erich von Däniken and Graham Hancock.

The word "mica" is derived from the Latin word *micare*, meaning to shine, in reference to the brilliant appearance of this mineral (especially when in small scales). Mica has a high dielectric strength and excellent chemical stability, making it a favored material for manufacturing capacitors for radio frequency applications. It has also been used as an insulator in high voltage electrical equipment. Sheet mica is used today as an insulating material and as a resonant diaphragm in certain acoustical devices.

The Anunnaki, Sitchin claims, utilized some form of spacecraft. In the Vedic literature of India, there are many descriptions of ancient flying machines that are generally called Vimanas and may be equated with the craft of the Anunnaki. Some call them ancient Atlantean craft. Interestingly, these craft utilized mica in a profound way.

The Vymanika Shastra (sometimes given other spellings) is a text of disputed age that deals heavily with the operational features of these flying vehicles. According to "Aakaasha-tantra," by mixing black mica solution with neem and bhoonaaga decoctions and smearing the solution on the outer body of the vimana made of mica plates and exposing to solar rays, the plane will look like the sky and becomes "cloaked."

Sitchin was perplexed by the presence of this mineral beneath the pyramid at Teotihuacán. Then he remembered the water flowing from the San Juan River and how it was artificially channeled to this site. What he proposed is that the river was channeled along the Avenue of the Gods and underneath the pyramid. Through a chemical reaction caused by the mica (or, I wonder, could it have been a harmonic process?) gold was pulled from the river water.

Drainage holes are spread throughout Teotihuacán. Sitchin theorizes these were used to sluice the gold into chambers where the Anunnaki could collect it.

"Just like you see here," said Ted, pointing to one of the massive square alabaster basins or sluices at Abu Ghurob. Those basins, it turns out, were decanters.

"I was thinking about Sitchin's theory," said Ted, "because here's the pyramid here. Now, keep in mind that 10,000 years ago this area was a lush jungle with water everywhere."

Indeed, the Abu Ghurob site was beginning to look a lot like the Teotihuacán lay out. The only thing missing was the mica.

It didn't take very long before we found huge sheets of mica in front of the pyramid. The pieces were falling into place.

As Ted explained, "the theory is that, like Teotihuacán, Abu Ghurob was a gold refining facility. What they would do," Ted proposed, "is bring gold laden water in from the Nile. It would flow over the mica sheets (which may have covered this entire site). Through the piezoelectric effect produced by the mica electricity was produced. The water would be channeled into the basins and would be spun around inside and flow up and out through the round holes in the sides. The gold would filter down and remain in the basins to be scooped out at the end of the day."

Is Abu Ghurob a stargate/power plant of the Anunnaki? Is it connected to Teotihuacán? No one can, as yet, say for sure. On thing is certain, this place of the gods is not only one of the greatest treasures of ancient Khemet, but of our whole world. It deserves further investigation.

This article first appeared in *Atlantis Rising* #59 (September/October 2006).

13

THE RETURN OF THE DJEDI

The Knights of Star Wars Were Preceded Long Ago by Egyptian and Persian Orders

BY MARK AMARU PINKHAM

The Jedi Knights of *Star Wars* were not simply the figment of George Lucas's most fertile and provocative imagination. Those who have grown up coveting the powers of the Jedi will be pleased to learn that Masters of the Force did indeed once exist. Records of them survive in certain countries, such as Egypt and Persia, where they were magician priests and the guardians of powerful priest kings similar to the "Emperor" of Star Wars, albeit without his predilection for the "Dark Side."

In ancient Egypt, the surviving histories reveal that the Jedi manifested as the Djedi (hence the name "Jedi") which was a sect of the priesthood and Masters of the Force that protected the Pharaoh; and in Persia they were the Narts, guardians of a Holy Grail called the Nartmongue, and the protectors of enlightened priest kings who lived at least one thousand years before King Arthur and his Knights of the Round Table.

The remarkable history and wisdom of these two early sects of "Jedi" Knights was first introduced to the West by the Knights Templar, who upon returning from the Middle East in the 13th and 14th centuries, distilled "Jedi" histories learned from the Sufis into a series of lengthy Holy Grail legends. Within these pithy legends, the Templars synthesized the powerful emperors and priest kings of the past into the enigmatic figure of the Fisher King, the resident of a Grail Castle and the owner of various manifestations of the Holy Grail. His well-being and the safekeeping of his castle's Holy Grail relics was given over to an order of Knights of the Grail, who were a distillation of the early "Jedi" Knights from Egypt and Persia. But the Knights Templar let it be known that they were not just historians of the ancient Masters of the Force; they were themselves a latter day version of "Jedi" Knights. This truth was boldly and authoritatively proclaimed in Parzival by Knight Wolfram von Eschenbach when he specifically referred to the Fisher King's Holy Grail Knights as Templars. Parzival, as well as other historical references put forth in the Middle Ages regarding the Templars, implied that the Knights had inherited wisdom of the Force that had been passed down to them almost directly from their ancient, antecedent "Jedi" Knights. Thus, from at least one perspective, the formation of the Knights Templar in AD 1118 could be historically entitled the "Return of the Jedi"! But if this is true, what happened to the Templars' "Jedi" wisdom? Does it still exist?

Art from Randy Haragan

In recorded history, the Secrets of the Force of the "Jedi" Knights' were first taught among the Egyptian "Jedi" or Djedi, who may have received them from a much earlier prehistorical "Jedi" Knight order, perhaps one from Atlantis. One Djedi priest mentioned in the Egyptian's Westcar Papyrus is said to have possessed the key that opened the "secret chambers of the sanctuary of Thoth," who many esoteric historians believe was a missionary and Master of the Force from Atlantis. Within his sanctuary were books authored by Thoth that covered in detail the physics behind activating and developing the Force through alchemy—the art that Thoth-Hermes would eventually become the recognized patron of throughout the world. Through Thoth's alchemy, the esoteric symbol of which is the caduceus, a future Djedi could awaken the normally dormant "serpent" power, the fiery Force at the base of his spine, and then move it upward to his head where it would culminate in supernatural powers and intuitive, gnostic wisdom. The proof that a Djedi had accomplished this alchemy is intrinsic to his name, which was, essentially, an honorific title. The *Djed* of Djedi denoted "column," while the root word or sound *Dj* denoted "serpent." Thus, a Djedi was one who had awakened the Dj or serpent at its seat and then raised it up his or her Djed "column" or spine to the head. Those Djedi that succeeded in this inner ascension could potentially become immortal, which is yet another meaning of Djedi. As the Serpent Force rises up the spine, its alchemical fire of transformation moves within every cell of the body and raises the frequency of human flesh to that of "immortal" pure energy. Because of the spine's association with immortality, the Djed column or pillar became for the Egyptians a symbol of immortality, and they traditionally covered their mummies and sarcophagi with symbolic Djed images in hopes of achieving immortal life in the hereafter.

Through raising the inner serpent power, the Djedi acquired an abundance of Force which could be used to perform supernatural feats similar to those associated with Lucas's Jedi. For example, the Djedi of the Westcar Papyrus who possessed the key to the secret chambers of Thoth were said to have acquired the power to reattach the severed heads of animals at will. Other Djedi are mentioned in Egyptian history as traversing the scorching Egyptian sands with only their magical staffs, and/or becoming powerful magicians in the service of the Pharaohs. Some Djedi are found in the service of the Pharaoh that Moses and Aaron confronted in order to demand freedom for the Hebrews. At the Pharaoh's command, his Djedi magicians turned their staffs into live serpents, which represented the serpent power that each Djedi possessed. But Aaron's staff also turned into a snake, albeit a much larger snake than those of the Djedi, and it proceeded to consume their smaller serpents, thus proving the superiority of his serpent power to theirs.

The wisdom of the Djedi that the Knights Templar learned about may have first entered the Middle East as early as the Exodus, since Menetho tells us that the Hebrew leader Moses had been initiated into all the secrets of Egypt's priesthood during his formative years in the country. The wisdom of Djedi may have also arrived many years later when Dhul-Nun al-Misri traveled from Egypt to the Middle East after spending many years studying the alchemical hieroglyphs covering the temples and obelisks of Egypt. With the esoteric wisdom he discovered, Dhul-Nun al-Misri founded the Al-banna, the Sufi sect of "Freemasons." According to the Sufi Idris Shah, the Al-banna were teachers of the Templars during the years the Knights resided in the Al-Aqsa Mosque on the Temple Mount. Much of the wisdom of alchemy and the Force that resulted from the Templar-Al-banna intercourse was later taken into the continent of Europe by Templars who assimilated it into fledgling Speculative Freemasonry.

The order of "Jedi" Knights known of by the Templars was the Order of the Nart Knights, Masters of the Force of the ancient Persian Empire.

Possibly as old or older than the Djedi of Egypt, the Narts may have existed as early as King Jamshid, one of the incipient Persian kings of legend who ruled during the time of "Airyan Vaejahi," the Persian Golden Age that some historians have placed as early as 20,000 BC. Jamshid was a classic example of the Fisher King of Grail legend in that he suffered a fall from pride and lost his Force, or "Farr" as it was called in Persia, although he had previously adhered to a righteous path and been a renowned Master of the Force. Jamshid engendered a lineage of Farr-empowered priest kings that culminated in the highly spiritual Kayanid Dynasty founded by King Key-Khosrow, the "Persian King Arthur." Records state that, like King Arthur, Key-Koshrow possessed knights (the "Narts") who were associated with a Holy Grail (the "Nartmongue") and conducted their meetings around a table similar to Arthur's Round Table.

The mystical legends of Key-Khosrow and his Narts were eventually compiled into the Nart Sagas during the later Persian Empire and have since been regarded as Persian counterparts to Europe's Holy Grail legends. According to From Scythia to Camelot, the Nart Sagas may have first entered Europe with bands of Persian Sarmatian warriors who were in the hire of the Roman legions. The authors of this theory, Littleton and Malcor, make the interesting observation that King Arthur and his Knights may have themselves been Sarmatian soldiers and members of a Roman legion stationed at what was Hadrians Wall with orders to protect England from the marauding Pics of Scotland. According to this possible scenario, following the downfall of the Roman Empire, Arthur and his men would have been released from their Roman service, at which time Arthur would have become king of the newly liberated land of Britain and his fellow soldiers would have been transformed into the Knights of the Round Table. This alternate history of Arthur and his Knights was recently made into a major motion picture entitled *King Arthur* (2004) staring Clive Owen as the British monarch.

What little we know today of the Persian Narts suggests that these neo-Jedi Knights were continually seeking to increase their Force in order to become warrior adepts with a high level of spiritual purity and enlightenment. Only those whose dedication to king and country was immaculate could hope to increase their Farr to the degree needed in order to drink from the Nartmongue when it was passed around the Persian Round Table. Certain Narts increased their Farr to such a degree that they became the obvious choice to succeed an outgoing king. Some, like King Key-Lohrasp of the Kayanid Dynasty, became endowed with a mystical temperament and an abundance of gnostic insight. The mystical Key-Lohrasp eventually abdicated his "Fisher King" throne in favor of leading a purely mystical existence deep within the lofty mountains of Persia.

The "Jedi" Secrets of the Force possessed by the early Persian kings and their Narts were preserved within Persian civilization as popular leg-

Hasan-i-Sabah

end for many hundreds of years. Then, in the 11th century AD, Hasan-i-Sabah, the founder of the Order of Assassins that was to become a huge influence on the Knights Templar, revived the ancient Nart tradition. He resurrected the Secrets of the Force and founded a cadre of knights to serve him. Hasan chose for his court the castle of Alamut, the "Eagles Nest," which was located high in the Albourz Mountains, the region of northern Persia that had anciently been the seat of the Persian kings.

Hasan learned the Secrets of the Force both by studying the Nart legends and by traveling to Cairo in his younger years for the purpose of mastering nine mystical degrees of a Sufi mystery school centered within the city. After his graduation, Hasan left Egypt and returned home to quickly establish himself as one of the greatest alchemists that Persia had ever seen. He subsequently founded his own mystery school of nine degrees, which eventually became known as the Order of the Assassins. The degrees of alchemical purification of Hasan's school—which Hasan cryptically referred to as the nine steps of ascension up the mystical mountain of Kaf—assisted his Assassin Knights in awakening the inner Force and acquiring gnosis. Hasan's manual for his mystery school, the Sargozast-i-Sayyid-na, provided a step-by-step guide to the alchemical practices that would lead an aspiring knight to the summit of Kaf.

Hasan's alchemical Secrets of the Force were passed down to successive generations of Assassins, during which time they became known as the Teaching of the Resurrection. The greatest promoter of these teachings, and a fully enlightened Master of the Force in his own right, was the later Assassin Grand Master Rashid al-din Sinan of Syria. Sinan began his career

The Ruined Fortress of Alamut in present-day Iran.

as a common Assassin knight in Persia but eventually achieved enlightenment and an abundance of supernatural powers by adhering closely to
Hasan's alchemy. After being sent to govern the Assassins' outpost in Syria,
Sinan is said to have acquired the power to be able to see into the past or
future, and for being able to go for indefinitely long periods without eat-
ing or drinking. His psychic ability was also legendary. When a letter was
delivered to him it was said that Sinan would hold the unopened letter
against his third eye for a moment and then promptly write down and
dispatch a reply to the sender.

Through their encounters with Sinan and his knights the Templars,
who had nearby castles in Syria, learned some of the Assassins' Secrets
of the Force. The Templars felt an affinity with the Assassins since they
were both renegade orders of knights aspiring to alchemy and gnosis while
being ostensible members of a fundamentalist religion. Sinan, whom the
Templars came to call the "Old Man of the Mountains," awed the Knights
with his powers and they coveted his alchemy, which they eventually
learned from both him and his knights, as well as from various other Sufi
sects. As a complement to what would eventually become the prodigious
amount of Sufi teaching they acquired, the Knights Templar also inherited
the gnostic teachings of the Johannite Gnostic Church, which had been
passed down to them from a series of grand masters beginning with John
the Baptist, Jesus, John the Apostle, and Mary Magdalene.

The Knights Templar would subsequently create their own Holy Grail mystery school tradition comprised of numerous levels. The Force, the Knights Templar were to discover, was the true "Holy Grail." Although the Knights may have possessed certain physical objects which were ascribed the power of a Holy Grail, including the Holy Shroud and perhaps even the cup from which Jesus drank during the Last Supper, they discovered from their Sufi teachers that what made an object a Holy Grail was its accompanying Force or Holy Spirit power. It was this Force that activated and drove the process of alchemy within a Knight and eventually opened him to his inner gnostic wisdom and supernatural power.

The Templars' Secrets of the Force eventually passed into some of the Secret Societies of Europe, including the Rosicrucians and Freemasons, and for a while this wisdom survived in its purity. But it would eventually become grossly distorted, hidden, or completely forgotten, and the era of the "Jedi" Knights would come to a grinding halt. But now, certain Templar organizations are making a concerted effort to resurrect the "Jedi" Knight wisdom of Egypt, Persia, and the early Templars. The old gnostic and alchemical rites are beginning to be observed again and the hidden alchemical texts are being pursued in places like Rosslyn Chapel and Languedoc in France.

This article first appeared in *Atlantis Rising* #74 (March/April 2009).

14

THE GREAT PYRAMID & THE WORLD AFTER DEATH

Is the Great Pyramid a 3-dimensional Representation of the Duat?

BY PHILIP COPPENS

What happens to us after death? Science does not address the issue, but for the ancient Egyptians, it was a carefully mapped region, called the Duat—very close to the word death. The Duat is the realm experienced by the soul once it is detached from the body. In Sumer, this realm was called Nibiru, "Crossing"; in Greece it was symbolized by Charon, the ferryman, who would transfer the soul to the other side of the River Styx. In Egypt, the symbol for this mode of transport was that of the Henu Bark, the boat that transported the soul to the Land of the Dead—the equivalent of the Magur boat of the Sumerians.

The Apkallu, or Anunnaki, were the Sumerian equivalent of the spirit aides that helped the soul in its negotiations of the Duat, or Nibiru—the neteru, the gods, of the ancient Egyptians. Equally, the Pyramid Texts were said to be written on the "Henu Bark," and because they were written on the walls of the burial chamber inside the pyramids, it is clear that the chambers were envisioned as the Celestial Bark—thus explaining the presence of boats next to the pyramids, such as the Great Pyramid. Equally, the Coffin texts were the same text written on the coffin of the deceased, the wooden coffin being another—smaller—version of a bark.

The Pyramid Texts state how "I am a soul . . . a star of gold." In Egyptian symbolism, the soul was placed on a boat, led by a navigator—the boat would be the instrument for the soul's exploration of the Duat. The Papyrus of Nu, from the 18th Dynasty, says that the original text was indeed present in the Shrine of the Sacred Boat. The *Book of the Dead* was literally a map for travel in the Duat.

But what was the Duat? Eastern religions speak of a state following death that is literally a "state of nothingness"; they have called this the "bardo," which is identical to the Christian concept of Purgatory.

The Egyptian Book of the Dead is a book for the living as well; it aims to concentrate the mind of the living on their continual preparation for the afterlife, with liberation from the cycle of life and death as the ultimate goal. However, reincarnation is deemed to be the most likely outcome for the majority of human beings who have not attained sufficient spiritual advancement during their life, and preceding past lives.

Wooden boat found buried next to the Great Pyramid, now displayed in the adjacent museum. It is generally believed to have been intended for the soul of the pharaoh in the afterlife.

Some authors, in particular Andrew Collins, have argued that the Duat, the Egyptian Underworld, must have been physically represented beneath the Giza complex. This idea has led to various theories, specifically those of Edgar Cayce, who claimed a chamber existed underneath the Sphinx, which would hold evidence of the lost civilization of Atlantis. In more recent years, the discovery of a small door leading from an "air shaft," the so-called Gantenbrink door, has fuelled speculation that there are as yet undiscovered chambers inside the Great Pyramid.

Though this is certainly a possibility, most, if not all, of us have missed the point. If we were to ask the question whether anyone doubts the fact that we have identified the core chambers and corridors of the Great Pyramid, the answer would be "no": it is clear that the current known passages are the main arteries inside the highest building in the world, until the Eiffel tower was finished in the 19th century.

The next question to ask is what these passages mean, if anything. For many Egyptologists, they are merely the visible evidence of a Pharaoh who repeatedly changed his mind, from being buried in the subterranean chamber, to a new room, which is now known as the "Queen's Chamber," and eventually the King's Chamber. Anyone familiar with project management will know that project owners often change their minds, and either request changes, or even alter the scope of the project. But if you were project manager of the biggest building project the world had ever seen, and would ever see for the next 5,000 years, would you agree with these changes? The answer would be "no"—especially since it is known that Khufu, or Cheops as the Greeks called him, was not a tyrant as Herodotus would have it, but instead an apparently nice man. His father Snofru was easily swayed in his opinions and ideas, but nevertheless successfully managed the construction of three pyramids. Equally, because the granite was a key ingredient for the construction of the King's Chamber, it is clear that the time required to prepare those blocks means that the King's Chamber must have been an integral part of the pyramid's original design.

If the design was always intended to incorporate three chambers, what would that mean? What was Khufu trying to do? As leading Egyptologist Mark Lehner has pointed out, the Egyptian word for pyramid, *mer*, is possibly derived from *m*, meaning "instrument" or "place," and *ar* meaning "ascension." Therefore, the pyramid is either the place of ascension or the instrument of ascension, or both. I. E. S. Edwards also identified *mer* or *mr* as "instrument/place of ascension," but added that the interpretation was "open to justifiable doubt." What the word meant, nobody knows for sure, as the *m-er* conjunction is unusual in Egyptian grammar. In Egyptian hieroglyphs, the mer is written as a pyramid, which is definitely capturing the essence.

Again, "ascension" has been interpreted as taking off in a rocketship. But the "ascent to Heaven" should perhaps be looked upon in a metaphysical context. After all, though Egyptologists might not have been perfectly able to explain the meaning of the pyramid, it is a matter of fact that the Pyramid Texts speak of a metaphysical journey, of the soul on his way through the Duat to reach the afterlife.

Charles Muses (1919–2000), a man who walked the fine line between New Age and solid research, realized that in the museum of Torino, in Italy, there was a coffin from the Egyptian village of "Two Hills" (Gebelein), which depicted the plan of the Duat, as written down in the Coffin Texts, spell 650.

It visualizes the three paths of the soul at death, at the Duat, the Crossing: floating about, return, or voyage. It is depicted as a fork in which the central path leads to regeneration (the voyage) and the other two diverge from it, postponing the regeneration.

The Egyptians visualized this in the concept of the Henu Boat, where the navigator guided the soul: once it set off, where did the soul want to go to? Float about? return to shore? or go to an undiscovered country?

Muses identified each path with the types of couch, or bier—or coffin—on which the deceased, and Osiris, the god who had died and had had to face the same trial, laid. The central path (resurrection) was identified with the lion couch, the hippopotamus couch with return to the shore (reincarnation), and the cow couch with the floating about in the Duat.

There are various depictions of the "lion couch," as this was the path obviously favored by all those who were buried—and definitely path desired by the Pharaoh. After all, if the Pharaoh did not go on the voyage, who would? Examples of a hippopotamus bier and a cow bier were found in the tomb of Tutankhamun, and his tomb shows that each couch was furnished. To a large extent, what would happen after death could only be confirmed once the Pharaoh was deceased—it was then that the choice had to be made. As Tutankhamun died at a very young age, it is clear that it was not at all clear that his "mission in life" had been fulfilled and that he would have gotten enough brownie points to enter the afterlife—the realm of the gods, the "First Time," a point beyond creation, beyond time.

The state of the bardo is therefore identical to the encoffined Osiris: though dead, he is not "*dead* dead": there is still potential, not for an Earthly life, but for a life "elsewhere." The soul is in a "land of nothingness," a gateway, a crossroads, where the soul is also in need of a guide.

Let us go through each option one by one. At death, the easiest path was the path of reincarnation: one body was exchanged for another and the cycle of life continued. In nature, this cycle was visible in the snake shedding its skin, the sun rising and setting, the seasons repeating, the deer renewing its antlers—symbols and "physical evidence" that has been found at many sacred sites. It was the path chosen by most souls, it seems, for a variety of reasons: the *sahu*, the Egyptian term for soul, might have had too much fear to go on a voyage or even dwell in the Duat for too long; the life review might have been specifically negative—life was not led properly, and hence a successive incarnation is required for the soul to grow before it might be ready to return to the Source.

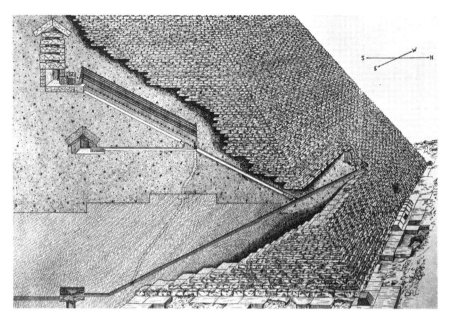

John Greaves' 1638 diagram of the passages in the Great Pyramid.

The second option, the path of the Cow, was to sail about in the Sacred Boat in the Duat. It is believed that this was literally "biding time": the soul was undecided as to what to do. It is this state that in popular parlance is known as a ghost: the soul is literally in a state of "nowhere;" it has not gone on. It could also be the state during which certain séances, particularly popular in Victorian England, could contact the "dead" and receive information from "the beyond." But at some point, the soul could either reincarnate, or the boat could set course toward the "Lion's Path Gateway"—the third option.

Central to the imagery of the Duat is a central path, a tunnel, from the world of the living into the darkness of the Duat. In that tunnel, the soul is given three paths, each leading to a specific destiny, and identified, at least at the time of Tuthankhamun, with three different couches: a cow, a hippopotamus, and a lion.

This imagery translates straightforwardly to the Great Pyramid: the entrance leads down into a dark, low tunnel. By default, the path descends to the Lower Chamber. However, there is an entrance toward another tunnel, leading to the "Queen's Chamber" or the "King's Chamber." A lot of ink has been spent on how the stone blocking of this tunnel was put in place and whether or not it could pivot. That is less important than the observation that there was a "guarded" entrance in this fork in the road. Once in the ascending passage—an apt description for those trying to attain heaven—a further fork occurred, one leading to the Queen's Chamber, another that continued to climb, toward the King's Chamber.

Did each of the tombs symbolize a path? The path of reincarnation, of the hippopotamus, would be the Underground Chamber: easiest to reach, but very "basic," earth to earth. The path of the cow would be to the Queen's Chamber: in between both, specifically there for a soul stalling to make the final ascent to the King's Chamber. The lion's path would be the continued ascent toward the King's Chamber, where the "tomb of God," the coffin, was the symbol of resurrection—initiation in the Divine Abode.

This interpretation of the Great Pyramid as the three-dimensional visualization of the Duat would explain many anomalies, too many to list here. But one intriguing anomaly is the "Well Shaft," a roughly hewn path connecting the Lower Chamber with the fork in the tunnel toward respectively the Queen's and King's Chambers. This path was the "loop" from the second path, that of the cow, either to reincarnation or regeneration. It would, by default, have to bypass the original "choice" (the original fork in the road), but it would have to lead to both other chambers. For the architect, this presented a problem, but I believe the shaft and its execution display exactly the nature of the path: rough, "unhewn." To some extent, the architect had made the passage from the Queen's Chamber to the Lower Chamber more difficult than the passage toward the King's Chamber. It was a reminder that the seeker "had come so far, why not go all the way"?

The Well Shaft is not open to the public and few people officially enter it, though it seems that the guards on the Giza plateau must occasionally practice climbing it, as they normally act as descent guides for those who do enter it, such as Mark Lehner. Its purpose is unknown and whatever scenario has been proposed for its function, it has always failed. I believe that the theory of the Great Pyramid as the three-dimensional representations of the Duat, and the paths within, not only makes sense of the number of chambers, but specifically illuminates the reason behind the presence of the "Well Shaft." It would also firmly set into place the presence of the Sphinx, the guardian of the Duat—and above all, why the Sphinx was in the form of a lion with a human head. Was it because those who entered were humans on the Lion's Path, toward the Abode of Osiris?

Mark Lehner states that the Duat, the Netherworld, was written as a star in a circle. He states that "in the Pyramid Texts the Duat is connected to the Earth or to a darker region lying primarily beneath. Aker, the Earth god in the form of a double Sphinx, was the entrance—already the Sphinx is a guardian of gateways." In this case, it is quite clear how the Duat is entered: via the Sphinx. Or rather, the Sphinx is the guardian of the entrance, of the gateway, which from the depiction of the Duat as a star in a circle, is quite literally a "star gate," although not in the concept of an entrance to Heaven, but to the Underworld. It is, furthermore, not an opening to an Underground Chamber which would hold evidence of Atlantis, but it is an entrance into the Duat. The Great Pyramid was a three-dimensional representation of the soul's journey in the Duat. Visible and clear . . . built to last, finally understood.

Excerpted and adapted from *The Canopus Revelation: The Stargate of the Gods and the Ark of Osiris*, by Philip Coppens (Adventures Unlimited Press, 2015). This article first appeared in *Atlantis Rising* #76 (July/August 2009).

PART FOUR

TRACKS OF THE TEMPLARS

15

THE UNDERGROUND STREAM & RENNES-LE-CHÂTEAU

The Da Vinci Code Barely Scratched the Surface

BY STEVEN SORA

MILLIONS WHO HAVE READ Dan Brown's book *The Da Vinci Code* or seen the movie adaptation of the same name, have been intrigued by the story of the Priory of Sion, a mysterious secret society which some believe operated for centuries behind the scenes of European and American history. As has been argued recently in British courts, most of the ideas in Brown's book were allegedly taken from the 1980s best-seller *Holy Blood, Holy Grail* by Michael Baigent, Henry Lincoln, and Richard Leigh, but the actual facts behind both these works were laid down decades and centuries earlier. Today researchers continue to comb the archives of the world in a tireless quest for the secrets of a forgotten order. Not the least among them is our own Steven Sora, who here discusses his foray into the secrets of Rennes-le-Château.—Editor

A secret society does exist, sharing knowledge among its members, blocking knowledge from others who are not among the initiated. In the greatest cities in the world, hints of deeper mysteries are out in the open. In smaller villages and towns, the secrets may be just as noticeable, especially to an insider. And on occasion, an outsider may just stumble across a secret meant to be kept secret.

That may describe the unusual story of Bérenger Saunière.

In June of 1885, Father Saunière arrived in his new posting, the tiny village of Rennes-le-Château. It was not a great posting, as the young priest would find out. At first, his income was barely enough to keep him from starving. Soon, the generosity of parishioners came to the rescue and eventually he was able to lead a peaceful life reading, learning languages, hunting, and fishing. In his employ was a young village girl, Marie Denarnaud, who caused a few eyebrows to be raised, but in general life was quiet. That is until he found some mysterious parchments hidden in an old altar.

One of the four coded parchments mentioned a painting entitled, "Shepherds of Arcadia," by Nicolas Poussin; and one phrase in the same line said "Teniers held the key."

Father Saunière visited his bishop in Carcasonne to show him the parchments. The bishop sent him to St. Sulpice in Paris where he bought prints of the paintings. St. Sulpice had been a center of unusual politics for centuries. It held several mysteries and concealed several, secretive orders. One of them was the Priory of Sion.

Oddly enough, St. Sulpice was right on the zero degree line, the meridian of Paris. On one particular day each year, the sun emerged through a church window on what is called the Roseline.

Henry Lincoln, one of the three authors of *Holy Blood, Holy Grail*, has described the area around Rennes-le-Château as the Holy Place.

After his visit to Paris, Father Saunière returned from St. Sulpice to Rennes-le-Château. Soon, inexplicably, he was a wealthy man. He eventually spent the equivalent of millions of dollars on public works, an unusual villa, and a downright bizarre church. Along the way, he would run afoul of his bishop and be accused of selling Masses. The accusation was more likely a guess, as his wealth could simply not be explained. Intercession by the church kept him from being removed, and it was speculated that the parchments he discovered may have provided legitimacy for the Hapsburg dynasty to rule as Holy Roman Emperors.

Saunièr's Chapel at
Rennes le Château

SECRET KNOWLEDGE

"The Shepherds of Arcadia"
(Nicholas Poussin)

The story was much greater than the rustic priest. He had simply found himself in the middle of it. Did he uncover secret objects or precious metals held by the Cathars who were nearly annihilated centuries before? Did he find a hidden treasure brought from Jerusalem to Rome by Titus, and then in turn looted from Rome and brought to the south of France? No gold or silver was found; after the priest's death, his housekeeper had in her possession only bank notes, which pointed to only an earthly and modern horde.

ET IN ARCADIA EGO

Part of Saunière's discovery was a tomb with the Latin inscription "*Et in Arcadia ego*." This tomb and the Nicholas Poussin painting were linked by the expression.

The inscription itself roughly translates to "And in Arcadia I am."

The "Shepherds of Arcadia" painting depicts a tomb with three shepherds and a woman standing beside it. The men are all pointing at something, which they appear to be showing to the woman. While most art historians claimed the tomb was a mystical representation of an idyllic Arcadia where the shepherd's tomb was situated by the underground river Alpheus, the tomb was actually discovered to be a real tomb six miles from Rennes-le-Château near a village named Arques. There are no records of the construction of the tomb, and it is said to have been there from at least 1709. By the time of father Saunière, it was on the property of an American, Louis Lawrence.

The Poussin painting, however, dates to 1620–1640. The painter did not invent the depiction in his painting nor did he invent the saying "*Et in Arcadia ego.*" The tomb and descriptive saying were themes that reached back to Virgil who wrote of Arcadia as an Eden. The theme was modernized through Jacobo Sannazaro who wrote in 1504 of an idyllic Arcadia. It was an Eden or a paradise that existed in an age of purity. The tomb of the shepherd was where other shepherds went to make sacrifice to the river god. The actual phrase first appeared on a work done by Guercino, just before 1621. Sannazaro's theme was followed by Sidney's *Arcadia*, Montemayor's *Diana* and Belleau's *La Bergerie.*

THE MIRROR IMAGE

Far from the south of France, at Shugborough Hall in Staffordshire, England, lies the ancestral home of the Earls of Lichfield. Their home, like the St. Sulpice Church in Paris, had been a hotbed for Masonic activity; and when Charles Radclyffe, an alleged grandmaster of the Priory of Sion, escaped from Newgate prison, his cousin, the current earl, protected him.

The Priory of Sion, under one name or another, might be one thousand years old. It is believed that the organization operated within, or in control of, the Knights Templar. It took on the name Company of the Sacred Sacrament during the colonization period in America and operated out of St. Sulpice in Paris. Today, the Priory operates in Barcelona, barely a couple of hours from Rennes-le-Château; while the Sulpician priests operate in several countries, including the United States.

Around the time Poussin painted his famous Shepherds of Arcadia, the Anson family bought the Staffordshire lands. The date was 1624, and the purchase would soon include the titles. William Anson was the name of the buyer as well as the name of his son and grandson. Next came Thomas Anson, who continued the upgrading of the famous hall that was started in 1693. Then finally, a George Anson went to sea in 1711. He was the second English privateer to circumnavigate the world. The first, Sir Francis Drake, was doubtless a hero of his. When Drake came home, he gave his Queen enough money to start the Royal Navy. He bought a great house owned by a rival and brought a water supply system to his village. Anson had returned home from his epic voyage in June of 1744. He paraded through London with 32 wagons of treasure and with his cronies, who would later band together to sack Havana.

With his newly established fortune, Anson bought 17,000 acres of land in North Carolina in the New World, and upgraded London's docks. It was just part of his ostentatious expenditure.

Sir Francis Drake has long been speculated to be the man who hid an immense treasure on Oak Island in Nova Scotia (see "Knight Templar Treasure in America," *A.R.* #20). Anson, too, would be named by some as a man who had motive and means to construct the major complex shaft on Oak Island, complete

Shepherd's Monument at Shugborough

with the booby traps which would vex treasure hunters in the centuries ahead. Enjoying, as they did, the support of the crown, Drake and Anson spent their fortunes openly. While there is no evidence for Drake, there is evidence of Anson landing at Halifax, just a short hop to Oak Island. Members of the Anson circumnavigation expedition who looted Havana had the means, and greater motivation, to conceal their loot.

Some of the two-million pounds Anson brought home, an immense fortune in his time, would go to making additions to Shugborough, such as a Pagoda (no doubt inspired by his visit to Asia) an imitation of the Arch of Hadrian, a Doric Temple, and a monument also based on Grecian mythology—the House of Winds. Last, and inscribed in cipher text, was the Shepherd's Monument.

Many believe it signifies that Anson was connected to a shadow Templar group, now surviving in a Masonic context. They further believe the Holy Grail is preserved at The Shepherd's Monument.

The most interesting thing in the Shepherd's Monument at Shugborough is the recreated Poussin painting. It is close to an exact depiction with one dramatic difference, it is horizontally reversed. The woman on the right is now on the left. And why is this important? The positioning of the figures and the tomb was never explained. To outsiders, this is just a coincidence. To the initiate it means something much greater.

When Admiral George Anson died in 1762, a poem was read in Parliament to his honor. It included lines about Arcadia's blessed plains and ended saying "Reason's finger pointing at the tomb."

Why was the tomb in Staffordshire related to the tomb at Rennes-le-Château? Did they hold an important message related to Jesus, Arthur, or to a secret underground society? It is very likely. The theme of an underground stream of knowledge stretched from Italy to France to England and spanned centuries. A secret society held and protected a secret knowledge from the Catholic popes and kings who claimed a monopoly over education and learning. Members of such secret societies used certain themes as a backdrop. Pre-Masonic groups often formed attachments to tombs. Virgil's tomb, the tombs of Solomon, Hiram, and others were very important; and for some reason, the tomb of the Shepherd might have been important as well. Another strong theme is Fog. From books and plays to early motion pictures, fog is usually depicted surrounding tombs. Fog and mist hovering over a tomb or a sacred place in the woods was meant to point to the chaos of birth and death. The passage was through the worlds of birth, death, and possibly resurrection. It was a theme in religion from Ireland to India.

Evelyn Waugh's most popular work, *Brideshead Revisited,* has a chapter entitled "Et in Arcadia Ego." Traces in other works suggest a meaning is recognized, understood, and secretly preserved by a select few. George Sand wrote a letter to Gustave Flaubert saying, "In any case, today all I am good for is writing my epitaph! You know, Et in Arcadia ego."

Maurice Barrès wrote "The Mystery in the Open," as well as other essays on the tombstone and the motto, "Et in Arcadia ego." Both he and Jules Verne were connected by Rosicrucian thought and "Angelic Society."

Shugborough is nearest to the town of Great Haywood. During the winter of 1916–1917, the *Lord of the Rings* author, J. R. R. Tolkein, stayed in Great Haywood. In his *Tale of the Sun and the Moon,* he mentions seeing a great house of one hundred chimneys. Shugborough has eighty chimneys. Similarly another borderline occult writer, Jules Verne, goes well beyond Tolkein in mentioning Rennes-les-Château names in his works. Clovis Dardentor refers to the Merovingian king Clovis and the title given to Dagobert. Captain Bugarach, another important character, is taken from a village of the same name. According to author Henry Lincoln, the village of Bugarach forms one point of the star on the geographical face of the Rennes-le-Château area. In the Jules Verne story, this is where the protagonists kill time at the chalk hill of St. Clair.

THE NEW ARCADIA

The Sinclair family, of course, plays a central role in the Priory of Sion, in the break-up of the Knights Templar, in carrying away a treasure to their realm in Scotland headquartered at Roslyn. In 1398, the Sinclair navy crossed the Atlantic, nearly one hundred years before Columbus. They landed in a place that would become Nova Scotia, although they had no name for it. When asked the name of the place they had landed, a native, most likely a Micmac, answered, "Acadia."

The Sinclair family stayed and briefly established a colony or two in the New World. When the Verrazano brothers went looking for their colony, they placed Arcadia on the map, near to another name, Refugio, the refuge of the Sinclair Templar organization. They further depicted a "Norman villa" on their map, although most likely the Verrazano family was aware of the building style as a Templar baptistery. The structure in the New World would be similar to structures from Damascus to Ireland. Some of these structures measured the lunar and solar year.

The Verrazano expedition's last European port was left on January 17. This day is the feast day for St. Roseline, whose name is recalled in the Roslyn home of the Sinclairs and the rose-line marker in St. Sulpice. The same day is the feast day of St. Sulpice. Saunière's documents revealed that Teniers painting of St. Anthony "holds the key." January 17 is the feast day of St. Anthony. A purported grandmaster of the Priory of Sion, Nicholas Flamel, said he discovered the method to transmit base metals to silver and gold. The date of his discovery was January 17, 1361. Possibly last in this chain of messages, *Holy Blood, Holy Grail* was dedicated by Henry Lincoln on January 17.

Works of architecture and art, poetry and rhymes, sculpture and literature have conveyed concealed secrets for centuries. Some are in plain sight, many are undecipherable even in plain sight. Except for an initiate.

This article first appeared in *Atlantis Rising* #73 (January/February 2009).

16

THE TEMPLARS' GREATEST SECRET

*What Did the Vatican Know about the Knights Templar
and their Johannite Beliefs?*

BY MARK AMARU PINKHAM

According to one esoteric tradition, after nine years excavating the foundations of Solomon's Temple, the Knights Templar left the Middle East with five "caskets" or cases full of treasure they had collected in the Holy Land. These cases, the story goes, were eventually deposited in Kilwinning, the Mother Lodge of Scottish Freemasonry, before being transported to Roslin Castle, ancient home of the Sinclair Barons of Roslin, where they were kept safe until a fire broke out in the building. The cases were then quickly removed from the castle and very soon afterward the construction of Rosslyn Chapel officially began. Thus, it appears that the chapel may have been built specifically to hold the five cases.

This notion was ostensibly corroborated in the 1990s by Andrew Sinclair, who conducted ground scans at Rosslyn and discovered five rectangular objects or boxes in the crypt underneath the Chapel. Sinclair's discovery has fueled speculation about what might be in the cases, including notions of artifacts associated with Solomon's Temple or Herod's Temple, and possibly some ancient scrolls. It has been conjectured that some of the imagined artifacts in the cases were discovered by the Knights via clues they found while studying obscure Essene texts, a theory recently corroborated by the discovery of the Copper Scroll, one of the Dead Sea Scrolls. Clues found in the Copper Scroll (see chapter 28 of this book) have led archaeologists to empty pits in close proximity to Templar symbols and weapons, thus ostensibly revealing that the Knights had overseen the secret excavations and then absconded with whatever treasure they found. The hypothetical scrolls that may exist within the five cases have been theorized to include genealogical information regarding a family spawned by Jesus and Mary Magdalene, or, assert authors Christopher Knight and Robert Lomas in *The Hiram Key,* possibly Essene information regarding the origins of Freemasonry. But at present all that can be said for certain about the scrolls is that one of them contains a diagram with symbols recalling the mysterious Johannite Heresy, a gnostic belief system into which the Templars may have been initiated in the Holy Land.

Copied by Lambert de St. Omer, a retired schoolmaster, when the Knights Templar passed through Flanders as they moved through northern Europe, this diagram—today entitled the "Heavenly Jerusalem," it hangs on a wall within a museum in Ghent, Belgium—is a map of the New Jerusalem as described in the Book of Revelation. Johannite heretical wisdom is evident in the design via the iden-

Heavenly Jerusalem

tification of a Messiah—the figure prophesied to found the holy city of the future—as being not Jesus but John the Baptist. Such a designation is consistent with the ancient Johannite heresy, which stated that John was both Messiah and founder of the gnostic Johannite path that leads to the intuitive vision of the Heavenly Jerusalem. According to this heretical tradition, there were two Messiahs or Chosen Ones, with John, the Priest Messiah, one rung above Jesus, the incarnated King Messiah. If the Johannite Heresy is truly the key to understanding the Templar scroll now in Belgium it must be allowed that the Knights were Johannites and embraced a greater veneration for John the Baptist than Jesus. Furthermore, if they were Johannites, then they practiced a gnostic path comprised of heretical rites that culminated in an inner revelation regarding the nature of the universe and the goal of human existence. This would explain why the five cases with their Johannite scrolls ended up in Rosslyn Chapel. The Sinclair builder of the Chapel considered himself to be a caretaker and preserver of the Templar's gnostic wisdom. Earl William Sinclair was a Grand Master Freemason of the developing Scottish Rite, an order that had descended directly from the Templars who had fled France and later made their home in Scotland. According to Niven Sinclair, a contemporary patriarch of Clan Sinclair, rather than risk death by exposing the gnostic secrets in his possession Earl William imbedded them within his stone edifice. Perhaps he knew at the time that the secrets he was hiding for posterity—secrets which would prove that the Templars were Johannite gnostics and heretics—were indeed the Templars' "Greatest Secret."

THE DISBELIEF OF POPE CLEMENT V

According to conventional history, the first intimation that the Vatican had regarding the Templars gnostic and Johannite predilections came to the surface during the Knights' depositions for allegations of heresy in 1307. Then, in 1308, Pope Clement V disbanded the ruthless Inquisition so that he could privately interview the Knights Templar himself. At stake was his own private bodyguard of knights, which since the time of Pope Honorius II and the Council of Troyes in 1128 had been the Holy See's personal militia. The Knights had been accused of a litany of heretical offenses, any one of which could have been reason to cast them into the holy fires

of the Inquisition, but since many of the Knight's confessions had been extracted under extreme torture, their credibility had been compromised. Therefore, having himself never fully believed the damning allegations against his beloved Templars, Clement V confidently called for 72 Knights to be transported from Paris to his villa in Poitiers in southern France where he was sure they would recant their previous testimonies. Imagine his surprise when, after insuring the Knights safety in his home—no matter how

The execution of Jacque De Molay

SECRET KNOWLEDGE

damning their confessions might be—the Templars refused to discredit the confessions previously extracted from them in the dark and dank torture chambers of Paris. Pope Clement, who was essentially a pawn put into office by King Philip, could only scratch his head in disbelief and lament that his Knights had somehow strayed from the straight and narrow. To his dismay he had found out conclusively that all the vile allegations against the Templars were indeed true. The Pope was finally forced to accept the fact that he had lost his knights. Later, within the silence of his quarters, the distraught Pope must have wondered whether the Templars had ever truly been a Christian army of the Church.

WHAT THE VATICAN REALLY KNEW

Since the time of Templars' private audience with Clement V, a body of evidence has been forming to prove that although the Pope was blind to the Knight's heretical activities, other informed Church officials within the Vatican did indeed know about their heretical propensities. For example, according to testimony given during the Templar trials from one Father Antonio Sicci, some of the Knights' gnostic activities had been witnessed by Vatican spies in Palestine well before 1307. It also became clear during the Templar trials that both the Vatican and King Philip of France had had their spies overseeing the Knights' activities in Europe before 1307 because some of them were later chosen as witnesses for the prosecution. It was because of the evidence uncovered by these early spies that, months before the Templars' mass arrest, King Philip knew exactly what heretical activities to instruct his 12 specially selected spies to look for when he had them infiltrate certain Templar preceptories. The monarch may have also known what heresies to look for from studying information contained within a secret Templar document. This document, entitled "Baptism of Fire of the Brothers-Consulate," and often referred to by Templar historians as the "Secret Rule of the Templars," was later discovered in 1780 in the Vatican Library by a Danish Bishop. Said to have been written in AD 1240 by a French Templar Master named Roncelinus, it appears to give a green light to all the heretical offenses that the Knights were accused of in the 14th century. Permission to indulge in all manner of Templar heresy can be found in this document, including defilement of the Cross, denial of Christ as the Savior, sexual liaison, and the worship of the idolic head known as Baphomet. There is even a passage within the document that gives the Knights permission to initiate other gnostics into their order, including Cathars, Bogomils, and even Assassins. If the "Baptism of Fire of the Brothers-Consulate" was indeed in circulation beginning in AD 1240, it would have been an easy task for a Church or Royal spy to procure a copy for their employers.

THE KNIGHTS OF ST. JOHN

A more substantial bit of evidence in support of the notion that the Vatican was aware of the Templars heretical Johannite affiliations came in the mid 1800s when Pope Pius IX gave his famous "Allocution of Pio Nono against the Free Masons." In fact, this address implies that the Vatican may have known all along about a heretical Templar-Johannite relationship.

At the time of his momentous address, the Pope was receiving immense pressure to take a stand against the uprising of numerous heretical gnostic sects forming in France, one of which was the Johannite Church of Primitive Christians. This sect claimed to be a direct descendant of the early Knights Templar, and the chief of the sect, Bernard Fabre-Palaprat, claimed to be a Templar Grand Master in line from both Hughes de Payen and John the Apostle. Pope Pius' subsequent denigration of the sect during his address proved that the Church had ostensibly known for hundreds of years about an intimate Templar-Johannite association: "The Johannites ascribed to Saint John [the Baptist] the foundation of their Secret Church, and the Grand Pontiffs of the Sect assumed the title of Christos, Anointed, or Consecrated, and claimed to have succeeded one another from Saint John by an uninterrupted succession of pontifical powers. He, who, at the period of the foundation of the Order of the Temple, claimed these imaginary prerogatives, was named Theoclet; he knew Hugues de Payens, he installed him into the Mysteries and hopes of his pretended church, he seduced him by the notions of Sovereign Priesthood and Supreme royalty, and finally designated him as his successor."

Pope Pius' address was soon corroborated by some highly respected esoteric historians of the 19th century. In *Isis Unveiled*, Madame Blavatsky revealed, "They [the Knights Templar] were at first the true Knights of John the Baptist, crying in the wilderness and living on wild honey and locusts," while her contemporary, the self-styled Templar descendant and Kabbalist, Eliphas Levi, volunteered in *The History of Magic*, "The Templars had two doctrines: one was concealed and reserved to the leaders, being that of Johannism, the other was public, being Roman Catholic doctrine… The chiefs alone knew the aim of the Order the Subalterns followed without distrust."

Thus, Levi confirmed the Templars' affiliation with the gnostic Johannites but he went one step further in pointing out that it was principally the Grand Masters and chiefs of the Order who were aware of the Knights' heretical activities. This notion has been corroborated by transcripts compiled by the Papal Council during the Templar trials that show that when the Knights were questioned regarding one of their most important Johannite rites, that of worshiping an idolic head called Baphomet, only the chiefs of the Order knew anything about it. The caretaker of the head was, at the time, Hughes de Peraud, the second in command under Templar Grand Master Jacques de Molay, who secretly carried the head from one preceptory to the next whenever an initiation or ceremony called for its presence.

WHAT WAS BAPHOMET?

Who or what was Baphomet and how did it connect the Templars to the Johannites? The contemporary Johannites, who became separated from mainstream Templarism in the mid 19th century, claim to know. Suppos-

edly their church, the Apostolic Johannite Church, is in possession of secret wisdom descended directly from the chiefs of the Knights Templar. According to James Foster, former Primate of the Johannite Church, Baphomet of the Templars was the decapitated head of John the Baptist, the "Messiah" of the Johannite tradition. This would explain the extreme sanctity the Templars ascribed to the head and why it was in the sole possession of

Salome views the head of St. John the Baptist.

the Order's second in command. According to the Templars at their trial the head possessed special power and could make "trees blossom and the land to produce." Legend has it that when John's head was found by the Templars in the Boukoleon Palace in Constantinople during the Fourth Crusade, the head had been used to keep an 11th century emperor of the Eastern Roman Empire vibrant and alive through daily passes near his body. This power, known as the Holy Spirit in the West and Kundalini in the East, is the same power John was saturated with during his lifetime in the Holy Land. It is this power that can awaken itself as a normally dormant evolutionary energy at the base of the spine and culminate in gnostic awareness.

This article first appeared in *Atlantis Rising* #56 (March/April 2006).

17

THE REAL SECRET SOCIETY BEHIND
THE DA VINCI CODE

*Was the Priory of Sion Actually a Cover Story for an
Even More Elusive Secret Order?*

BY MARK AMARU PINKHAM

As known by anyone who has read Dan Brown's *The Da Vinci Code,*
the plot revolves around the clandestine activities of an ancient
secret society known as the Priory of Sion. The actual existence
of this society, claims Brown, is one of the few irrefutable truths woven
into his fictional novel. This may have been true when he was writing his
manuscript, but the authors of *Holy Blood, Holy Grail*, the non-fiction book
that introduced Brown to the Priory, publicly stated that the organization
appears to be a hoax. They confessed to having been led astray by some
dubious documents they discovered in Paris' Bibliothèque Nationale, an
admission that for awhile deterred most researchers from further pursuing the legitimacy of the Priory. Then researchers Lynn Picknett and Clive
Prince published *The Sion Revelation* (2006), within which they examined
all arguments for and against the Priory. Their surprising conclusion was
that there has indeed been a secret European organization with an agenda
similar to the Priory's, and that the Priory of Sion may have been invented
to act as a cover for this legitimate organization.

Picknett and Prince were never able to conclusively identify this elusive order, perhaps because the secret society they apprehended is not
very secretive anymore. The order they sought is commonly known as
the Rosicrucian Order, although it has also been known by other related
titles, including the Order of the Rose or Rosy Cross and the Brotherhood of the Rosy and Golden Cross. Although seemingly innocu-
ous today, in the past this organization has preserved many secret rites
and passed among its members many heretical secrets that are just as

The Rose and the Grail,
Atlantis Rising art

explosive as any information regarding the sacred Bloodline of Jesus and
Mary Magdalene.

The Rosicrucian Order, which we can now call the *real* Priory of Sion,
first made its presence known in the 17th century through public documents known as the *Fama Fraternitatis* and *Confessio Fraternitatis*. These
manifestos claimed that the Order of the Rosy Cross was moving into a
new public cycle although it had already been in existence as a secret
society for hundreds of years. Then, in 1785, one of the Order's Paris
representatives, Baron de Gleichen, penned an oft-quoted letter claiming
that the members of the Order of the Rosy Cross had been the "Superiors and Founders of Freemasonry," while additionally maintaining that its
Grand Masters "were designated by the titles John I, II, III, and so onward,"
thereby ostensibly aligning them with John the Baptist, John the Apostle,
or both. These revealed characteristics of the Rosy Cross were later woven
into its alter-ego, the Priory of Sion, which was similarly reputed to award
its Grand Masters with sequential "John" titles.

Perhaps the most conclusive evidence in favor of the Priory of Sion
being a cover name for the Order of the Rosy Cross is simply that the Priory once called itself the *L'Order de la Rose-Croix Veritas*, "The True Order of
the Rose Cross." Supposedly the Priory once adopted both this epithet and

that of "Ormus," a name that also irrefutably ties the Priory to the Rosy Cross because Ormus is the name of the founder of an early Rosy Cross sect that existed in 1st century Alexandria. The information regarding Ormus and his sect first originated in the 18th century with the Rosicrucian historian Baron von Westerode, who claimed that Ormus, a disciple of St. Mark and a gnostic priest of the Alexandrian deity Serapis, was the founder of an early Rosy Cross sect that he denominated the "Sages of Light."

THE ORDER OF THE HOLY GRAIL

There is, however, one crucial difference between the Order of the Rosy Cross and the Priory of Sion. The Order of the Rosy Cross never designated itself as the guardian of the bloodline of Jesus and Mary Magdalene, which was the sole *raison d'être* of the Priory of Sion. Upon deeper inspection, however, it becomes evident that the two orders actually mirror each other in their fundamental missions, which for both has been the search and protection of the Holy Grail. If they diverge, it is over their understanding of what the Grail is. While the members of the Priory of Sion contend that the Holy Grail is the body of Mary Magdalene, the Rosicrucians take a much broader approach. For them the Holy Grail is a subtle power that any human or object can possess. This power has been known by many names worldwide, including the Holy Spirit, Shekinah, Baraka, and Kundalini. A seeker must simply find the right cup, sword, spear, rock, person, and so forth, that is endowed with this power and then absorb it into themselves, thus initiating a process of alchemical transformation that leads to enlightenment and even immortality.

Those human Holy Grails who possess the greatest abundance of this power are most commonly fully enlightened masters, and those objects that are ascribed the power of Holy Grails, such as the Cup of Christ or Spear of Longinus, are normally items that have been in close contact with such masters or held a part of them, such as their blood, and then absorbed their power. This sought-after Holy Grail power can also be acquired via the head or relics of a deceased saint, such as John the Baptist, whose head was discovered in Constantinople during the Fourth Crusade and became one of the prized Holy Grails possessed by the Knights Templar. The Knights Templar were, by the way, also linked to the Order of the Rosy Cross. According to Baron von Westerode, they are known in Rosicrucian history as the "Disciples of the Rose Cross." Their definitive red

The Rose Cross and alchemical symbolism

cross of eight points was an ancient alchemical symbol of the Rosy Cross Order. And similar to other branches of the Rosy Cross, the Templars also entitled their Grand Masters as John I, II, III, and so on.

BACK TO THE GARDEN

Besides finding the Holy Grail, the goal of both the Priory and Rosy Cross has been its protection. For the Priory of Sion this means the protection of Mary Magdalene and her descendants. By contrast, the far-reaching Rosicrucians have been rigorously protecting a lineage of Holy Grail masters and their alchemical teachings that can be traced all the way back to the Garden of Eden. According to the historian Arthur Edward Waite in *The Brotherhood of the Rosy Cross*, it was not unusual for certain branches of the Order of the Rose Cross to maintain that their "Rosy Cross" wisdom was first taught by God to Adam in the fabled Garden. This secret wisdom was then passed down a lineage of enlightened "Sons of Wisdom" that included Moses and Solomon, as well as the alchemist Hermes Trismegistus.

Could the Order of the Rosy Cross have literally originated in the Garden of Eden as Rosicrucian historians maintained? A body of surprising evidence supporting this notion can be found in the archives of the Order of the Garter, Britain's most prestigious knighted order founded by King Edward III, who synthesized elements of the Templars, the Knights of the Round Table, and the Sufi Order of Al-Khadir to create his 14th century chivalrous organization. The Order of the Garter and its symbols, which include a rose and a rosy cross, was, according to Frances Yates in *The Rosicrucian Enlightenment*, initially linked to the Rosicrucians. St. George, the Garter's patron saint whose symbol is a rosy cross embedded in an eight-pointed star, also links the Order of the Garter to the Rosy Cross, while in addition he also connects both orders to the Garden of Eden. Today, St.

George is known as Al-Khadir by the Middle Eastern Sufis who maintain that his true home is Kataragama on Sri Lanka—the island paradise currently recognized by Moslems worldwide as the original site of the Garden of Eden.

Thus, St. George ties the Rosy Cross to Eden—but he also does so in a more direct way. According to the Hindus (who also venerate St. George at Kataragama albeit as their deity Skanda-Murugan), in very ancient times St. George was physically incarnate as a great spiritual leader who first taught the knowledge of alchemy to humanity. He was also full of the alchemical power of transformation, which he passed to his students, thereby founding lineages of adepts full of Holy Grail power. One of these lineages was taken west by the Nasurai Mandeans, who eventually merged with the Jewish Essenes to produce the sect of the Nasoreans or Nazarenes, the sect that John the Baptist and Jesus were born into. John received the Holy Grail power and wisdom from his Nasorean teachers before passing it to Jesus and other masters who founded gnostic sects, including the founders of the Alexandrian sect that produced Ormus. Jesus eventually passed the power and wisdom to his successors, John the Apostle and Mary Magdalene, who in turn transmitted it down a line of Holy Grail masters that culminated with the Knights Templar. Thus, in the end, the power and secret teachings of the Holy Grail came into the possession of many branches of the Order of the Rosy Cross, the real Priory of Sion.

This article first appeared in *Atlantis Rising* #58 (July/August 2006).

18

THE TEMPLARS & THE SHROUD

Were Two of the Greatest Enigmas
of the Middle Ages Intertwined?

BY JOHN WHITE

According to tradition, the Shroud of Turin is the burial cloth of Jesus. It resides in the Cathedral at Turin, Italy (and can be viewed online at its official web site: *http://sindone.torino.chiesacattolica.it / en/welcome.htm*). The provenance of the Shroud has now been established well enough to say with some certainty that it did indeed cover Jesus in the tomb.

Prior to its placement in the cathedral, the Knights Templar had possession of the shroud and kept it folded in a wooden container with a viewing window, so that the face of the Man in the Shroud was visible as an object of worship for them. (They were, after all, the Poor Knights of Christ and the Temple of Solomon.) The viewing window was framed with wooden latticework. This is based on the research of Frank Tribbe, whose book *The Holy Grail Mystery Solved* (2003) builds on the work of Noel Currer-Briggs' *The Holy Grail and the Shroud of Christ*. Tribbe's more recent book *Portrait of Jesus?* (2006) is an account of the shroud in history and science, and was published posthumously a year after he died at age 91.

According to Tribbe the term "Holy Grail" originated with the Templars and that the Old French word *greille*, which referred to the lattice frame or grillwork on the shroud's container, was transliterated over time into the English "grail." (The transformed word's meaning was corrupted, however, because "grail" etymologically means cup or bowl, and the various grail-story authors wrongly told the public that the Holy Grail is the cup of the Last Supper, or a bowl which caught Jesus' blood while he was on the cross.) The wooden frame itself was not holy, of course. Naming it "the holy greille" was simply a shorthand way of referring to the tangible evidence of holiness which it displayed—the cloth imprinted with the image of the risen Christ formed at the moment of resurrection. So the true Holy Grail, by this reckoning, is the Shroud of Turin.

The shroud itself is now, arguably, the most important religious relic in the world because it has been subjected to such rigorous scientific testing and its authenticity, we are told, has been established. Although a carbon-14 test in the late 1980s apparently showed that the shroud was no older than the 13th century—and therefore was a hoax—it has now been shown that those test results were badly flawed due to several factors. First, the piece of shroud used for testing was taken from what is

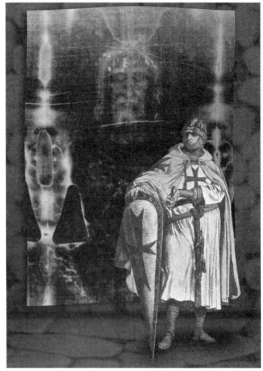

A Templar Knight protects the shroud. (Illustration by Randy Haragan)

now recognized as a 14th century "patch" or repair of the shroud, woven "invisibly"—that is, not immediately visible to the naked eye. Second is the presence of biological material—mold or microorganisms—growing on the fibers of the piece of fabric tested. These materials skewed the carbon-14 data toward a more modern date.

New chemical tests move the age of the shroud back in time to the first century AD. Furthermore, the weaving of the linen Shroud is now recognized as consistent with the weaving of first century Palestine, and not 14th century Europe. Moreover, new research has identified pollen grains on the shroud which could only have come from the vicinity of Jerusalem during the months of March and April—the time of Passover—when such vegetation is in bloom. For these and other research-based reasons, the shroud is now clearly established as an authentic first-century relic from the Near East, precisely as legend holds.

THE MAN IN THE SHROUD

As for the image of the Man in the Shroud, research likewise indicates it is no hoax. The blood stains are real (type AB) and contain human male DNA. Tribbe notes in his book *Portrait of Jesus?* that the closest science can come to explaining how the image of the Man in the Shroud got there is by comparing the situation to a controlled burst of high-intensity radiation, similar to the Hiroshima bomb explosion, which "imprinted" images of incinerated people on building walls. Shroud researcher Ray Rogers, a physical chemist from Los Alamos laboratory, said, "I am forced to conclude that the image was formed by a burst of radiant energy—light if you like." In other words, the image is recorded on the cloth as if by a photoflash of brilliant light radiating from the body of the Man in the Shroud. Another researcher, Prof. Alan Adler of Western Connecticut State College, concluded that the shroud image could have been created only by a form of energy that science cannot name.

The image of the Man in the Shroud was venerated by the Templars because it visibly demonstrated the central fact of Jesus' teaching: the conquest of death. The face-image was created by a mysterious—call it miraculous—process which science does not understand but nevertheless can recognize. The Templars understood it, however. At least, they understood that the shroud seemed to be mute testimony to the notion that Jesus transubstantiated himself in the grave through an act equivalent to a self-controlled nuclear explosion, which transformed his flesh, blood, and bone into a body of light—the resurrection body—and thereby conquered death. He attained enlightenment to the ultimate degree; he actually became light and is now revered as the Light of the World. That was the object of Templar worship.

The Shroud of Turin Web site (*www.shroud.com*) was created in 1996 by Barry M. Schwortz, the official documenting photographer for the Shroud of Turin Research Project (STURP) since 1978. An orthodox Jew, Schwortz says he is still involved with the Shroud of Turin because "knowing the unbiased facts continues to convince me of its authenticity."

THE SUDARIUM OF OVIEDO

Additional confirmation of the shroud's authenticity is the recent research on the Sudarium of Oviedo, an ancient bloodstained linen cloth the size of

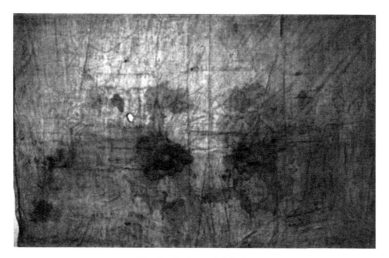

The Sudarium of Oviedo

a small towel which is claimed to have covered the head of Jesus after his crucifixion (see John 20:5-7). *Sudarium* is Latin for "face cloth." The cloth has been known historically as the Sudarium Domini, and has always been associated with Jesus. It has been kept as a holy relic in the cathedral at Oviedo, in northern Spain, since the 8th century and dated back to the 7th century by historical documents. It seems highly probable, from other historical records, that it goes back to first century Jerusalem. Pollen on it comes from Palestine, Egypt, and Spain, confirming the oral tradition that the sudarium was taken from Jerusalem through North Africa to Spain.

The sudarium is severely soiled and crumpled, with dark flecks which are symmetrically arranged but form no image, unlike the markings on the Shroud of Turin. Only disconnected bloodstains are visible to the naked eye, not a complete image of a face. When the sudarium was placed on the dead man's face, it was in a folded-over condition. Counting both sides of the cloth, there is a fourfold stain in a logical order of decreasing intensity. The cloth was draped over the face temporarily, but apparently was removed in the tomb and placed aside. (The Gospels state exactly that.) Thus the sudarium was not in contact with the face of the man when the resurrection event occurred; perhaps that is why the image of a face is absent. Nevertheless, the bloodstains correspond precisely with those of the shroud and reveal typical facial features, a prominent nose and pronounced cheek-bones.

Research since the 1980s shows that the sudarium's blood stains are type AB, matching those on the shroud. One type of pollen found on it is identical to that found on the shroud; it grows only east of the Mediterranean Sea as far north as Lebanon and as far south as Jerusalem. Scientific studies validate the ancient claim that the cloth had covered the head of a long-haired, bearded man with bleeding scalp wounds who died in an upright position. Residue of what is most likely myrrh and aloe have been discovered in the sudarium, in accord with the Jewish burial custom of Jesus's time. The sudarium and the shroud have so many bloodstains which match up—70 on the face side and 50 on the rear side—that the only possible conclusion is that the Sudarium of Oviedo covered the same face as the Shroud of Turin.

Both tradition and science indicate the sudarium was used to cover the head of the dead body of Jesus. No evidence points away from that conclusion except for one radiocarbon dating to the 7th century, and the researcher who obtained that age of the cloth acknowledges that his results are questionable. (See the 2001 book *Sacred Blood, Sacred Image: The Sudarium of Oviedo* by Janice Bennett.)

When the Templars were violently suppressed in AD 1307 by Philip IV of France, the principal charge against the knights was the accusation that they worshipped the head of a bearded man. The charges against the Templars include "adoration and worship of an idol—which was said to be the image of the true God." The charges were trumped up by Phillip to disband the Templar organization so that he could take possession of the Templar treasure in their Paris headquarters and elsewhere. However, in an irony totally lost on their accuser, we now know that the principal charge was actually true! As noted above, according to Tribbe, the Templars had come into possession of the burial cloth of Jesus. It was central to Templary. Today, according to Tribbe, more than 80 Templar churches and asylums remain, and nearly every one of them contains an image of the face of Christ which is a drawn (via painting, mosaic inlay, or sculpture) from the original image of the face of the man in the shroud. Yes, the Templars did indeed worship the head of a bearded man and called it the image of the true God.

The Templars sought to follow in the way which Jesus taught. However, because of their experience with the corruption of the Old World, they apparently set in motion a long-term project for the creation of a new and uncorrupted society in the New World. Over time, the suppressed Order of the Temple gave rise to modern Freemasonry and to the Freemasons who had such a strong role in the foundation and formation of America.

Is it possible that America is the result of a Templar/Masonic experiment intended to create a New Israel or New Jerusalem in the New World—not a Jewish nation but a universally God-centered society? John Adams and Benjamin Franklin spoke of that possibility. Here is the argument for that Templar project.

Several books about the Knights Templar and the Holy Grail indicate that the African kingdom of Mali should be credited with two momentous facts bearing profoundly on Euro-American history. According to Michael Bradley in his 1988 book *Holy Grail Across the Atlantic* and, building on that, William F. Mann's 1999 *The Labyrinth of the Grail*, by the 14th century the emperor of Mali had ships going to the New World, and other Africans had crossed much earlier. Pre-Columbian stone statues in Central America of men with negroid features appear to testify to this extraordinary achievement.

Transatlantic travel could not have been done well without the development of a method to measure longitude. That means Africans solved the problem of determining longitude at sea long before Europeans did. However, the knowledge was lost and apparently had no influence on the solution developed by Europeans in the 18th century.

Why it was lost and why Malian seafaring culture declined are topics for research. The Bradley-Mann thesis contends that knowledge of longitude measurement was passed from Mali to Arabic culture, and thence to the Knights Templar, whose interactions with Arab Muslims in the Middle East were more often friendly than hostile. (Sufi mystics and Christian mystics would tend toward friendly contact, wouldn't they?) The Knights Templar, in turn, kept that knowledge—and knowledge of a great land mass to the west—secret, using it for their own purposes.

Those purposes may have included voyages to the New World a full century before Columbus, through Prince Henry Sinclair of Scotland and Orkney. Sinclair's forebears had granted shelter in Scotland to fugitive Knights Templar when Philip arrested Grand Master Jacques de Molay and hundreds of other knights, and suppressed the Templar Order. The Sinclairs of Scotland were related to the St. Clairs of France, a Templar family.

A fleet of Templar ships fled La Rochelle, France in 1307 on the eve of King Philip's hostile action and sailed around Ireland to Scotland. (The fleet may have carried great Templar treasure; at any rate, when Philip entered the Treasury in Paris, it was empty.) Those exiled Knights Templar made Roslin Castle, the ancestral home of the Sinclairs just south of Edinburgh, their center of operations.

Rosslyn Chapel was begun there in the mid-1400s and completed before the end of that century. Its floor plan is identical to that of Solomon's Temple in Jerusalem. It contains carvings of maize (Indian corn), aloe, and other plants that are native to the New World. (For more on this see The *Lost Treasure of the Knights Templar* by Steven Sora and *The Hiram Key* by Christopher Knight and Robert Lomas.)

"Rosslyn Chapel" (Alexander Nasmyth, 1789)

How did knowledge of New World vegetation get to Scotland before Columbus? The probable explanation is this.

In 1398, Henry Sinclair led an expedition which reached Nova Scotia and the East Coast of America. (A 15th century text called *The Zeno Diary* recorded the event.) In Nova Scotia, there is a modern monument to Sinclair and the expedition; there is also a museum containing evidence of a nearby 14th century Scottish settlement, including a 14th century bronze cannon found there. In Westford, Massachusetts, there is an ancient engraving of a 14th century Scottish knight on a rock ledge which, experts say, indicates a Templar presence there also. The knight's shield markings identifies him as a member of the Gunn clan, which owed allegiance to Prince Sinclair. And in Newport, Rhode Island, the so-called Viking Tower likewise indicates the presence of the Sinclair expedition because it is based on 14th century Scottish architecture and has nothing at all in common with Viking stonework. *Templars in America* by Tim Wallace-Murphy and Marilyn Hopkins (2005) gives an excellent photo-illustrated summary of all this evidence, as well as commentary on the link between the Templar/Freemasons and the Founders of America.

It is speculated by Templar/Masonic scholars that, because of their harsh experience with the political corruption of the Old World, the Templars conceived a secret plan for creating a new and better society in the American wilderness. Over several centuries, the Order of the Temple was transformed into Freemasonry (see John Robinson's *Dungeon, Fire and Sword*) and the plan was carried forward through Freemasonry and its influence over the founding of America. Francis Bacon, who was a driving force behind the creation of the Royal Society for scientific research and exploration, was connected to the Templar remnant. He also wrote *The New Atlantis,* about a mythical land to the West, and his account of that land shows remarkable parallels to later historical developments in the New World, as if his book were a kind of coded blueprint for Masonic endeavors in the vast and virgin continent.

Is it mere coincidence that the first evidence of Freemasonry in North America appeared in Nova Scotia? A stone engraved on the top with a square and compasses—the premier Masonic symbol—was found on the shore of Goat Island in the Annapolis Basin in Nova Scotia, where Prince Henry Sinclair had first voyaged to the New World. In the center of the flat slab was the date 1606. (Dr. Charles T. Jackson of Boston wrote about it in 1829, calling it the "Annapolis Stone." The stone is said to have become a part of a wall for a building; it was covered with cement and never found again.)

Perhaps there is a secret history to America, much like what has been alleged by Manly Palmer Hall in *America's Secret Destiny* and by others who claim there is an occult (meaning hidden) or esoteric (meaning not publicly disclosed) foundation to America. Perhaps, just perhaps, America is in part a Templar/Masonic effort to advance human society on the basis of secret knowledge and secret activities.

I am not qualified to judge the validity of the evidence mentioned above for a Templar project in America; I simply report it. However, if there is anything sacred about America, it is the idea that God is the author of our being and the source of our freedom, our sovereignty, our rights, our justice, and our human dignity. The four references to Deity in the Declaration of Independence collectively express those ideas. They are very Masonic ideas, injected into the social-political institutions and worldview of America by those Freemasons who were among its founders. Moreover, the fundamental value of America is freedom, the same value expressed in the prefix of Masonry. Was it purely chance, or has a hidden hand been guiding American affairs through the centuries and working through barely visible means which carry the symbols and substance of Freemasonry?

If so, it is a benevolent counterbalance to the dark forces of the world seeking to destroy freedom and god-oriented society.

This article first appeared in *Atlantis Rising* #67 (January/February 2008).

PART FIVE

MARKS OF THE MASONS

Constitution/Masonic Collage (*Atlantis Rising* art)

19

THE TEMPLE IN WASHINGTON

What Was the Spiritual Intention
of the Nation's Founders?

BY WILLIAM HENRY

The United States Capitol, rising atop Capitol Hill in the monument city of Washington, D.C., may well be the most famous building in the world. To Americans, the cast-iron Capitol dome, dressed in pure white sandstone, is a symbol of strength and democracy. Radiant. Luminous. Shining. Freedom rings from this beautiful bell. Yet how many recognize the Capitol is really a temple?

Thomas Jefferson called it "The first temple dedicated to the sovereignty of the people."

An anonymous essay of 1795 described the Capitol building as a "Temple erected to Liberty."

Specifically, the founders of the Capitol Temple likened it to Solomon's Temple in Jerusalem.

On September 18, 1793, at the laying of the cornerstone of the Capitol, Maryland Grand Master Joseph Clark remarked, "I have every hope that the grand work we have done today will be handed down…to a late posterity, as the like work of that ever memorable temple to our order erected by our ancient Grand Master Solomon."

On November 22, 1800, opening the Second Session of the Sixth Congress in the new Capitol building, President Adams declared, "It would be unbecoming the representatives of this Nation to assemble for the first time in this solemn Temple without looking up to the Supreme Ruler of the Universe and imploring His blessing."

These words are more than poetic. The U.S. Capitol has numerous architectural and other features that unquestionably identify it with ancient temples, including stone construction, an underground entrance, chapels, an image of a deified being, religious imagery, symbols, and inscriptions, divine proportions, massive columns, palpable spiritual energy, acoustic trickery, terrifying guardians, mystic visitors, closed doors, private members, secret chambers, and orientation to the Sun.

It is crystal clear that the builders viewed the Capitol as America's sole temple (a solemn, Solomon's Solar Temple to be exact).

THE DOME AT THE HEART OF AMERICA

The dome of the Capitol ices this connection. Domes have been called the perfect architectural shape: the circle, symbol of the universe, executed in three dimensions. In religious architecture, domes proclaim the glory of God. The word dome comes from Latin *domus*, a "house," via Italian *duomo*, a "house of God," that is a church (from *kirk*, meaning "circle"). The temple is a "house of the holy." Temple is also a word for the flat part on either side of the human head—called a dome in slang—above and beyond the eye.

The oculus, or eye of the dome, is considered the Gateway of the Sun. From this gateway at the top of the dome rises the World Axis, the link between Heaven and Earth. Domes, therefore, are the threshold or gateway of the spiritual world.

Designed in 1854 by Philadelphia architect Thomas Walter, the cast-iron U.S. Capitol dome (its second) features stunning columns, pilasters, windows, and is crowned by a statue of the goddess Freedom. When funds ran low during the Civil War, Abraham Lincoln encouraged continuing the controversial construction of the New Dome as a symbol of unity.

The Capitol Rotunda is a large, circular room located in the center of the Capitol on the second floor. Ninety-six feet in diameter, it is the symbolic and physical heart of the U.S. Capitol. It is the ceremonial center of the United States of America.

More directly, it is a place of American ritual. Rites are performed here. Statues, such as the one of Eisenhower, are unveiled here. Inaugurations take place here. Eminent citizens lay in state here. It was the body of Abraham Lincoln, the first president to be assassinated, lying in state which has forever hallowed the spot.

GEORGE WASHINGTON IN THE SUN (OR STAR) GATE

Hanging 180 feet above the floor of the Rotunda, in the canopy of the interior Dome is the single most important work of alchemy anywhere in the world.

Brumidi's masterpiece in the dome of the Capitol: "The Apotheosis of George Washington."

Painted in true fresco, it's called "The Apotheosis of George Washington." The Italian painter, Constantino Brumidi, painted it during the Civil War. A renowned Vatican painter, Brumidi came to the United States in 1852, after he had received a papal pardon for his role in Italy's republican revolution. He was inspired by Michaelangelo's last great work, the Dome of St. Peters, and is in fact called "the Michaelangelo of the Capitol."

Floating in the center of the "Apotheosis," a uniformed Washington sits enthroned on a rainbow in front of a Sun gate. Liberty, holding her *fasces* (a goddess symbol of transformation), and a combination of Victory and Fame sounding trumps, flank him.

Apotheosis is a Greek word that means "to raise to god-like stature" or the glorification of a person as an ideal. Indeed, this fresco depicts Washington as a god-man. Christian art portrays Jesus sitting on a rainbow and enthroned exactly the same way. The sun is a symbol of Christ from the

prophecy of Malachi 4:2 "But unto you that fear my name shall the Sun of righteousness arise with healing in his wings."

Tibetan artists use identical imagery to portray their high holy ones (called lamas) who have achieved "The Great Perfection" (Dzogchen). The aim of the Great Perfection is to awaken the individual to the primordial state of enlightenment, which is naturally found in all beings. The initiate's goal is to integrate enlightenment into all his or her activities and to unite the physical body with the energy of Nature, the supreme realization of which lies in the manifestation of the "Rainbow Body" or body of light.

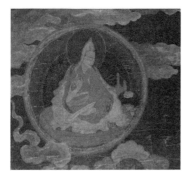

This is the meaning behind the symbolism of both Jesus and George Washington sitting on the rainbow. Washington is a perfected human, not only a Grand Master, but also an "American Christ," in tune with his divine nature. He is now somewhere over the rainbow and is a bridge between Heaven and Earth.

Perfection is the foundation tantra of the European Enlightenment thinkers—Locke, Voltaire, and Rousseau— who inspired the deeply spiritual, even mystic, founders of America (many of whom were Freemasons and Rosicrucians). Human beings are not inherently depraved or sinful; Enlightenment thinkers reasoned; we are naturally good.

Top: Detail of Jesus enthroned on a rainbow with celestial beings all around him. Note the "sun gate" behind him.

Center: A lama rides in a rainbow.

Bottom: Washington enthroned on a rainbow with, sun gate behind him.

Tearing a page from Plato's Republic, they saw enlightenment as a process of revealing what is already inside the person:

self-perfection into the Gnostic "Man of Light." The enlightened ones of Tibet say the same thing only adding that perfection or holiness is the natural state of every living being whether they know it or not and that we also have the capacity to manifest perfection—that is to say, the Rainbow Body.

The Founders had a vision of America as a psychological space and a place where individuals were free to perfect themselves, or in Jefferson's multi-layered language, to form "a more perfect union."

The circle or "gate" of 72 stars surrounding George Washington affirms this philosophy. Seventy-two is a powerful esoteric number with numerous correspondences in the Mysteries. Seventy-two represents the number of years on one degree of a zodiacal age. Manly P. Hall's *The Secret Destiny of America* has an interesting interpretation of the 72 stones in the pyramid of the Great Seal. He sees them corresponding to the 72 arrangements of the Tetragrammaton, or the four-lettered name of God, in Hebrew. These four letters can be combined into 72 combinations, resulting in what is called the Shemhamforesh, which represents, in turn, the laws, powers, and energies of Nature by which the perfection of man is achieved.

Thirteen female figures encircle Washington, each with a star above her head. They are thought to represent the thirteen original states. However, this is not an earthly scene. They are 13 star beings.

Surrounding Washington are seven mythological figures that correspond to the seven stages of alchemy. Included is Poseidon, the ruler of Atlantis, and Mercury and Vulcan, two gods synonymous with alchemy.

THE STAIRWAY TO HEAVEN

An imaginary vertical line descending from the Sun gate in the dome travels through a golden dot at the center of the Rotunda, then through a star in a large circular room called the Crypt one story beneath the Rotunda. The Latin *crypta* means "hidden" or "secret." A crypt is usually found in cemeteries and under public religious buildings, such as churches and cathedrals. It's a burial place, but also, importantly, a meeting place.

The star in the crypt marks the literal ground zero in Washington, D.C. It divides the city into four quadrants, and every address in the city tells you where you are in relation to that precise point in the U.S. Capitol building. This is just another open (yet hidden) hint as to the significance of that particular gold dot.

Architectural historians link the crypt with the unconscious and the chthonic, subterranean, or earthly realm. This is based on the medieval belief that the cathedral was the body of Christ and a symbol also of Man. The body and spirit, encased in a coffin or casket, is "planted" in the crypt to resurrect or rise.

A crypt is also an entrance to a tomb. Indeed, the Capitol's Crypt provides an entrance to Washington's Tomb, which is located one story beneath the Crypt.

Washington's Tomb is empty. Why? We know the tomb was never used to inter Washington's body. We know the plans to place his casket there were scuttled by a legal issue in Washington's will. We know his grave is at Mount Vernon, the President's home. But perhaps a more compelling answer is because Washington is on the ceiling of the dome . . . in the heavens above. Washington has risen. Just like Jesus' tomb (and the King's Chamber of the Great Pyramid) Washington's tomb is empty because the man is now a deity.

This perspective conjures the image of the Capitol as a temple of transformation or even a casket.

THE TEMPLE OF MAN

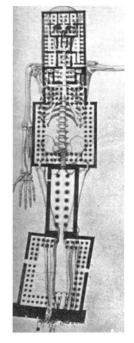

The work of the French explorer of Egyptian alchemy, Schwaller de Lubicz, as presented in *The Temple In Man: Sacred Architecture and the Perfect Man*, leads a to major breakthrough in our understanding of the Capitol-is-a-casket story.

De Lubicz's work centered on the Temple of Luxor, located two miles from Thebes, Egypt's equivalent of the Vatican. The plan for this temple, he demonstrated, is based on human proportions and designed to symbolically represent the human body. Luxor is an open book containing the secrets of human spiritual anatomy. In this temple he found the form of a human being embodied in the geometry of the Temple's architecture. This, he concluded, is Pharaoh, symbolic of the Perfect Man.

The Temple of Man was built by Ramses II in the 13th century BC as a setting for the rituals of the Festival of Opet. The word *opet* means "secret chamber." So it is "the Festival of the Secret Chamber."

During this festival the king would make a ceremonial precession from Karnak along the avenue of Sphinxes to the temple of Luxor, located two miles away. The king would make his way to one of the innermost chambers of the temple. There, the king and his divine essence (called the *ka*, and created at his birth), were united and the king was transformed into a divine being. The crowd, waiting anxiously, their belly's full of bread and beer provided by the king for the rite, would cheer wildly upon the king's emergence as the transformed, or transfigured god-man.

The festival affirmed and renewed the king's Divine Right to Rule. It assured the people that the power of the Cosmos was renewed in the king.

Projecting the image of the Temple of Luxor onto the U.S. Capitol, which is divided into seven chambers that correspond with the seven chakras, reveals a provocative match. The House of Representatives corresponds with the feet. The Rotunda is the womb. The Senate is the head.

It is ironic that the U.S. Capitol mimics the sacred layout of the Temple of Luxor, considering that America was founded to abolish the Divine Right of Kings. Nonetheless, the spectacle of the Opet Festival is echoed in the inauguration ceremonies of U.S. Presidents as *head* of state or *head* of government, a position that indicates that the President is above party politics.

Below: Projection of the Temple of Luxor and human skeleton upon Latrobe's plan of the U.S. Capitol.

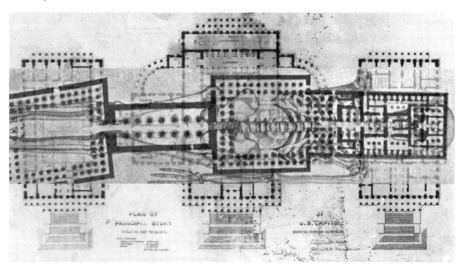

The word *inaugural* comes from ancient Rome, where priests, called augurs, interpreted the will of the gods by reading the flight patterns of birds. The word *augur* is thought to be derived either from the root *aug*, "to increase, to prosper" or from the Latin *avi* and *gero*, "directing of birds."

In this lavish American ceremony, initiation, or rite, politicians stand at the gate of the Secret Chamber, the Capitol Rotunda, in front of hundreds of thousands of spectators (and millions more watching on TV) to take the oath of office and to renew the office of the President. It is strikingly similar to coronations and enthronements. The crucial difference is that the *people* elected the individual being sworn in to be their head ("president," or "present Id" to use a Freudian term for the instinctual aspect of our psychic apparatus).

Originally, the word inauguration referred to the sacred marriage, the symbolic mating of the new king with the goddess of the kingdom. Scholars point to the Irish Feast of Tara, at which the king married the goddess Medb.

In America the goddess is named Freedom, Liberty, and America. Her statues are abundant on the Hill and in the Capitol. She stands on top of the Capitol. Why? It could be because, symbolically, she "owns" it.

Traditionally, the swearing in takes place on the East Portico. For the first time ever, an inauguration took place on the West Terrace of the Capitol when Ronald Reagan took office in 1981. The west side would accommodate more visitors. Reagan's second inaugural ceremony in January 1985 took place in the Rotunda due to weather.

President Barack Obama also chose the West Terrace. After being sworn in at noon, the newly anointed President enters the Capitol Temple. He ascends 33 steps into the Rotunda. He looks up. He first sees Mercury; then, he sees the deified Washington peering down at him, challenging him to be an enlightened American leader.

This article first appeared in *Atlantis Rising* #74 (March/April 2009).

20

PHOENIX: MASONIC METROPOLIS?

Were the Pioneers Who Built This Desert City Following a Hidden Agenda?

BY GARY DAVID

Turquoise swimming pools, when seen from above, shimmer like a squash blossom necklace on a jet setter's tanned breast. Imported palm trees tower over a surrendering army of native saguaros, while skyscraper mirages of steel and glass gleam in the distance. This western metropolis pushes out more than up, though, sprawling over 450 square miles.

With the sixth largest population in the U.S., Phoenix, Arizona—the "Valley of the Sun"—attracts all kinds: retirees golfing their way into oblivion, snowbirds fleeing subzero winters, young construction workers cashing in on frenzied economic growth. Shopping malls, parking lots, concrete cloverleafs, subdivisions, and apartments relentlessly eat away at the mesquite and ironwood at the rate of "an acre an hour."

Summer temperatures routinely soar over 100 degrees. Before air conditioning, the Sonoran desert must have been unbearable. Where once rattlesnakes, scorpions, centipedes, tarantulas, and gila monsters reigned over the sand, now new dangers have crept in: gang wars, drug money, prostitution, and lots of asphalt. In other words, an aura of the foreign and bizarre pervades Phoenix. What exactly attracted early settlers to this hard and uncompromising landscape?

A LOCAL HABITATION AND A NAME

In the autumn of 1867, Bryan Philip Darrell Duppa and other founding fathers of the fledgling city were picnicking on the platform mound at Pueblo Grande near what is now the intersection of East Washington and 44th Streets near Phoenix Sky Harbor airport. Someone asked what this future municipality should be named. A Southerner in the party wanted to call it Stonewall, after the Confederate general. Another idly offered the appellation Salina, meaning "salt marsh," but that too was voted down. Then Duppa spoke: "This canal was constructed in an age now forgotten. Prehistoric cities lie in ruins all around you. A great ancient civilization once thrived in this valley. Let the new city arise from its ashes. Let it be called Phoenix."

Both the platform mound and the canal had been built by the Hohokam who inhabited the basin as early as 300 BC. The flat-topped mound (shaped like a Mayan pyramid) measures 300 feet long, 150 feet wide and 20 feet high. Lacking draft animals and wheelbarrows, these industrious Native Americans also dug 500 miles of aqueducts to irrigate over 25,000 acres. The main channels were 75 feet across and 12 feet deep. H. M. Wormington, one of the first archaeologists in the region, believed that the construction of this extensive system rivaled the architectural achievements of the Egyptian pyramids or the Mayan temples. Duppa would have probably agreed.

Darrell Duppa

Born into English landed gentry, "Lord" Darrell Duppa was one of the best-educated men in the American West. Classically trained in Paris and Madrid, he knew French, Spanish, Italian, Latin, and Greek. The library that he carried with him into the wilderness included Ovid, Juvenal, and Homer in the original. An eccentric and a loner, he occasionally was given to fits of eloquence and could quote Shakespeare by the hour, especially if facilitated by a shot or two of red-eye.

Months earlier, Duppa had been seen in Prescott, the new prospecting town one hundred miles to the north. His ostensible business was to check up on some gold mining claims owned by his prosperous uncle, whose New Zealand sheep ranch he had helped to establish. Before arriving in Arizona, Duppa had traveled extensively throughout Australia and was the sole survivor of a shipwreck off the coast of Chile. Although water rather than fire was the threatening element, this event may give a clue to his personal choice for the name.

Duppa was alluding to the description of the mythical phoenix by the Greek historian Herodotus. At the end of each temporal cycle this brilliantly plumed male bird flies to Heliopolis in Egypt and builds a nest of cassia twigs in a myrrh tree as his pyre upon which he will be resurrected. Thus a new cycle is initiated. All this scholarship must have impressed the settlers, because the name began to be used officially. Or so the official story goes.

Birds of a Feather

Perhaps it is no accident that most of the first citizens of Phoenix, including Duppa, were Freemasons.

John T. Alsap, for instance, was an attorney, judge, first territorial treasurer, and first mayor of Phoenix. He also served as the first worshipful master of Arizona Lodge No. 2 as well as the first grand master of the Masonic Grand Lodge of Arizona. Even earlier, he had been first master of Arizona's first Masonic Lodge called Aztlan, located in Prescott, the first territorial capital. (A lot of "firsts" here.)

Aztlan is a Nahuatl word meaning "place of the heron." The Aztecs inhabited this mythical land after emerging from the Seven Caves located in the bowels of the earth. The heron is thought to be the naturalistic model for both the phoenix and the bennu bird. In the Egyptian sun cult the Bennu was found perched atop an obelisk or sometimes upon a pyramid-shaped stone of meteoric iron called a Benben.

Seen as an Egyptian symbol of morning and new life, the heron passes with flying colors (no pun intended). Likewise, the bennu embodies the morn-

Bennu bird

ing star Venus, appearing each dawn on the laurel tree in Heliopolis. This ornithological curiosity is also the incarnation of the heart (*ab*) of Osiris and the soul (*ba*) of Ra, two primary deities related by a simple palindrome. In addition, the heron and the bennu were among a small number of animals, including the hawk and the serpent, in which a discarnate soul could inhabit for as long as it wished.

The hieroglyph for bennu means both "purple heron" (*Ardea purpurea*) and "palm tree." One denotation for the word "phoenix" is "purple-red;" consequently, the Phoenicians were known as "red men." Even today residents of Phoenix are known as Phoenicians.

In a tome called *Morals and Dogma of the Ancient and Accepted Scottish Rite of Freemasonry*, 33rd-degree Mason Albert Pike states that the phoenix

Phoenix and Firebird

was a quintessential alchemical icon. In this regard J. E. Cirlot's *Dictionary of Symbols* remarks, "In alchemy, [the phoenix] corresponds to the colour red, to the regeneration of universal life and to the successful completion of a process." Some Arizona prospectors may indeed have been seeking spiritual gold.

Is it more than mere coincidence, then, that the phoenix, whose center of worship was the pre-dynastic City of the Sun, should lend its name to what would become the largest city in the Valley of the Sun? Is the name something more than the whim of some erudite settler, misplaced in the hinterlands of America?

Aztlan is furthermore conceptualized as an island, and some speculate that the name even refers to the legendary continent of Atlantis. According to comparative linguistics scholar Gene D. Matlock in *The Last Atlantis Book*, the Aztlán of Nahuatl mythology was really called Aztatlán, referring to the village of Nayarit on Mexico's western coast. The Sanskrit word *Asta* apparently means "Place of the Setting Sun." Matlock suggests that this could actually be the westernmost boundary of what was once Atlantis.

Did Lord Duppa and Judge Alsap consciously try to merge Egyptian and Mesoamerican mythologies in the wilds of Arizona? Alsap's Bachelor of Law and Doctor of Medicine degrees prove that he was no dummy himself. Was the establishment of Aztlan (Masonic Lodge No. 1) and Phoenix

(Masonic Lodge No. 2) an attempt to symbolically merge Prescott (the heron) and Phoenix (the bennu) in the same way they would soon actually be linked by stagecoach? Was it a clandestine Masonic intent that a new Atlantis (Aztlan) should rise in Arizona and a new Heliopolis (Phoenix) should be its heart?

WHOSE STORY?

Other questions about the initial territorial capital come to mind. Why was Prescott named to honor the prominent 19th century historian William Hickling Prescott, who never set foot in the town? Were the run-of-the-mill settlers really all that interested in his book *History of the Conquest of Mexico*? According to its author, "The inhabitants, members of different tribes, and speaking dialects somewhat different, belonged to the same great family of nations who had come from the real or imaginary region of Aztlan, in the far north-west." In other words, the Arizona Territory. Is this why two major thoroughfares in the town of Prescott are named Cortez Street and Montezuma Street?

Why did the territorial capital suddenly shift in 1889 from Prescott to Phoenix? The mercantile owner, postmaster, and territorial representative John Y. T. Smith greatly influenced this movement. He, too, was another "pioneer Mason" of Phoenix. After governmental authority had finally rested with the southern city, spiritual symbolism superseded natural potency. Did secret powers dictate that instead of the heron the phoenix should arise?

Whatever the reason, Columbus H. Gray, who served as a territorial senator and member of Maricopa County's Board of Supervisors, began during Phoenix's early years to construct a Masonic hall at the corner of Jefferson and First streets. Before it was completed, he sold it to Mike Goldwater, grandfather of Arizona Senator Barry Goldwater, himself a 33rd-degree Mason. Incidentally, Phoenix is located at 33 degrees north latitude.

By 1890, a number of the fraternal organizations were operating in the city: Masons, Odd Fellows, Knights of Pythias, Ancient Order of United Workmen, Grand Army of the Republic, Chosen Friends and Good Templars.

Darrell Duppa spent his last days in the Valley of the Sun and died in 1892. He was initially buried in the Odd Fellows Cemetery but was later reinterred in Greenwood Memorial Cemetery. "Membership in both the Masons and Odd Fellows has been common as evidenced by numerous pins showing the square and compass conjoined with the three link chain." The Odd Fellows' symbol of three links represents the principal tenants of Friendship, Love, and Truth, whereas Freemasonry's square and compass signify Earth (matter) and Heaven (spirit) respectively.

Further evidence of Duppa's Masonic association comes from one source that connects him to Jacob Waltz, the famous Lost Dutchman, by identifying both men as Masons. This German prospector supposedly discovered a fabulous gold mine in the Superstition Mountains east of Phoenix. As with many lost treasures of the Wild West, its location remains a mystery.

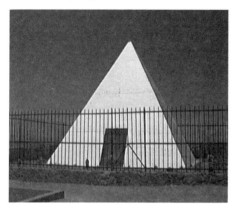

Mausoleum of Arizona's first governor, George W. P. Hunt, Papago Park, Phoenix

Masonic influence in Phoenix continued well into the 20th century. Arizona's first governor, George Wiley Paul Hunt, served seven terms between 1912 (the year of statehood) and 1932. He was also a prominent and long-standing Freemason. As a populist and supporter of trade unions, he spoke and wrote in a simple and sometimes grammatically incorrect style. Nonetheless, like Duppa, he loved classical literature, which gained him the moniker "Old Roman." A man of contradictions, Hunt had also been known to address Theosophical Society meetings.

His final resting place in Phoenix's Papago Park is within sight of an archaeo-astronomical observatory once used by the Hohokam but now called Hole-in-the-Rock. Oddly enough, Hunt's family mausoleum was constructed in the style of a white-tiled Egyptian pyramid.

This article first appeared in *Atlantis Rising* #57 (May/June 2006).

21
─────

SAN FRANCISCO & PHILADELPHIA

The Masonic Connection

BY STEPHEN V. O'ROURKE

F reemasons and Philadelphia are as American as apple pie (see Steven Sora's article "The Heretics Who Lit the Way for America" in *Atlantis Rising* #63). Even before America's independence, as Sora indicated, there was a strong Masonic community thriving in the "City of Brotherly Love." Ben Franklin, the city's great Revolutionary War hero, was also a prolific Freemason and in 1754 he dedicated the very first Masonic building in America, the Philadelphia Freemasons' Lodge.

Another of the city's revolutionary Hero's and Freemasons was Francis Hopkinson, the designer of the first United States flag, a signer of the Declaration of Independence, as well as a composer of sacred and secular music. Hopkinson was also a specialist in heraldry and seal designs, and in the 1770s he helped design the Great Seal of New Jersey with famed artist Pierre Eugène du Simitière.

Two designs that Hopkinson had used for early American currency, the all-seeing eye (on a $40 note) and a stepped pyramid (on the $50 note of 1778) would be incorporated by du Simitière and William Barton when the Great Seal of the U.S. was officially sanctioned in 1782. Hopkinson is also credited with designing the Seals of Admiralty and the U.S. Treasury; he died suddenly (of an epileptic seizure) in 1791 at the age of 53, leaving behind a wife and a large family.

Of Hopkinson's nine children, his son Joseph (born 1775) was to carry on his father's legacy as a lawyer, composer, and Freemason. It was Joseph's son, also named Francis Hopkinson, who seems to have passed down information regarding the reverse seal and its purpose in the development of the United States. Francis Hopkinson the younger was born in 1796 in Philadelphia, and had five children, the first of whom was named Alexander Hamilton Hopkinson, in honor of the first U.S. Treasury Secretary.

The reverse of the Great Seal of the United STaets

In the 1840s Francis Hopkinson II employed the architect Gordon Parker Cummings to design and build a new home for the family in the rare Egyptian revival style. Although little else is known about the building, it is probable that much of the imagery used to design it came from freemasonic imagery passed down within the family. Cummings himself was a Freemason and a highly educated architect. He also is the one person most likely to have been privy to the San Francisco/Great Seal agenda (see my article, "San Francisco's Pyramid Saga" in *Atlantis Rising*, #55) and was perhaps initiated into the secret meaning of the reverse of the Great Seal at Philadelphia Masonic meetings of the day.

G. P. Cummings is a mysterious and now forgotten figure of the 19th century. Born circa 1809 somewhere in the northeast U.S. (some sources say Boston, one says New York), Cummings made his home in Philadelphia by the 1830s. In 1845, already an accomplished architect and knowledgeable Freemason, Cummings began teaching at The Carpenter's Company in Philadelphia. In 1850, he designed his first major building, the Penn Mutual, the first iron-fronted building in the U.S., outside of New York City. A year later, Cummings' Masonic standing grew as he designed a Gothic style structure known as the Prince Hall Freemasons of Philadelphia, the black Freemasons of the city.

ESTABLISHING THE TALISMAN—PHILADELPHIANS IN CALIFORNIA

Whatever secrets Cummings learned in his Philadelphia days he would soon bring them with him to the west coast. In 1852, he suddenly appears with an office at 152 Montgomery, San Francisco, the very same street where the first freemasonic meeting had been held in California in 1849. San Francisco counted among its pioneers at least two Philadelphians. One was George Hyde, a Philadelphia educated lawyer and an early political leader in Yerba Buena, the original name for San Francisco. Hyde's friend and fellow civic leader was Jasper O'Farrell, a dedicated Freemason and surveyor. Together Hyde and O'Farrell put the first names on San

Francisco's streets, taking a few from the City of Brotherly Love—Market, Sansom, and Filbert. At least one source claims that O'Farrell in fact hoped to design San Francisco in a style similar to that of his former hometown, which he deemed was a well laid out city.

With Cummings, the new Philadelphia arrival, in town, San Francisco was about to incorporate elements of the reverse of the Great Seal into its street design. The seal would provide the proper feng shui to ensure prosperity and growth for survival in the post-Gold Rush days that lay ahead. It would ensure that the city stood tall, as a beacon of Manifest Destiny. From atop Montgomery Street, the All-Seeing Eye would radiate; from the base of the pyramid the cornerstones of the U.S. Army (at Black Point Ridge) would be matched by the center of local politics the circular tower of old City Hall (named enigmatically as the Hall of Records).

Mind you, the reverse of the Seal was not a common sight in the mid-19th century, and anyone knowledgeable of its meaning and symbolism needed to be learned and well read. Despite being officially designated as

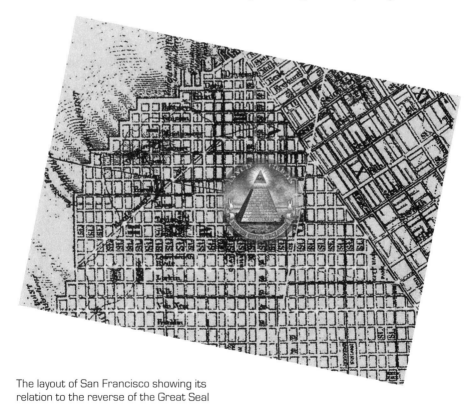

The layout of San Francisco showing its relation to the reverse of the Great Seal

an official U.S. symbol in 1782, the reverse Seal of the United States had yet to be used on any official documents and had rarely been seen since its creation. It is probable that only highly initiated Freemasons and members of certain governmental departments had seen it at this point in time. Whether any of the San Francisco Masons were aware of the reverse seal at this point is unknown, but it is known that Cummings soon began designing a strategically based building in that city; and soon after, a diagonally placed street was incorporated into the city's alignment that emulates well the imagery of the Great Seal's reverse.

MONTGOMERY BLOCK—THE MASON'S MARK

Under the direction of future Civil War general Henry W. Halleck, whose wife was the granddaughter of Alexander Hamilton; G. P. Cummings constructed the building known as the Montgomery Block in 1852 and 1853. Montgomery Block was situated almost precisely at the site of the first Masonic meeting and would become a legendary melting pot for the bizarre, witty, and literate. Mark Twain, Ambrose Bierce, and in later times Jack Kerouac, would squat there. The building now sitting where the Montgomery Block was (the Transamerica Pyramid Building) seems to confirm the Masonic theory regarding San Francisco's founding, yet even in the 19th century that spot on the San Francisco map was intriguing.

PATH TO PORTER'S LODGE—AKA FORT MASON

The road that later became known as Columbus Avenue was first officially incorporated into the San Francisco street map circa 1872 and was originally called Montgomery Avenue, an offshoot of Montgomery Street. (Montgomery Street had been named in honor of Captain John B. Montgomery who had taken Yerba Buena in 1846 in the name of the United States, and had come ashore at a spot later numbered as 552 Montgomery; it is not known if Montgomery himself was a Freemason.) In the early days of San Francisco, Montgomery Avenue served as a link between the army headquarters at Black Point Ridge and the Montgomery Block building. Prior to becoming the U. S. army headquarters, Black Point Ridge was the site of a Masonic structure known as Porter's Lodge, and was owned by early California pioneer and Freemason John C. Fremont. In the 1880s the army facility that incorporated Black Point Ridge was renamed Fort Mason.

The Philadelphia Masons Open a Lodge

In the years prior to the publication of the 1873 map of San Francisco, the first map that officially listed Montgomery Avenue, the Freemasons of both San Francisco and Philadelphia made alliances of no small significance. In 1868, just as the cornerstone for the great Freemasonic Temple of Philadelphia was being laid, the Grand Lodge of Pennsylvania chartered a new lodge for San Francisco, the Mosaic Lodge #38. Almost immediately a new Masonic temple in San Francisco was also constructed at 200 Montgomery Street. In 1875, directly between the Masonic Temple and the Montgomery Block, the U.S. Mint and sub-treasury was built, further ensuring that this portion of San Francisco would embody the pillars of an enlightened society. The arts and free press (Montgomery Block), the financial world (the U.S. Mint), and society's progressive thinkers (the Masonic Temple) all now inhabited an area on the map that corresponded with the All-Seeing Eye of the U.S. Seal's reverse side.

G. P. Cummings—The Architect of the Seal?

Perhaps the main Mason behind much of this was none other than Gordon Parker Cummings. After completing the Montgomery Block in 1853, Cummings returned to Philadelphia in 1855. His work over the next decade is unknown and in 1865 he was back in California, overseeing the construction of the famed Capitol Building of Sacramento. Cummings later also reopened his San Francisco office, and in 1875 designed the California Hall for the Centennial Exposition. All of these happenings lend credence to the view that Cummings was highly regarded as an architect and also possibly as a Freemason. We have very little tangible information regarding Cummings, but some of the information that we do have about him tends to confirm that he was a high initiate in Masonic, and perhaps other, circles. In something that would not have seemed too far out of place, in the film *National Treasure* (2004), we learn that at his death in 1889 at the Philadelphia Masonic Home (he had returned again to that city in 1877), Cummings left to his friend John Baird a "walking cane with a gold quartz head" that he had received from "the workmen on the Capitol Building of California."

Another fact about this mysterious figure is that Cummings had his portrait painted by Emanuel Leutze, painter of the iconic canvas, "Washington

Crossing the Delaware." Leutze was a highly regarded portrait painter of his day—to have one's portrait made by him was an honor of no small significance. One of Leutze's other famous paintings may leave us another clue as to why San Francisco was created as a talisman of the reverse Seal of the United States. The painting "The Way of the Empire Is Going Westward," which Leutze completed in 1861, includes in it's background imagery a sunny, inviting view of the San Francisco bay and embodies much of the romantic sentiment associated with Manifest Destiny. Those same sentiments seem also to lie behind the founding of the city of San Francisco, and may well have led to the incorporation of imagery from the mysterious reverse Seal of the United States onto that city's map.

This article first appeared in *Atlantis Rising* #63 (May/June 2007).

22

HIDDEN AGENDA?

NASA is Keeping Many Strange Secrets

BY JOHN KETTLER

G oing dark, in espionage parlance, means hiding and ceasing to communicate, as when a spy goes to ground until things calm down. To "take it dark" means to remove something from public view, meanwhile clandestinely continuing to operate whatever the asset may be. This can be as simple as moving a suddenly sensitive discussion from an open radio channel to an encrypted one, or the more complicated faking the breakdown of a satellite, or even reporting its loss, but continuing to clandestinely receive the data. According to Richard "Dick" Hoagland, the maverick space expert, in his 2007 book *Dark Mission* (a best seller with both the *New York Times* and *amazon.com*) coauthored with Mike Bara, these are the least of NASA's "sins," dating clear back to its beginning.

Hoagland, a recognized authority for over 40 years on astronomy and space exploration, in the early 1990s authored *The Monuments on Mars*— which first discussed the enigmatic "face" on the Mars Cydonia plain. At various times he served as a space consultant for all of the major broadcast networks. Among his many contributions to history and science, the best remembered is probably his conception, along with Eric Burgess, of *Mankind's First Interstellar Message* in 1971: an engraved plaque carried beyond the solar system by the first manmade object to escape from the sun's influence, Pioneer 10. Carl Sagan acknowledged Hoagland's contribution in an article for *Nature*. The latter's friendly relations with NASA, however, ended some time ago.

"There has been a consistent, conscious effort by NASA, since its inception," Hoagland told *Atlantis Rising* in a recent exclusive interview, "to find and then conceal verifiable evidence of mankind's ancient past, starting with the moon."

That's a grave charge to level against a purportedly transparent and benign civilian agency, but Hoagland says he has the proof. We are referred to the National Aeronautics and Space Act of 1958, the law which created NASA, Section 305(i), "The National Aeronautics and Space Administration shall be considered a Defense Agency of the United States for the purpose of Chapter 17, Title 35 of the United States Code." Further, Section 206(d) explicitly states, "No [NASA] information which has been classified for reasons of National Security shall be included in any report made under this section [of the act]."

Richard Hoagland (top) and Ken Johnston (bottom)

These revelations put the famous and oft pooh-poohed Brookings Institution Report into an entirely different light. The report, issued in the early days of NASA, had recommended that the space agency's Administrator "seriously consider suppressing" evidence of extraterrestrial civilizations or technology found during NASA's exploration of the moon and planets. Thus, Hoagland argues, NASA not only has the standard array of bureaucratic tools to hide what it has found, but it can now invoke "National Security" and wrap itself in layers of classification, some so deep that outright lying is permitted to protect the secrets!

On Tuesday, October 30, 2007, at the National Press Club in Washington, D.C., The Enterprise Mission—a private research and public policy group led by Hoagland, held what was called a "review" of "NASA . . . its 50 years of cover-ups and hidden solar system data." Among the questions raised were: Why does NASA continue to represent itself and its programs as "civilian space research?" Why did a NASA official direct Ken Johnston—a former NASA contractor in charge of Apollo photos in NASA's Lunar Receiving Laboratory during the Apollo Program—to destroy copies of official astronaut photographs taken on the moon? Did Apollo astronauts discover and bring back to Earth bona fide "ET artifacts" salvaged from the moon? And, was one of those artifacts an amazing "robot head"—immediately classified, under NASA's charter, because of its enormous national security implications? At the press conference it was revealed that Johnston had been fired from NASA for, it was said, his cooperation with the *Dark Mission* book project. Johnston, it was asserted, had secretly preserved missing Apollo moon photos, which he had been told at the time to destroy. The photos that were displayed at the press conference appear to show previously undisclosed artificial structures on the moon and other anomalies.

NASA, WE HARDLY KNEW YE

According to Hoagland, to appreciate his message it is necessary to understand a concept which he says informs all of NASA's policies: "The lie is different at every level." Hoagland tells us he heard this from an individual he independently confirmed as being an intelligence officer, and he has made the statement a kind of analytical springboard for determining what's really going on at NASA. Bluntly characterizing what the authors call "coverup city from top to bottom, the book breaks open the lie at every level." Hoagland seems quite serious!

If he is right, those steeped since childhood in the warm, fuzzy, safe view of a public NASA could be in for quite a shock. The real agency, he proclaims, is decidedly not that way. Rather, at its core, it has been carrying out a whole series of hidden agendas—and all at taxpayer expense.

THE PLAYERS

While Hoagland is careful to point out that most NASA employees are both innocent and clueless as to what's being done by their agency to subvert its mission, he does identify three main, albeit shadowy, groups as running NASA for their private, and often bitterly contested, benefit. They are, he tells us: the "Magicians," the "Freemasons," and the "Nazis." Strange as it may sound, Hoagland is in earnest. He has no problem calling the lot a "priesthood" adamantly determined to reserve whatever they choose for themselves, deeming only themselves worthy and initiated via bloodlines tracing, in some cases, clear back to Atlantis.

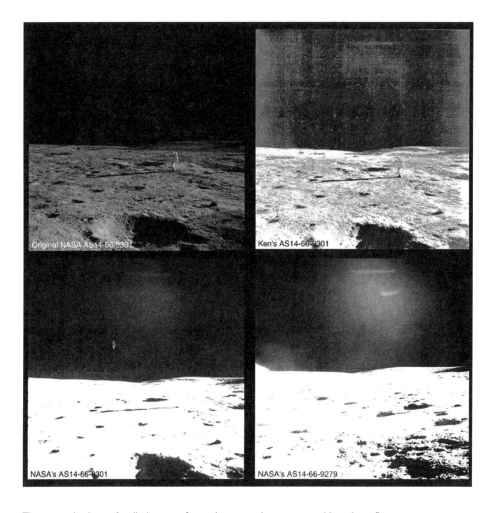

The mass in these Apollo images from the moon is not caused by a lens flare, says Hoagland. The astronaut's shadow in the first three images shows that the sun is coming in at a right angle to the camera axis—thus eliminating the potential for such a mundane explanation. (www.enterprisemission.com)

Consider rocket scientist Jack Parsons, cofounder of the Jet Propulsion Laboratory (JPL) in Pasadena. Hoagland declares emphatically that Parsons was handpicked by the notorious black magician Aleister Crowley to head the Pasadena lodge of the O.T.O. (Ordo Templi Orientis—Order of the Eastern Temple) and ultimately ran the entire U.S. branch of the O.T.O. Moreover, he says that the JPL was founded on Halloween, 1936, the time when, in occult tradition, the veil between this world and the next is thinnest, letting spirits roam for a time. And the man whose rocket technology to this day flies as the SRBs (Solid Rocket Boosters) on the Space Shuttle, it is alleged, was involved in occult doings so "out there" that Crowley himself was seriously disturbed by them. Parsons, says Hoagland, performed the Babylon Working with the goal of creating the very Whore of Babylon, as in the Book of Revelation. Objective? Bring forth the End Times!

Consider Farouk El-Baz, the expatriate son of an Egyptian who was expert in the ancient Egyptian gods and their ritual worship by the priests. How did a man working for NASA contractor Bellcom, Inc. as a field geologist wind up the most powerful single individual in the American space program?—as Hoagland puts it, "the guy who picked the landing sites, controlled the dissemination and analysis of all the photography, and directly oversaw and managed the astronauts' geological training, preparing them for what they would actually observe on the lunar surface"? And how did mission after mission in which he was deeply involved just "happen" to align in such a way that one or another of these gods/goddesses was worshipped/honored/communicated with via exquisitely careful placement of landings with the stars overhead in particular parts of the heavens associated with the clearly defined Egyptian deities Isis, Osiris, Horus, and Set?

Consider SS Major (yes, the title is correct) Werner von Braun, who per President Truman's own decree didn't qualify for admission to this country under Operation Paperclip. The same applies to a slew of Braun's colleagues who went on to control many key slots in NASA. Their records on projects involving V-2's, slave labor, forced human experimentation, even executions, were all sanitized, but their continuing values may have been revealed by a swastika left on a sign in El Paso, Texas, as the group visited from the nearby White Sands Missile Range. Hoagland describes the "outrageous" hijacking of no less than three NASA landings which he says were carefully timed to celebrate Hitler's birthday, April 20—while the star positions were aligned for "resurrection."

And as for the Freemasons? Hoagland says they were and are so prevalent at NASA as to be practically ubiquitous and have been occultically "signing" missions left and right with their trademark numerology for decades. They particularly favor, he says, the transformative, Great Work signifying 33, while serving what Hoagland calls their ancient Egyptian gods, a "crafty" worship conducted in the earthly, lunar, and planetary skies, with the ignorant masses utterly unaware.

As Hoagland and his colleagues argue, these precise alignments must fall at exact times and geometries, and at no other, and amount virtually to standing a mission's publicly stated purpose and its exacting calculations of celestial mechanics squarely on its head. In *Dark Mission*, the authors cite many such cases.

THE PLAY

As detailed by Hoagland, Bara, and other similarly persuaded investigators, NASA used and continues to use the best technology and means available to hide one blockbuster discovery after another, though not always well. Some Russian researchers have recently claimed to have carefully confirmed NASA's manual stripping in of black segments to hide something in a 1960s vintage lunar surface shot, as well as the use of airbrushing. The capabilities of Adobe Photoshop, it is pointed out, were simply beyond imagining in the early days of manual image alteration. Hoagland and colleagues claim to have documented many examples of NASA's digital paste-in of poorly chosen cloned background imagery on Mars. They cite the agency's refusal to provide requested images of some areas, while freely providing other images which cover up critical data—digital processing conducted in such a way as not only to remove vital data but make what remains appear to be something other than what it is. Hoagland and Bara liken what NASA did to the Cydonia imagery (the face on Mars, shown as what has been called the "cat box" image) to be akin to taking your grandmother's picture, stretching it horizontally, flattening it, turning it upside down, and reversing the color palette, thus making her unrecognizable even to her kin! The list does not include the deliberate misrepresentation of already provided imagery as either completely black or so dark as to be useless; the collection of imagery without reporting it; stonewalling the release of imagery, and apparently making a host of embarrassing transcripts, records, imagery, even whole satellites, disappear from public view.

So, what exactly could NASA be hiding, anyway?

TOO SECRET FOR US!

At this point, we can only scratch the surface, but here is a sampler of offerings from *Dark Mission*.

Remains of gigantic glass lunar domes, which Hoagland believes once covered entire craters, as well as evidence of covered and partially covered craters and underground lunar structures. Concerning the last, Hoagland notes that both the Russian and Chinese probes currently surveying the moon are equipped with "deep penetrating radar" to find such things, and he wonders why the Apollo Long Wave Radar tests were never made public. He goes on to inquire regarding what has been termed "Chapel Bell" on Apollo 17. Then there's the "small" matter of something called "Data's Head," (as in Commander Data of *Star Trek: The Next Generation*). Actually, though, the apparently robotic head, imaged in lunar crater Shorty, more nearly resembles C3PO's from *Star Wars*. If you wish to dismiss it as a rock, you'll need a cooperative geologist who can also explain the prominent bright red band running below the apparent nose, while simultaneously addressing the remark-

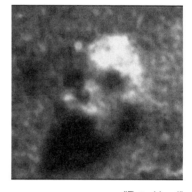

"Data Head"

able bilateral symmetry of the apparent head, eye sockets, eyes/cameras, nose, and mouth.

Things are even wilder on Mars, where NASA bitterly contests pretty much everything Hoagland has put forward, from evidence of water flow to the artificiality of the Face. For engineering on a gigantic scale, Hoagland and Bara argue Mars is the place to be, complete with one stupendous critical geometry/tetrahedral (hyper-dimensional signifying) 19.5 degree geometry embodying one structure after another, arcologies straight out of *Blade Runner,* underground structures, glass underground tunnels, ruins of cities far vaster than Los Angeles. Mars landing sites were littered with so much technical debris from a long-dead civilization that NASA had to censor images shot less than a yard from Pathfinder. Hoagland says he has evidence that this incredibly advanced civilization was swept away by a solar system cataclysm, which destroyed Mars as a habitable planet. Astronomer Tom Van Flandern and other maverick scientists have drawn similar conclusions from careful analysis of Martian photos.

The explosion of Mars' neighbor, it is argued, blew away most of the planet's atmosphere, causing the oceans to slip their moorings in a titanic deluge as the gravitational forces holding them in check failed, and as the exploded planet's debris turned the exposed side of Mars into not merely a ruin but a buried one. If, as the celebrated Brookings Report suggests, the mere evidence of extraterrestrial civilization could bring down society, how much more, we are asked, would the story of one wiped out within days at most? And what technology has NASA quietly recovered and not shared with the people who paid for the missions? What would "Data's Head" be worth? Were samples of the lunar domes retrieved? Considering that Hoagland has found that the famous gold-flashed astronaut visors were spectrally optimized to see best in the blue range precisely occupied by the domes, it could be argued that NASA was looking for them? Hoagland doesn't buy NASA's lunar landing purported "take" as being no more than 88 pounds of rocks. He thinks artifacts were brought back.

On the other hand, Astronaut Edgar Mitchell, a moonwalker from Apollo 12 and a bit of a maverick himself, who carried out telepathy experiments while on the moon and later founded the Institute for Noetic Sciences, which openly pursues paranormal research, told *Atlantis Rising* that he considered Hoagland a "flake." Anybody who says that there were any undisclosed structures on the moon said Mitchell "is crazy." In his book, *The Way of the Explorer,* Mitchell tells how he experienced a great spiritual awakening on his way back to earth from the moon. He reminds us the entire mission was shown live, and that it would be impossible to alter the pictures in real time, as Hoagland suggests.

As for Mars, officially we're still trying to get there. Some say there is evidence, though, that we're already there—not via conventional rocketry, either. And then there are those who say we never went to the moon at all—that the moon landing was a hoax. But those are all other stories.

BLACKOUT BY MAJOR U.S. MEDIA?

The October National Press Club briefing was remarkable in at least one other respect: how it was covered and how it wasn't. *NBC Nightly News* wanted an interview the night before, but Hoagland was stuck in flight from Albuquerque, New Mexico, to Washington, D.C. FOX wanted to do an interview on *The O'Reilly Factor,* then was never heard from again. The *Washington Post* had a reporter at the briefing—who published nothing. "*Wired* got a review copy" and has said nothing, but, we are told, the "editor of a major national magazine has a copy and plans an article." We should, says Hoagland, compare our "free press" with the tightly controlled Russian media, involved, in his view, in a "political background conversation between [then president] Bush and Putin."

Four Russian networks were there, he says, and some taped the entire briefing. The Russian equivalent of CNN, RTTV, did a three-hour interview, and NTV had scheduled two days of interviews, to be boiled down and presented to its 120 million viewers.

But meanwhile even more strange things are happening on earth.

The blog, *The Space Review,* ran a blistering two-part attack by Wayne Day in "the truth, it is out there" (*www.thespacere-view.com/article/1022/1*), which portrayed Hoagland as a commune-living nutty stud and his "Deep Throat," Dr. Ken Johnston, as some bureaucratic nobody. Johnston, by the way, is the man who was Manager of NASA's Data and Photo Control Department during the Apollo program. On another front, former NASA employee and current CSICOP member James Oberg has made what Hoagland calls "absolutely unrelenting" attacks. Hoagland views the backlash as a sign the Dark Mission scenario is "gaining political traction within NASA." Interestingly, at *Amazon.com's Dark Mission* page, former NASA mission controller Dr. Ali Fant confirms some of the key claims. Hoagland continues to look for "some break on the national scene here" and says he wants congressional hearings.

In the meantime, a multinational stampede (U.S., Russia, China, India, Japan, Germany) is underway to get to the Moon/Mars. If NASA is hiding nothing, why go there and why now? And why did neither NASA nor JPL have any official comments to offer on *Dark Mission* when formally contacted?

This article first appeared in *Atlantis Rising* #68 (March/April 2008).

PART SIX

ALCHEMICAL HINTS

23

SECRETS OF THE CATHEDRALS

*What Does the Strange Mix of Christian
and Masonic Symbolism Mean?*

BY JAN WICHERINK

Gothic cathedral architecture originated in France in the early 12th century during the heyday of the Knights Templar. The Templars, officially called the "Poor Fellow-Soldiers of Christ and of the Temple of Solomon," formed a knight's order of priests who ostensibly protected the pilgrimage routes to Jerusalem.

Founded in AD 1118 by Hugo de Payens, the order of the Knights Templar originally included nine brave knight-priests. The group eventually became one of the richest and most powerful in history. With its vast wealth, collected from financing the crusades, the Templars were able to build Europe's gothic cathedrals. The cathedrals, with twin towers facing west, resemble the Temple of Solomon with its two pillars Jachin and Boaz standing in front. This explains why, in many cases, a statue of Solomon is placed at the West portal of the French cathedrals between the twin towers.

Much has been written about the mysteries of the French Gothic cathedrals and the sacred geometry employed in their architecture. One famous book, *Le Mystère des Cathédrales,* was written in 1929 by Fulcanelli (1839–1953), the mysterious French alchemist. According to Fulcanelli, a cathedral is an alchemical book written in stone.

THE END OF TIME

Upon entering a French cathedral, a visitor is immediately confronted with "The Last Judgment" displayed at the tympanum (mural) above the entrance. In the tympanum, Jesus is surrounded by the four beasts of the Apocalypse. These four beasts, as mentioned in John's Revelations and by Old Testament prophets, have been equated with the four apostles of

The Porch of Chartres Cathedral shows Jesus in the Vesica Pisces Surrounded by the Four Beasts of the Apocalypse.

the four canonical books of the New Testament, Matthew, Mark, Luke, and John. They also have an astrological significance. The beast with the human face correlates with Aquarius (Matthew), the lion with Leo (Mark), the ox with Taurus (Luke), and the eagle with Aquila (John). The sign Aquila is often takes the place of Scorpio in ancient zodiacs.

In Christian art, Christ is often portrayed inside a Vesica Pisces along with these four zodiac signs, and surrounding his head is a halo resembling the Sun. The cross in the halo in reality could therefore be a reference to these four signs of the Apocalypse, since Taurus, Aquarius, Scorpio, and Leo together form a perfect cross in the zodiac.

CHARTRES CATHEDRAL

One of the oldest French Gothic cathedrals is Chartres, which is aligned to the summer solstice. On that day, the Sun shines through the window of "Saint Apollinaire" (which depicts the Roman sun god Apollo), and its rays fall straight on an iron nail in the floor.

Strangely, within the cathedral can be found a zodiac—peculiar since in Christian tradition, astrology is regarded as pagan. Moreover, this particular zodiac seems to be saying something extraordinary. First the cross connects the four signs Taurus, Aquarius, Scorpio, and Leo. As in the "Last Judgment," this zodiac cross seems to emphasize the importance of these four signs and presumably must be associated with The End Times as well.

The reason might be that these four signs rise heliacally (before the sun) during a Great Celestial Conjunction at the solstices and equinoxes. They are thus symbols of the true Galactic Cross determined by the places in the zodiac where the ecliptic and the Milky Way cross. The importance of the Great Celestial Conjunction of 2012 was that it marked the event after 6,480 years when the equinox and solstice axis of the zodiac cross merged again with the Galactic Cross. This was when the 26,000-year precession cycle concluded and a new cycle commenced. This event is what in John's Revelations has been called The End Times. (For more on this phenomenon, see "Rosslyn Chapel & 2012" in *Atlantis Rising* #71.)

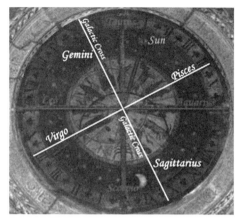

Chartres Zodiac. The axis of the Vesica Pisces coincides with the axis of the Galactic Cross during the current Great Celestial Conjunction of 2012.

The next thing that attracts one's attention in the Chartres zodiac are two semicircles intersecting to form a Vesica Pisces. The Vesica Pisces is an important ancient, pre-Christian symbol, later adopted by Christians to represent Christ. When vertically depicted, the Vesica Pisces once represented the vagina of the goddess mother and as such was associated with fertility and birth. Christ is often depicted inside the Vesica Pisces in a vertical position as in the "Last Judgment" of the tympanum above the

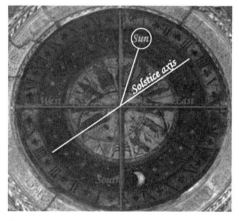

The zodiac corresponds with the summer solstice. The Sun is depicted in the northeast (summer solstice sunrise). Notice that a line drawn from the Sun to the center of the zodiac connects the Sun with the birthplace of the Sun, meaning inside the Vesica Pisces (the female birth canal) and at the center of the Galactic Cross!

West Royal Portal of Chartres cathedral. This symbolism therefore refers to the rebirth or Second Coming of Christ at the End of Time.

When the Vesica Pisces in the zodiac of Chartres is carefully inspected, something even more interesting is revealed. Its intersection aligns with the zodiac's Pisces-Virgo axis, hinting that it should be associated with these signs. Esoterically, the astrological significance is that Pisces stands for Christ (the fisherman) while Virgo stands for Mary (the virgin mother). It was the virgin mother Mary (Virgo) who gave birth (Vesica Pisces) to Christ (Pisces).

GREAT CELESTIAL CONJUNCTION

Astronomically, there is only one rebirth taking place in Pisces around the year 2012 and that's the rebirth of the Sun in the precession cycle on the Galactic Cross. This moment denotes the start of a new precession cycle. Could it be that the Chartres zodiac was meant to denote this astronomical event?

In the years of the Great Celestial Conjunction (1978–2017), the 5° Pisces to 5° Virgo axis of the Galactic Cross will align with the equinoxes, while the 5° Gemini to 5° Sagittarius axis (sidereal zodiac) of the Galactic Cross will align with the solstices. The Galactic Cross therefore occurs in the Chartres zodiac and is defined by the Vesica Pisces.

The cross—Taurus, Aquarius, Scorpio, Leo—corresponds in addition with the cardinal directions. If this cross is interpreted this way, interesting new insights come to light. The Sun depicted in the upper-right corner of the zodiac is now situated in the northeast at the place where the Sun rises during the summer solstice.

The symbolism used here suggests that the Christian doctrine of the End Times is not about the rebirth of Christ at all, but actually about the rebirth of the Sun. This could be why Jesus is placed inside the vertical Vesica Pisces surrounded by the four beasts of the End Times in the "Last Judgment" in the first place.

BLACK MADONNA

Are there more reasons to suspect that the biblical End Times is, in reality, about the rebirth of the Sun? There is actually a very convincing clue left in Chartres, again dealing with the very same symbol, the Vesica Pisces.

Chartres cathedral is well known for its Black Madonna veneration. The Black Madonna however has nothing to do with Mary. She actually represents the pagan Egyptian mother goddess Isis. In her arms she's therefore not holding Jesus but the immaculate conceived son, the sun god Horus. Isis, like Mary, was a virgin who gave birth to a son on December 25. This is exactly four days after the winter solstice, the moment of the rebirth of the Sun in the annual cycle after the Sun has "died" on the cross of the zodiac at the winter solstice day.

In the Freemason's tracing board, Mary's Immaculate Conception is depicted. She's placed inside a Vesica Pisces, in between the two pillars of the temple of Solomon, with the All-Seeing Eye of Horus watching over her. The meaning is that the birth of Christ in reality is mimicking the birth of Horus, the Egyptian Sun God.

Notice that the Virgin Mary in Chartres is placed on a pillar in a Vesica Pisces shaped cavity. In Christian traditions, the origin of this custom, to place the virgin mother on a pillar, stems from the legend of Our Lady on the Pillar—the appearance of the virgin mother to the apostle James in the early days of Christianity on top of a column or pillar carried by angels.

In Masonic tradition this pillar however represents the Milky Way. The symbolism of placing the Black Madonna with Jesus on a pillar must therefore be equated with the Sun (Horus) on the Milky Way. The Sun entered the Milky Way at the "End of Time" during the summer and winter solstice of 2012.

ZODIAC WINDOW

In the Chartres cathedral ambulatory, a stained glass window contains the twelve signs of the zodiac. On top is a four leaf clover, representing a form of cross, Christ is shown between the Greek letters alpha and omega. In Christianity, Christ's birth is represented by the letter alpha and his Second Coming at the End of Time with the letter omega. The letters alpha and omega in this zodiac are therefore most likely representing the beginning and end of the precession cycle. The Great Celestial Conjunction of 2012 is the alpha and omega point in the precession cycle, the moment when one cycle ends and another begins.

The four signs (Leo, Taurus, Aquarius, Scorpio) associated with the Galactic Cross appear similarly to Christ in a four-leafed clover. All of the other zodiac signs are depicted in ordinary circles. There is however one

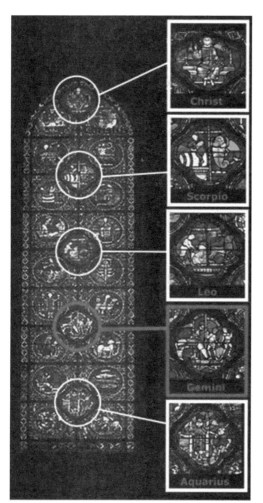

On June 21st 2012 (Gemini) the Sun resides on the Galactic Cross. Taurus is deliberately replaced by Gemini introducing an error in the zodiac sequence.

seeming error in this zodiac. Taurus of the Galactic Cross (Aquarius, Scorpio, Leo, and Taurus) has been deliberately replaced by the sign Gemini. The summer solstice of June 21 takes place during the last day of Gemini (May 22–June 21). By exchanging Taurus with Gemini—Gemini must be associated with the summer solstice Sun—the summer solstice Sun is placed on the Galactic Cross. The summer solstice Sun at June 21, 2012, was in Gemini at the Galactic Cross where the ecliptic and the Milky Way cross.

So this zodiac window in Chartres is clearly a reference to the summer solstice Galactic Alignment of 2012, the Great Celestial Conjunction of 2012.

CROSS RIB VAULTS

In my previous writings (see my Rosslyn Chapel article published in *Atlantis Rising* #71), I argued that the architecture of Rosslyn Chapel contains a secret message concerning 2012. This secret in my opinion is the best kept secret by the highest degrees in Scottish Freemasonry, the Royal Arch, which has connected its name with this secret. The 2012 message has been cunningly embedded in the architecture by using cross symbols in the arches and cross rib vaults. These arches are not only found in Rosslyn Chapel but in most of the Gothic cathedrals as well.

The ground plan of a Gothic cathedral is a cross. This cross comprises a nave in the East-West direction (aligned to the solstice Sun) that is bisected by the transept that is perpendicular to the axis of the nave. From a bird's eye view the cathedral forms a huge cross aligned to the solstice Sun.

The vaults of the Gothic cathedrals are for the most part four-pointed cross rib vaults with the exception of the vaults of the apse that form a semicircle. The only exception to the four pointed cross rib vaults is the eight-pointed cross rib vault of the Crossing. The Crossing is the heart of the cathedral where the nave and the transept intersect.

On top of the Crossing, in most cases, a tower is placed. This tower is shaped in the form of an octagon, such as in the cathedral of Coutances en Conques (France). Other examples are the cathedrals of Amiens, Auxerre, Laon, Rouen, Senlis en Toulouse—all have eight-pointed cross rib vaults at the Crossing of the cathedral.

An interesting detail is that the four main pillars on which the vaults of the Crossing rest are named after the Four Evangelists. The Four Evangelists as mentioned before represent the four signs of the zodiac, Taurus, Aquarius, Scorpio, and Leo.

It is important to realize that the eight-pointed cross is at the *heart* of the cathedral. It is the only eight-pointed cross in the cathedral since the rest of the vaults are four-pointed crosses. In my opinion the four- and eight-pointed crosses of the cross rib vaults that are part of the design of the cathedral have been intentionally introduced to leave a message about the End of Time. The ground plan of the cathedral, in the shape of a huge cross, has thus, most likely, very little to do with the cross of Christ. It is far more likely that this cross represents the zodiac cross, which explains why the cathedrals are aligned to the solstices.

The Notre Dame of Amiens, just like the Notre Dame of Rouen and the Notre Dame of Paris are aligned to the winter solstice. The axis of the cathedral runs from northwest (azimuth 295°) to southeast (azimuth 115°). The azimuth of 115° of the cathedral corresponds exactly with the azimuth of the sunrise at the old Celtic New Year's Day Samhain at 9–10 November.

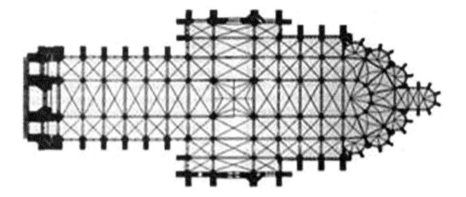

Ground plan of a cathedral with the eight pointed cross at the Crossing. (Center of the cathedral)

The angle that the length axis of the cathedral makes with the east-west cardinal axis is 25°. Due to this angle, the Sun at the summer solstice will reside exactly one hour before sunset at azimuth 295° (270° for the West plus 25°). This means that the Sun is facing the west portal of the cathedral to shed its last light on the "Last Judgment" in the tympanum. The setting Sun symbolizes the ending of an era, the "End of Time."

In the nave of the cathedral an octagonal labyrinth is situated so that during summer solstices it aligns with the setting Sun along with the "Last Judgment." In the center of this labyrinth is an octagon with two different crosses inside.

The first cross is formed by four angels; the second cross by four human figures, among them the king, the local bishop, and the architect of the cathedral.

The cross of the angels aligns with the four cardinal directions and hence with the equinox axis. The intriguing fact about the octagonal labyrinth is that it aligns to the equinox (cardinal directions) and the solstice axis (with an accuracy < 2,5°) at the same time.

It's of course no coincidence that the summer solstice evening Sun aligns exactly with both the "Last Judgment" and this labyrinth. In my opinion the message of this labyrinth, with its eight-pointed cross consisting of two separate crosses, is that it is a reference to the Great Celestial Conjunction of 2012 when the zodiac cross, after 6,480 years, aligned with the Galactic Cross—indicating the end of an era.

On top of the apse of the Cathedral de Notre Dame de Paris an eight-pointed cross is aligned to winter solstice sunrise since the cathedral has an azimuth of 115° (South East).

This is not unique for the Notre Dame de Paris since most cathedrals and churches have similar crosses placed on top of the apse, hence the cross symbolism is not restricted to cathedrals. At the spire of virtually every church a weather vane in the shape of an eight-pointed cross to denote the cardinal directions is placed. However it is completely impossible to tell the direction of the wind by means of this cross. There are two reasons. The first is that this cross is placed vertically and not horizontally so it is not aligned to the cardinal directions at all. The cross is placed perpendicular to the length axis of the church and in case the church (or cathedral) is aligned to the solstice (which is often the case), it means that this cross is aligned to the solstice Sun instead of to the cardinal directions, albeit in vertical position.

Since the function of the weather vane can't possibly be to tell the direction of the wind, it can only have a (Masonic) symbolic and/or esoteric significance.

The French Gothic cathedrals bear an astrological message about the End Times of the New Testament. As has been demonstrated here, the biblical End Times is the equivalent of the Great Celestial Conjunction around 2012. The Second Coming of the Redeemer at the End of Time must therefore be interpreted symbolically as the rebirth of the Sun, heralding in a new age.

This article first appeared in *Atlantis Rising* #73 (January/February 2009).

24

THE CELESTIAL ART OF KEEPING SECRETS

How Did the Ancients Protect Their Knowledge?

BY STEVEN SORA

There is little doubt that Freemasonry inherited a body of knowledge from remarkably early times. While Masons used such knowledge for practical applications in building cathedrals and bridges, they understood a concept of "As above, so below," that went far beyond the practical. They were not the only ones. From the most ancient times, mankind believed the heavens ruled the earth. Going against the will of the stars was inviting trouble. As *aster* was the Greek word for "star," a *dis-aster* was the result of such indiscretions.

In recent times we have begun to understand the extent of conformity to the heavens as practiced by both ancient and even surprisingly modern builders. The pyramids in Egypt were aligned to the three stars in Orion's belt, monuments in pre-historic Scotland calculate solar and lunar phenomena, city streets in Washington D.C. and Detroit were laid out in accordance with the passage of certain stars. Even these are dwarfed by the massive pentagram on the land of southern France, and the Maltese Cross that exists over Greece and Crete.

What we have not fully appreciated is the ability of the initiated to pass on such sciences concealed in poetry, in music and most visibly in architecture. Science was at all times guarded under the guise of religious myths, epic poems, and the tales of kings and heroes. Such knowledge was passed through select groups of initiates. Individuals were selected for their ability to learn and their ability to keep the secret from the masses. Druid schools passed down volumes of information through memorization. At other times, science had to be protected from religion as the Church regarded anything new as potentially heretical. Again the method of preserving science in times of intolerance required initiates that could be trusted.

Astrological teachers (*Atlantis Rising* artwork)

Just how far the knowledge of the stars was married to practical arts is unknown. When the massive mound-tunnel complex of New Grange was built in Ireland circa 3300 BC, it was created to serve as an astronomical calendar with stunning accuracy. There was no trial-and-error process, implying that even though it was older than the Sumerian and Egyptian monuments, an even earlier prototype must have existed. The "window" that allows the sunlight to light up the back wall of the tunnel is evidence of amazing precision. The fact that after 5,000 years the roof does not leak is testament to practical ability.

The Ring of Brodgar, Maes Howe, Clava Cairns, and other Scottish monuments measure the winter solstice sunset. The first two are in the Orkney Islands near Skara Brae. Discovered recently after a storm literally blew the roof off, this prehistoric complex had crude plumbing, indoor kitchens, stone furniture, and even hinged stone doors. It is believed the cells served as rooms for students practicing the ancient arts.

The Sumerians had understood the concept of measurement by determining the sun's rise along the horizon. The prefix "hor" in our word for horizon is linked to the French *heure* and the Greek *hora,* both meaning "hour." The horizon could be used to calculate time throughout the twelve-hour day. (The night was assigned a separate twelve hours.) Our word "survey" begins with the prefix "sur," another Sumerian word for "delineate." They used this word to mean "border" as well. Today we might hire a professional to survey our property and fix a line delineating our neighbor's property from our own.

The Egyptians adopted the same principles in constructing the pyramids. What were once believed to be simply passageways are now being understood to provide focused views to certain constellations—a virtual stargate. The stargate of ancient Egypt, as we understand it, might actually be a dumbed-down version of the information such observatories once provided. The "air shaft" in the King's Chamber of the Great Pyramid at Giza was discovered, in 1966, to point to Orion's Belt as it crossed the southern meridian at the time when the pyramid was built. Osiris was the most important god, the "opener of the ways." His myth is an early example of death and resurrection. A pharaoh had to pass the test of showing he could inherit the title and have his soul become part of Osiris. Thus the stargate allowed his soul access to achieving divinity.

Greek contact with the Near East brought to that civilization a multitude of ancient texts. Although the burning of the Alexandria library in 48 BC destroyed 150,000 texts, we have seen that many cultures never trusted writing to preserve their knowledge, rather the recitation of solar texts would be considered more likely to keep their science alive.

The author of the Greek epic the Argosy told a story that everyone could understand, yet within the text the movements of the heavenly bodies were preserved. Pegasus was from *pegasai* meaning "entrance" in the Greek language. The Argo, the ship of Jason, is derived from the constellation and first recorded by the Phoenicians. One who would take the sailing

The building of the ship Argo: Athena (left) adjusts sail; Tiphys (center) holds the yard; Argos (right) astride stern (first century Roman artwork)

directions literally would have the good ship Argo somehow crossing the Alps. The Phoenicians also brought to Greece the tales of Hercules. As a sun god first worshipped along the Atlantic coast of Europe and Africa, Hercules defeated the dragon, as represented by the constellation Draco. Later Christian theology had the Son of God facing the ultimate dragon, Satan.

The tale of the Argosy was then a body of knowledge concealed in the text of a popular tale. The teller of the tale was a predecessor to the Irish bard. He was adept in keeping an audience enthralled while his true mission served a much greater purpose. The early bards understood that every story and every symbol had more than one level of meaning. The exoteric tale was invented to convey the esoteric meaning, the truth.

Homer may have created the *Odyssey* to convey knowledge of Canis Major. Within that constellation one of the brightest stars is Cyon, the Dog. The 19 stars of the constellation are said to be the 19 years that Argo (Ulysses' dog) waited for his master to return from the Odyssey. Within the *Iliad*, the shield of Achilles is depicted as the heart in the shaggy beast, a clue to the star Sirius in Canis Major. The seven most visible stars in the

Ursa Major are called the "wain," which is the wagon that Priam used to carry home his son's body. Homer's "Catalogue of Ships," possibly the dullest part of the *Iliad*, is believed to be a record of 45 constellations to the initiated.

In compiling the stories of the Old Testament, much was drawn from the stargazing Babylonians. The story of Samson killing a lion is believed to be similar to a tale of Orion and taking place in the Constellation of Leo. The story of his slaying hundreds with the jawbone of an ass is absurd, although it is mirrored in texts around the world. In one case, the hero slays with the jawbone of a tapir. Psalm 18:2 in the Old Testament has a decidedly Masonic view saying "the skies proclaim God's glory, the vault of heaven betrays his craftsmanship."

Christianity, which had little use for astrology, also betrays some secrets even in the Gospels. John 3:30 has the Precursor (John the Baptist) say about Jesus "he must grow greater while I diminish." John's feast-day of June 24 is the longest day for the sun, then his time diminishes, Jesus' birthday, Christmas, comes after the shortest day, then the day grows longer, the sun becoming greater. Christian days mimicked the Roman Sol Invictus cult, which faded as Christianity grew. Aurelian, who had established the cult as religion, said "the sun appears as an infant at the Winter Solstice."

This would be understood by "pagan" Celts who passed along such astrological tales mirrored in the practical craft of agriculture. John Barleycorn is a tale of the seasons with poor old John losing his head in Midsummer, just as St. John Baptist did.

Later in the 5th century, when astrology and astronomy were forbidden sciences, Cassiodorus writing in a southern Italian monastery declared the law of the stars was created by God who put them in place.

The evidence of solar and lunar calendars and observatories has not been bound by time or distance. Medicine wheels in Wyoming, the Cahokia Mounds near St. Louis, temples of Uaxactun in Guatemala, and Chichen Itza in Mexico, megaliths at Stonehenge, Carnac, and the furthest northern islands of Scotland all point to a secret transmission of science that has occurred through time and distance. As Scottish and Irish astronomers could construct the Ring of Brodgar and Newgrange to reflect the equinox and the solstice, the Mayan builders of the central pyramid of Chichen Itza could create a 365-step stairway, complete with the illusion of a writhing serpent on the Equinox. Ancient Greeks and the more modern Algonquin Indians shared the same name for the Big Dipper, the Bear. A supernova outburst that occurred in AD 1054 is recorded in Sung Dynasty China and at two places in Arizona. Inheritors of the Mayan culture in Chiapas claim a god who is the Sun, and as such he dies and is resurrected.

It becomes clear that even in societies we regard as "primitive" a brotherhood of men and women kept alive, passed down, and spread knowledge of our universe. Such knowledge is exponentially greater than the uninitiated are aware.

Christian Europe served as a bushel over the lamp of learning until the Crusades woke Christendom from the Dark Ages. Greek texts that had been unknown, or thought to be lost or simply forgotten, emerged from libraries in Constantinople and even from Islam. During the centuries of fighting, there was more peace than war. At such intermissions in the hostilities, Arab scholars conveyed a great deal to Westerners. The Knights Templar helped bring such treasures back to the west, and wealthy individuals, notably Cosimo Medici, paid for their translation.

But some knowledge was kept from widespread exposure. As the Templars gave way to the Masons, the craft guarded such secrets. Linked to Freemasonry were the members of the Royal Society, a gathering of England's greatest minds. Even in Shakespearean times, Giordano Bruno was executed by the Church for his observations of the heavens. So it was important to keep science from the church. Isaac Newton, the society's most well-known member, believed the constellations were a cryptogram set by the Almighty.

Shakespeare himself borrowed strongly from the ancient tales that guarded the ancient science. Hamlet was based on the Icelandic Amlodhi, a story of a son dedicated to vengeance for his father. In the pre-Shakespeare version, Amlodhi owns a mill that grinds out peace and prosperity, but later only salt, bitterness, and misery.

As symbols are used to conceal and reveal they are present in some surprising locations. One is the capital of the United States. Both the capital building and the city itself is set to the east-west axis of the sun. Remarkably this is mirrored in the Egyptian pyramid of Khufu, which was built so the sun would trace the cross east-west axis on two key locations on Regulus day, the birth of Horus. From the earliest times, the Divine Child was a theme common to religion. That child is the product of the love between the male power, a sun god or a hero such as Baal, and a female power, a moon goddess, or female goddess like Isis, Aphrodite, and so forth. The child brought hope to the world. He could be named Horus or Jesus. The Federal triangle in Washington D.C. represents such a "trinity" concept. It is just one part of the Masonic philosophy.

Christopher Wren, the founder of the public Royal Society, mapped moons and comets as an accomplished astronomer and turned to architecture to express the nature of the heavens on earth. He publicly became a Mason in a ceremony conducted in one of his greatest works, St. Paul's Cathedral of London.

The Mason Pierre Charles L'Enfant organized the street plan of Washington D.C. to be like the plan of Rome. He organized it around certain monuments and further incorporated the ideas of Masonic astronomer Joseph Lalande. Lalande believed the constellation of Virgo to represent the goddess, the virgin, and the Blessed Virgin of Christianity. The prime star of Virgo was Spica. The positions of Spica, Regulus, and Arturus were all important as starting dates and dedication dates for the Washington monument, the Capitol, and the White House. Even the date, July 4, has significance in Egypt, in America, and in the heavens as Spica enters Draco, the Dragon's head. Twenty zodiacs and numerous other symbols can be found throughout the nation's capital.

Henry Lincoln, co-author of *Holy Blood, Holy Grail*, discovered more in the south of France than a priest who suddenly became extremely wealthy. He discovered that the odd geometry of the painter Poussin actually referred to a Pentagram built into the countryside. Three of the five geographic points hold a medieval castle. The remaining two, the high points of La Soulane and Serre de Lauzet, complete the massive pentagram. The circumference of this outline is fifteen miles. The pentagram is actually the symbol of Venus whose sacred number is five. In Christian theology she is the Magdalen. The pentagram is an earthly depiction of the travels of the planet Venus in the sky. As Above, So Below.

The Maltese Cross is another symbol taken from the skies, and its eight significant points are represented by eight significant temples and structures in Greece and Crete. The Greeks and their predecessors were not the only sky-watchers who had an interest in the symbol. The North American Lakota, who did not have an agricultural heritage, prized the Maltese cross as the yellow star. The single star was depicted as that cross, and other images, stars, suns and comets were all depicted on the shirts of those who performed the Lakota Ghost Dance. Their war shields also carried representations of the Little Dipper, the Pole Star and the Pleiades.

Transmission of greater secrets and deeper mysteries is then evident across a great deal of time and distance. A learned handful, initiated into secretive societies, is taught to preserve and protect such knowledge from the masses while at the same time keeping such knowledge alive.

This article first appeared in *Atlantis Rising* #68 (March/April 2008).

25

Icons & Soul Alchemy

Exploring the Secret Power of Byzantine Art

BY WILLIAM HENRY

The transfiguration of Jesus is one of the most transcendent, yet bizarrely neglected, events ever recorded in myth or sacred tradition. Perhaps this is because it sounds mystical in the extreme, even preposterous, like the story of a genie out of a bottle. Midway through his ministry, Jesus took three disciples, Peter, James, and John, and slipped off secretly to a high mountain on the borderland between the human and divine. He had something to show them. Suddenly, as recounted by Mark in his gospel, Jesus becomes radiant, his clothing shining white as light. He glistens. Elijah and Moses materialize beside Jesus, perhaps shimmering or translucent like him. They discuss events to come in Jerusalem. Through terrified eyes, the disciples see a cloud envelop the men with a brilliant haze and then the prophet and the lawgiver disappear. Jesus returns to normal human form, and he and his disciples walk back down the mountain.

Peter reflecting on this extraordinary event many years later recalls, "We were eye-witnesses of his sovereign majesty."

In the gospel accounts given by Matthew and Mark, the call it "The Transfiguration" or "The Metamorphosis."

TRANSFORMED

The word transfigured comes from the Greek verb *metamorphoo*, meaning "changed in form" or "transformed." It's the source of our English word metamorphosis. It is a change of form: like a caterpillar into a butterfly or a tadpole into a frog. They go through a metamorphosis, a change of their forms.

In the case of the transfiguration of Jesus, the term refers to his transformation or shape-shifting into a shining cosmic man, a light being, and back into flesh.

The Transfiguration. Russia. 17th century.

Apart from being taught in the Hogwarts School in the Harry Potter universe, the Transfiguration is utterly neglected in the prudent and plastic West, which predominantly worships the death and *resurrection* of Jesus—focusing on images of the bloodied and tortured Jesus, rather than an image of transcendence.

However, in the mystical East of the first six centuries AD (and later, magnificently, 14th through 17th centuries), astonishingly energetic and elegantly beautiful transfiguration icons of a levitating Jesus with rays of light beaming from his body entranced the imagination. These masterpieces were considered a visual counterpart to the gospels and were revered as holy. Whereas the gospels communicate religious truth through words, the artwork communicates through visible forms and symbols. Both equally are modes of revelation. In the magical-alchemical imagination of the icon makers, these images were designed to be actual doors to another world. Our world and "the spiritual world" are opened to each other through the icon. They were specially created to enable a visceral encounter with a holy being or to make present a spiritual energy. They are a form of "visual alchemy" that can help us in our own Transfiguration (if that is the chosen path). Nothing in art can compare, save perhaps for the complementary Tibetan depictions of the Great Perfection that portray a lama shifting the frequency of his body and transforming (by dissolving) into a spinning vortex called the Rainbow Body. These visual icons are engaging and instructive to believers and nonbelievers alike. They take us beyond the threshold, and through…

THE OPEN GATE

In Transfiguration images, Jesus is portrayed in front of an open gate, sometimes filled with stars, and composed of various geometric shapes, such as almond-shaped *mandorlas* (vesica piscis) or stars. Alternately, the gate is composed of concentric rings to indicate depth or dimension, and also vibration. (Today, we use the terms "stargate" and "wormhole" to denote such holes in space-time.) Strangely, the New Testament says

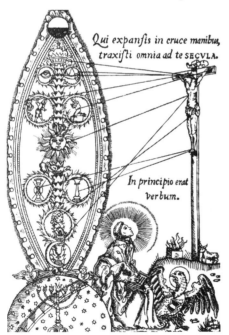

The almond-shaped gate or mandorla is shown in Kabbalistic art (left), and in icons of Transfiguration from Constantinople c. 1200 (right).

nothing about these rings or the opening of a (star) gateway. So, why are they there? Some propose the rings symbolize the Voice (frequency, or vibration) that came from the mysterious so-called cloud that appeared at the Transfiguration. Looking carefully, however, Transfiguration icons are actually maps that portray a two-step process, a transformative journey. As I discuss in my DVD *The Light Body Effect*, first (following the Tibetan model), Jesus unwinds or spins the human rig into a higher frequency. This "light body" is described in every sacred tradition. In Judeo-Christianity it is symbolized by the shiny, seamless white clothing known as the *pala* or miracle garment in the Book of Kings story of Elijah and his ascension in the whirlwind. It's woven of supramental threads of light.

With his light body wound up, Jesus then rips open a hole in the fabric of space-time, a stargate. Viewed this way, the opening of the gate is inferred by the story. It assumes prior knowledge of the understanding that Jesus was able to metamorphose and "toggle" between the worlds. He appeared repeatedly after his resurrection to the disciples, especially Mary Magdalene, giving detailed instructions for safe passage through the dimensions. (In fact, this is the difference between traditional Christianity and the Gnostics. The New Testament contains the words of the living Jesus. Jesus taught the Gnostics while in his resurrected or light body form.)

VISUAL ALCHEMY

When the icons were made, alchemy was the normal way of interacting with the world. Everything was viewed as being in the process of transmutation or changing into something else—like the acorn into the oak—simultaneously unraveling and being reborn. Everything was transmutable, including the human body, which was viewed as a pupal form of an ascended spiritual being, usually symbolized by the butterfly (earlier by the phoenix). All that was required to effect the transmutation was the Philosopher's Stone (which produces the pure tone or ring of the gate). I have concluded that this Stone causes the body to emit or secrete an elixir—the Secretion of the Ages—that purifies the body, transfiguring it to light. This is the key benefit of the Transfiguration icons. These images were designed not just to help the early Christians to teach about the Transfiguration through pretty pictures, but also to encourage them to reshape their lives in accordance with the hope or expectation of transforming into

Transfiguration. Greek, 14th century. Here the depiction of the transformation almost has a butterfly quality.

light (something our culture does not support). Unfortunately, in the 7th century, Byzantine Emperor Leo III banned icons (726–729) in response to criticism from adherents of the new religion of Islam who proclaimed that icons (i.e., "doors") were false idols (more later).

In recent years, there has been a sort of "rediscovery" of icons by Western Christians. This is concurrent with modern science's increasing awareness that stargates and wormholes permeate the universe. Before the Renaissance and Reformation, holy images were treated not as "art" but as objects of veneration, which possessed codes of the tangible presence of the holy realm. In this way, a Transfiguration icon is the same as a computer icon or a highway sign. It is *concentrated information* that symbolizes or points to something beyond itself. When we click on a computer icon it opens into a phenomenal inner world of enormous potential called a program, a set of coded instructions that enables one to do work. The program's icon is not the program, but it symbolizes it and opens the way to it. Strange as it may sound to our sensibilities, this is how devotees used icons to do the Great Work, the alchemy of the soul.

First, one would click on the icon in their imagination. With full focused attention (or devotion) they'd enter the slipstream of the fast-moving Jesus in the icon. Feel it right, and it might raise one's vibration and literally start a rush of chemicals in your bloodstream (at least according to a new neuroscience theory we will discuss momentarily). Absorb and become the energy of the Transfigured Jesus, drift in his wake, and one might open a gate to the cosmic realm right here on earth. The materials of the image become a channel or a bridge, a gate ("babel") between two worlds. In fact, to an Orthodox Christian the images are a medium through which the energy of the Transfiguration moment can be channeled, like a two-way mirror. Devotees could enter the cosmic realm through the icon.

MIRROR, MIRROR

The concept of the mirror explains the technology of icons. The word icon comes from the Greek *eikon*, meaning "image." In the New Testament, the Greek word "image" also means "likeness" and "portrait." Another term we might use is "projection." The Old and New Testaments use the word "image" to describe all of us being in the image of the God who made us (Gen. 1:26, Matt. 22:20, Col. 1:15). We are mirror images or icons of our creator.

When used as a verb, the word mirror means "to send back" or "form an image of," "image," "reflect." To mirror is also to reflect (and reflection produces insight or enlightenment).

A mirror does not create images; it only transmits them. In a similar way, icons function as transmission devices. They are stations, channels, or transmitters of the energy of a flashy being and a higher vibration (voice or sound), the ring of the Transfiguration that crosses time and space. Their message (programming, code) is designed to operate within the human biocomputer (transfiguration system). Also called a looking glass, a mirror is more than a communications tool.

Just as Alice ponders what the world is like on the other side of a mirror, and to her surprise, is able to pass through to experience the parallel world, a person who became adept at mirroring Jesus' experience of Transfiguration could reflect this process in their own body (itself an icon or mirror image of the Creator).

"I saw our Lord fastened upon the cross coming down toward me and surrounding me with a marvelous light. . . . Then there came down from the holes of his blessed wounds five bloody beams, which were directed toward the same parts of my body: to my hands, feet,

"Stigmatization of Saint Catherine of Siena," about 1630 (by Rutilio Manetti)

and heart." This was how, according to legend, Saint Catherine of Siena described receiving the stigmata wounds of Jesus upon the cross. She was praying before an icon, the image transmitted the marks as beams of light reflected in her body.

TRANCE-FORMATION

We know from research in psycho-neuroimmunology that feelings of helplessness weaken immune function, but that a sense of empowerment strengthens it. Redefining how we describe events with labels that promote helplessness to those that trigger empowerment can take a fearful reaction and inspire an ordinary person to perform extraordinary deeds.

So says Dr. Mario Martinez, who studied Stigmatics for the Vatican. He has shown that a woman in California exhibited the stigmata marks after obsessively reading about the Crucifixion. As he discovered, the Medieval Stigmatics showed wounds on the palm of their hands because all the paintings (which were based on cultural beliefs) showed Jesus' wounds on the palm. Then, science showed that Roman crucifixion specialists bypassed the main artery and hit a nerve in the wrist to ensure maximum agony (that lasted for days). More recent Stigmatics show the wounds in the wrist, because of cultural beliefs.

Martinez's theory of biocognition says we have a personal bio-informational field that has horizons that can be expanded. If you expand by interacting with the horizons of Jesus, then you'll identify with his suffering or his love. If it is with his suffering—and this is very rare—you may experience the occurrence of stigmata.

If you identify with the path of love, you experience healing or special abilities to do things, or just convey a sense of love. Taken to the extreme, through this process you could transfigure into a cosmic being.

It could be as simple as monkey see, monkey do.

MIRROR NEURONS

More than other primates, neuroscientists believe, humans are hard-wired for imitation.

The discovery of mirror neurons in the frontal lobes of macaque monkeys and their implications for human brain evolution is one of the most important findings of neuroscience in the late 20th century, says celebrated neuroscientist Dr. V. S. Ramachandran. Mirror neurons are active when the monkeys perform certain tasks, but they also fire when the monkeys watch someone else perform the same specific task. There is evidence that a similar observation-action matching system exists in humans.

Imitation learning via this cluster of neurons, says Ramachandran, holds the key to understanding many enigmatic aspects of human evolution, including our "great leap" in our ability to use the wetware between our ears.

Brain researchers at UCLA found that cells in the human anterior cingulate, which normally fire when you poke the patient with a needle ("pain neurons"), will also fire when the patient watches another patient being poked. The mirror neurons, it would seem, dissolve the barrier between self and others. Ramachandran calls them "empathy neurons" or "Dalai Lama neurons" because they demonstrated the interconnectedness of all things.

When we apply this science to the Transfiguration icons, it suggests a remarkable spiritual technology is active. The Transfiguration icon is a (nonreligious) spiritual invitation for us to mirror Jesus' transformation, to activate our latent potential, and to become enlightened ones, simply by using our imagination and reflecting what we see. So, how come images of Transfiguration aren't plastered everywhere?

THE AGE OF ICONOCLASM

As Linette Martin discusses in *Sacred Doorways,* the era during which the practice of icons was at its height in the Byzantine world was a time of grave military crisis, as well as domestic and economic instability. The Byzantine Empire was threatened by Persia (Iran), by steppe nomads, and by the final blow, the new power of Islam, a religion begun in AD 622 with the flight of the prophet Muhammed. For Muslims, to make a realistic picture of Muhammed was forbidden, because it implied that the craftsman was God, and God is the only image-maker.

To make an image of "Christ" was wrong to Muslims because they did not believe in the Incarnation (the bodily materialization of a cosmic being) as adopted by the Church at the Councils of Nicea in AD 325 and Chalcedon in 451, though Jesus was acknowledged as Prophet Jesus. With Islam's rapid spread throughout the Levant and North Africa between 622 and 722, Christianity lost valuable turf. In response to the new religion, the Christian emperors might have chosen to invoke the supernatural or cosmic powers or energies of the icons. They might have pushed the argument between Christianity and Islam over the Incarnation and the cosmic realm and promoted icons of this nature, especially of the Transfiguration.

Instead, Emperor Leo III ordered icons to be banned. To him the Byzantines were guilty of idolatry. He drew a sharp contrast between image-free Islam and icon-worshipping Christians. In effect, by standing against icons, they were standing with people who denied the reality of the Incarnation and the cosmic realm. With one imperial decision the destruction of sacred art began. Gradually, the Church took control of this practice and no longer taught that an icon was a door to another realm. In fact, to think this is potentially dangerous.

With today's world experiencing many of the same conflicts as Leo's world, perhaps it's time to correct his mistake by reopening the door of the icons and rediscovering the alchemy of the soul.

This article first appeared in *Atlantis Rising* #68 (March/April 2008).

PART SEVEN

THROUGH THE LABYRINTH

26

THE ROSWELL GLYPHS

Has a Secret Investigation of Jesse Marcel Jr.'s Strange Drawings Settled the ET Question?

BY LEN KASTEN

"Since it is virtually certain that these craft do not originate in any country on earth, considerable speculation has centered around what their point of origin might be and how they get here. Mars was and remains a possibility, although some scientists, most notably Dr. Menzel, consider it more likely that we are dealing with beings from another solar system entirely. Numerous examples of what appear to be a form of writing were found in the wreckage. Efforts to decipher these have remained largely unsuccessful."—Eisenhower Briefing Document, November 18, 1952

It's a controversy that refuses to go away. Now 65 years later, the mystery of Roswell continues to intrigue and fascinate and to provoke strong reactions, perhaps even more so lately than in the beginning. As with the Kennedy assassination and the Energizer bunny, the Roswell dispute just "keeps going and going and going." Mark Larsen, communications category manager for Energizer, says, "The Bunny has become the ultimate symbol of longevity, perseverance, and determination." But we would say that Roswell now trumps The Bunny. It wins hands-down in longevity, and dogged determination and perseverance is abundant on both sides of the debate. Just when it seems that public interest has waned and the incident has been relegated to the obituaries, something comes along to jolt it right back to the front page.

First, there was the Showtime movie *Roswell* (1994) starring Martin Sheen. Then there was New Mexico Congressman Steven Schiff's investigation and the outrage and renewed suspicion it provoked when it was found that the Air Force had destroyed all the relevant documents. Then came the blockbuster—the book *The Day After Roswell* by Colonel Philip Corso. In 1995, there was the television documentary *The Roswell Incident*. And keeping it in the news were the several clumsy efforts by the Air Force to explain it away, starting with the famous Mogul balloon gambit, and culminating in the notorious "crash-dummy" proposition, which, in terms of sheer absurdity, has now surpassed "swamp gas" and "planet Venus" as explanations of UFO phenomena.

One new theory, however, may even top those. In the book *Body Snatchers in the Desert: The Horrible Truth at the Heart of the Roswell Story* (2005), by British UFO writer, Nick Redfern, we are seriously expected to entertain the possibility that the bodies found at the crash site were not dummies at all, but were "deformed, handicapped, disfigured, and diseased" Japanese POWs, still in U.S. custody despite Japan's official surrender two years earlier, who were being used in experiments in high altitude survivability by the Air Force, thus supposedly explaining their oriental features and diminutive size. And so, the Roswell bunny continues to bang his drum.

PANDORA'S BOX

The stakes in this confrontation are very high. If it can be categorically proven that the Roswell crash did happen, then a cascading series of remarkable possibilities will become certainties. First it will mean that there is intelligent life on other planets with technology greater than ours. This has tremendous ramifications in terms of society, technology, weaponry, religion, economics, and so on. Then, the 65-year cover-up suggests the existence of a shadow government that continues in power from administration to administration to administration. Otherwise, how could the ongoing fraud be perpetrated so expertly? This, in turn, means that our democracy is an illusion, and that we really live in some sort of oligarchy. Then, it means that we have most certainly gained extraordinary knowledge about our place in the universe that has not been shared with the public and that could possibly revolutionize our life here on earth. Very possibly this knowledge could solve all our energy problems. And very possibly we now have the ability to travel to other star systems ourselves, which opens up vast vistas for the human race. These are all colossal developments, and they all hinge on the reality of Roswell. To prove Roswell is to open Pandora's Box and the stargate to our future at one and the same time.

The dramatic events of those first ten days of July, 1947, in that tiny, remote military town in the high plains of central New Mexico remained cloaked in impenetrable secrecy for more than thirty years! But interest had been slowly and unobtrusively building among UFO groups during that period. This activity culminated in 1978 with a historic two-hour presentation by researcher Len Stringfield at a monthly MUFON (Mutual UFO Network) meeting in Dayton, Ohio, in which he revealed the details of several crash retrievals throughout the Southwest, and presented strong evidence that all the wreckage and several dead alien bodies had ended up at Wright-Patterson Air Base right there in Dayton. Stringfield spoke of retrievals in Mexico, California, Nevada, Arizona, and Montana, and gave prominent mention to one particular crash near Corona, New Mexico, in July of 1947. His book *Situation Red: The UFO Siege*, published in 1978, filled in many of the sketchy details. Stringfield's work drew the interest of researchers William Moore and Charles Berlitz, and in the summer of 1980 they unleashed the first book on the subject, *The Roswell Incident*, which has now become a classic. Veteran ufologist Stanton Friedman was a key researcher on that project, although he did not get authorship credit. After 10 more years of research, he went on to write his own book about Roswell with Don Berliner, titled *Crash at Corona* (1992), and ultimately has emerged as the pre-eminent authority on the subject.

Since 1980, the drumbeat has picked up as dozens of other books have been written about Roswell, and the town itself has become a UFO mecca and world famous. But final proof of the crash has remained elusive as the government has continued to keep a tight lid on any information that could help researchers bolster their case, and has, apparently, deliberately led them down blind alleys with planted disinformation. There is one book however, that offers serious new evidence for ET involvement in the Roswell event.

The book, *The Roswell Legacy* (2007) by Jesse Marcel Jr. contains previously unpublished details of the intelligence career of his father, Major Marcel. It includes a foreword by Stanton Friedman and provides Marcel Sr.'s account of the events of that day in 1947 from the perspective of the base security officer. The most newsworthy part of book is the remarkable result of a recent scholarly study commissioned by Marcel Jr. of the curious alien markings on some of the debris carefully preserved over the years by his father. Though the "glyphs" on the debris have become public knowledge, this is the first time that Marcel Jr., himself, has taken on the challenge of interpreting them to the public.

We spoke with him about the events of that momentous summer.

"It Was Not a Weather Balloon"

From the outset, it was clear to all the investigators that Marcel was the central figure in the case. In fact, it was Marcel's involvement and testimony that first attracted Friedman, a nuclear physicist and professional ufologist, and convinced him that the crash really did take place, and

A young Jesse Marcel Sr. at the beginning of World War II.

drew him into the investigation. As an Army Air Force intelligence officer with a distinguished war record, Marcel's credibility was unchallenged. The 509th Bomb Group at Roswell was a top-secret facility and everyone there had a high-level security clearance. As the base intelligence officer, Marcel was especially security conscious. Just prior to the Roswell assignment in 1946, Marcel was in charge of security for "Operations Crossroads," the ultra-secret Nevada nuclear test program, for which he was awarded a commendation. The top brass knew they had no reason to be worried about such a loyal and dedicated officer, especially since they promoted him to Lt. Colonel immediately after Roswell, and spirited him away to a top Cold War job. Whether or not this was calculated to insure his cooperation can only be a subject of speculation. So it is not surprising that Marcel remained silent about Roswell for thirty-two years.

On the contrary, what was surprising was the fact that he agreed to the Friedman interview at all in 1979. Maybe it was because so much time had elapsed that he felt he could now speak freely. But more likely, good soldier that he was, Marcel nevertheless came to realize that his first obligation was to humanity. This was clearly the case, as you will see he may have already planted the seeds of revelation.

It was Marcel who had received the phone call from Chaves County Sheriff George Wilcox about the debris found on the sheep ranch of Mac Brazel that Sunday morning, July 6, 1947. And it was Marcel and counterintelligence officer Sheridan Cavitt who had driven out to the Brazel ranch and collected two carloads of the strange debris that stretched out over three-quarters of a mile. Of that discovery, Marcel said, "It was amazing to see the vast amount of area it covered. . . . It's something that must have exploded above ground, traveling perhaps at a high rate of speed…It was quite obvious to me . . . that it was not a weather balloon, nor was it an airplane or a missile. . . . It was something I had never seen before, and I was pretty familiar with all air activities."

ALIEN HIEROGLYPHICS

The material collected by Marcel and Cavitt was definitely not of this world. Marcel, "This particular piece of metal was . . . about two feet long, and perhaps a foot wide. See, that stuff weighs nothing, it's so thin, it isn't any thicker than the tinfoil in a pack of cigarettes. So I tried to bend the stuff [but] it wouldn't bend. We even tried making a dent in it with a sixteen-pound sledge hammer. And there was still no dent in it. And, as of now, I still don't know what it was." But strangest of all were the fragments he described as "like parchment." And among these parchment-like

pieces were small I-beams inscribed with strange characters that appeared to have been painted on in a purple-violet color. Marcel says that they were "symbols and we had to call them hieroglyphics because I could not interpret them, they could not be read, they were just symbols, something that meant something and they were not all the same." These fragments couldn't be broken or burned. There was other tinfoil-like metal that always returned to a smooth state after being crumpled.

Marcel with weather balloon debris.

The two men loaded up a Jeep Carry-All, and Marcel instructed Cavitt to drive that first load back to the base. He then went back out into the field and loaded up his 1942 Buick with more fragments. Even then he says, "we picked up only a very small portion of the material that was there." And then he drove the fragments home.

That night Marcel returned home late and woke his wife and son to show them what he had found. He spread the fragments out on the kitchen floor, and they all marveled at this strange stuff from space. Jesse Marcel Jr. was only 11 at the time, but he evidently appreciated the import of what he was seeing—and he never forgot that night. The next day, July 8, Marcel Sr. brought the debris back to the base, and was immediately ordered

Physicist and UFO Researcher Stanton Friedman with one of the famous headlines of 1947.

by base commander Col. William Blanchard to put it all on a B-29 and fly along with it to Wright-Patterson Air Base in Ohio, with a stop at the 8th Air Force Headquarters in Ft. Worth, Texas. And that same morning, Blanchard ordered base public information officer Lt. Walter Haut to issue a press release stating that the Air Force had recovered the wreckage of a "flying saucer." Haut released the report to Roswell radio station KGFL, and they, in turn, sent it to the United Press via Western Union and so the story broke in the evening papers in the Midwest and the West. And that's when the cold, clammy hand of official suppression descended on Roswell.

In Ft. Worth, Major Marcel was instructed by 8th Air Force commanding general Roger Ramey to pose with him for photos showing that the wreckage was from a weather balloon, and then was told to go home and forget the whole thing. A couple of days later, Army reconnaissance planes, reportedly, discovered the crashed disc itself, and four alien bodies, a few miles from the debris field.

THE DRAWINGS

Jesse Marcel Sr. died in 1986. His son went on to become a physician and a flight surgeon. In 1978, at the age of 42, Jesse Jr. joined the National Guard and was trained as a helicopter pilot and became certified as a crash investigator. In March of 1991, Marcel signed an affidavit (*Roswell in Perspective*, Karl Pflock, 1994) in which he described the material his father had brought home that night in 1947. About the I-beam, he said, "On the inner surface . . . there appeared to be a type of writing. The writing was a purple-violet hue and had an embossed appearance. The figures were composed of curved, geometric shapes. It had no resemblance to Russian,

Japanese, or any other foreign language. It resembled hieroglyphics but had no animal-like characters." In that affidavit, Marcel says that his father was certain the material was not from a weather balloon, and "may have mentioned the words 'flying saucer.' " In that document also, he drew a picture of the I-Beam about 18 inches in length and showing the characters as best as he could remember them, and in a postscript mentions that he showed the drawing to his mother, and that she concurred with his description.

While it is a rough drawing, each unique character is carefully delineated. It is a testament to the depth with which the entire event had been seared into his memory that the 55-year-old Marcel could recall such details so vividly; nevertheless his integrity and credibility as a witness has been clearly confirmed by a long and successful professional career. FBI forensic hypnosis has also backed him up and a new study of his drawings provides even further corroboration.

The alien glyphs found printed on Roswell debris as drawn by Jesse Marcel, Jr.

In his forthcoming book, Marcel explains that his father did more than simply gawk at the fragments arrayed on his kitchen floor that night; he discussed them with his son. As a seasoned intelligence officer, Marcel Sr., we can be confident, understood the implication of the artifacts. Later, when Jesse Jr. would make his drawings of the glyphs, his father's comments would come back to him. During a lifetime of military service Marcel has had little to say publicly about the glyphs, but now, almost 65 years later, retired, and outside the reach of military obligation, he has decided to make his case directly to the public. And now, finally, as Marcel explained to us, the mysterious I-Beam characters have been scientifically analyzed and explained.

As reported in the book, a year-long study by University of California at Berkeley professor Roger Weir, commissioned by Marcel, was concluded in 2005. Weir, a language expert, closely examined the glyphs and concluded that their construction was consistent with an essentially technical purpose of some kind, and that they could NOT have been concocted by an amateur. Weir discerns features similar to magnetic fields and speculates that they may have been related to the navigational guidance system in some way. An analogy might be the type of electro-magnetic fields used on earth to guide aircraft to a safe landing. According to Weir, the complexity and volume of information contained in the glyphs rules out counterfeiting and strongly supports their authenticity.

Could Dr. Marcel's book be the final word on Roswell? Probably not, but the fact that the glyphs now appear very likely to be of extraterrestrial origin certainly could lead to some very disturbing conclusions. It remains to be seen if the powers that be can construct a satisfactory counter argument. It may have taken 65 years, but Major Jesse Marcel, thanks to the diligence and independence of his son, seems to have reached out from the grave and circumvented the official suppression machine, of which he had intimate knowledge. Maybe Major Marcel will rest a little easier now.

Once again, it seems that, for the benefit of humanity, destiny has put the right person in the right place at the right time.

This article first appeared in *Atlantis Rising* #58 (July/August 2006).

27

THE LABYRINTHINE PATH

*Found in Ancient Caves and Gothic Cathedrals, but
What Do Labyrinths Really Mean?*

BY PHILIP COPPENS

The most direct path from A to B is a straight line. The most indirect path from A to B is likely to be a labyrinth. Not to be confused with a maze, which has several dead ends, a labyrinth is a unicursal voyage that leads from a point outside the design toward the center . . . in the longest of ways. Unicursal means a curve or surface that is closed and can be drawn or swept out in a single movement.

Though the labyrinth of the French Gothic Cathedral of Chartres is likely the most famous, labyrinths are of all times and civilizations. They have been found on rock art dating back thousands of years. Indeed, they may be as old as civilization itself. A labyrinth carved on a piece of mammoth ivory has been found in a Paleolithic tomb in Siberia. The site is more than 7,000 years old.

But what message do they convey? Though their interpretation has changed and been adapted by individual civilizations over time, and—whether intentionally or not—in origin, the labyrinth is best explained by its very shape. In the 1990s, British author Paul Devereux established a relationship between straight lines and the flight of the soul in its disembodied state. In folklore across the world, it is said that the disembodied soul within this earthly realm travels in a straight line. A labyrinth, however, is anything but straight; and it was therefore said that it could both catch the soul and keep it in one location or instead create a void, in which the person visiting the center would be "clean" of any outside spiritual influences, as such energies cannot penetrate the labyrinth. It's no wonder that some see the center of a labyrinth as a point outside of time. Such an observation has also been made by the Hopi Native American tribe of North America, who use the labyrinth shape as the symbol for what they call a place of emergence, where access to this—and other—realms becomes possible: a sacred space that creates a gateway through time, to communicate with the Creator God.

Because of the story of Theseus and the Minotaur, the birthplace of the labyrinth is popularly ascribed to Crete, where the Minoan civilization flourished in the second millennium BC, even though we know the story is far older.

The Minotaur is normally described as part man, part bull, a hybrid being, an abomination for which King Minos of Crete needed an enclosure. This was designed by the architect Daedalus and his son Icarus. Most identify the site of Knossos as the location. Though the palace held many puzzling compartments, the structure would clearly be more of a maze than a labyrinth. If there was a labyrinth here, it has, so far, not been uncovered. Most interpretations of the Knossos labyrinth, however, favor the story of a maze, as it seems more easily to explain the legend.

The key role in the story is that of Ariadne, the one who reveals the structure's layout to Theseus and the secret that he needs to tie a rope to himself at the start, so that, once having located and slaughtered the

Theseus and the Minotaur. Greek mosaic.

Minotaur, he can find his way out. But as labyrinths are unicursal, most researchers have thus concluded Knossos was a maze, if only because a labyrinth could not hold a beast, as it could simply follow the single corridor and come out.

Of course, this assumes the labyrinth was a real, physical structure and the Minotaur a "normal" beast. But if a soul were to enter the labyrinth, and since souls can only travel in straight lines, a cord would indeed be required to find the way out again. Remarkably, there are thousands of years of shamanic tradition that speak of such a cord—the famous silver cord through which the shaman remains connected to his body during journeys in the Otherworld and can find his way back. So it is therefore more likely that the Cretan structure was indeed a labyrinth but was not the palace itself, and perhaps not even a physical structure.

The inspiration for the Cretan labyrinth was said to have been built at Medinet el Fayum, circa 1800 BC, under Pharaoh Amenemhet III (12th Dynasty). Indeed, Daedalus is said to have studied there. The Egyptian "labyrinth" at Hawara was actually a temple of the dead and is a vast array of rooms, set on several floors, so that one could easily get lost. As such, it is on par with the Palace of Knossos. Indeed, both were possibly temples of the dead. Labyrinths were specifically identified as structures from which the dead could not escape.

The chief argument for Knossos being the labyrinth has been the number of rooms within the palace, and that the access routes to Knossos have several bends—there is no straight line in approaching the Palace. This latter fact is more important than it might at first appear. Spirits, remember, were said to be able to travel only in straight lines; and so, bends—like those for entering Knossos—guaranteed that spirits could not enter or leave such constructions. Seeing that the palaces of Crete were likely linked with a cult of the dead, this is a significant observation.

In hindsight, it seems that the term labyrinth was applied to two distinct structures. One was a design, unicursal and concentric, while the other was a structure. Both, however, were linked with the spirits of the deceased; it is likely that some confusion arose over time, leading to the current problems in identifying the "real" Cretan labyrinth. However, if the Palace of Knossos was indeed the residence of the infamous Minotaur, then its cell is still to be discovered, or identified.

Kathleen McGowan has recently popularized the Chartres labyrinth and its connection to Ariadne. McGowan argues that Ariadne is the ultimate divine feminine principle at work: "She represents the pure power and protection that can only come from love. It is through her love that she is able to shield Theseus from harm or death." Indeed, other myths that involve labyrinths underline the link between the design and a priestess or a virgin. The Greek poet Homer remarked that the labyrinth was Ariadne's ceremonial dancing ground, and she is obviously a key figure in guiding Theseus into the structure.

In fact, when we look at the story of Theseus, we find many shamanic connections. After slaughtering the Minotaur, Theseus became king of Athens; he would later enter Hades in an attempt to rescue the soul of Persephone. Hades, of course, is the Greek underworld and in Virgil's Aeneid, Aeneas found a labyrinth at the entrance to Hades, separating the living from the dead—once again underlining the psychical role of a labyrinth. Furthermore, Joseph Campbell speaks of many myths which relate that the approach to the Land of the Dead was halted by a female guardian, thus explaining the role of Ariadne.

The connection with Troy is also paramount. In Celtic tradition, there were Troy Stones, which were handed down by wise women from one to another and were used to communicate with the underworld. Nigel Pennick notes that "the wise woman would trace her finger through the labyrinth, back and forth, whilst humming a particular tune, until she reached an altered state."

According to the Roman author Virgil, after the fall of Troy, Aeneas popularized a processional parade or dance that became known as the "Game of Troy." This may have been identical to the Crane Dance, which is said to have originated with Theseus and his party after escaping from Knossos. The crane was the sacred bird of Mercury (Hermes), and rock carvings found at Val Camonica in northern Italy, dated around 1800–1300 BC, depict a crane standing close by a Cretan-style labyrinth, confirming the close connection between Troy, labyrinths, and the Crane Dance.

Indeed, in some regions, labyrinths are known as "Troy towns," while other traditions state that the center of the labyrinth was not occupied by a Minotaur, but that one needed to rescue a young woman at the center, often identified as Helen of Troy.

In Homer's *Iliad*, King Agamemnon, the commander-in-chief of the Greek army, is the brother of King Menelaus, who has lost his wife, Helen, to Paris of Troy. She is the one being held hostage in Troy and the key question, often unasked, is whether she was held in a "Troy town"—a labyrinth, from which she needed to be liberated. Was Troy, in fact, *not* a physical location but a celestial city—on par with the Christian concept of the New Jerusalem?

Florence and Kenneth Wood in *Homer's Secret Iliad* (1999) see the fall of Troy as an allegory for the decline of the constellation Ursa Major in the sky, and the end of one era making way for another, as identified by the precession of the equinoxes, a process that greatly influenced many myths and legends. They identify Helen as the constellation Libra, Menelaus the red-haired Antares, while Paris is Betelgeuse and Orion. It therefore seems that the concept of time is a key component of the labyrinth, too—at least in Greek mythology. Noting that the center of the labyrinth was often seen as a place outside of time, it was, indeed, a place of emergence and creation.

The identification of the Minotaur as Cretan, however, existed only from 400 BC onward. Previously, it was referred to as the "bull of Minos"—Minos Taurus. Furthermore, the story is likely to have originated in legendary encounters between gods-as-bulls and women, rather than that of a hybrid being. Such accounts were common in the Near East. As mentioned, there are earlier references to a labyrinth in Egypt. Egyptian etymology suggests *lapi-rohun-t*, or "Temple on the Mouth of the Sea," while the Cretan king Minos is a Hellenized Menes, the first Dynastic pharaoh of Egypt—which does not necessarily imply that the two are identical.

The sacred structure in Egypt connected with labyrinths and bulls was the Serapeum, which was a burial place for the Apis bulls. The Serapeum had more than 60 such mummies, collated over a period of thousands of years. Each tomb is a remarkable piece of engineering, believed by some to be beyond the technical capabilities of the ancient Egyptians. Each Apis Bull was linked with the beginning of a new era, as seen when Emperor Hadrian had to suppress a revolt in AD 138 in Alexandria; it marked the end of a Great Year when "bull fever" was even more intense than at other times.

When speaking of bulls and astronomical eras, we also need to consider Mithraism, in which Mithras takes on the role of Theseus and becomes the bull slayer. Interestingly, the bull in Greece was known as Asterion, which means "starry," or "ruler of the stars." In every Mithraic temple, the central focus was upon a tauroctony—Mithras killing a sacred bull—which was associated with spring. Remarkably, in Gothic cathedrals, the center of the labyrinth was often occupied by Theseus killing the Minotaur. Coincidence, or an inheritance of a sacred tradition? However, there seems to have been no room within Mithraism for labyrinths.

From the earliest depictions in Siberia, the labyrinth has been linked with shamanism, and hence altered states. The labyrinth, in short, should be seen as a shamanic device. This is also apparent in medieval labyrinths, even though these had, with the passage of time and cultures, received several more layers, including the intricate designs such as those of Chartres. But, in essence, the labyrinth remained a Way to Jerusalem. Often seen as a miniature version of a pilgrimage to Jerusalem, in truth, it was more a Way to a *New* Jerusalem: it remained a shamanic tool for the visitors who

The labyrinth design at Chartres Cathedral

entered it and performed a ritual walk, a practice often associated with shamanic traditions and visible in sites such as Nazca, Cusco, Chaco Canyon, and various other sites across the world.

Whereas Cusco and Chaco Canyon's ritual paths were linear, the labyrinth is . . . labyrinthine. The person walking the labyrinth is cleansing his mind, to enter at the center free from external thoughts, surrendering himself to God. Whether in Siberia in 5000 BC, or Chartres, in AD 1200, in essence, the labyrinth has remained a shamanic device. "Only" its complexity has transformed and moved along with the civilizations that have incorporated it in their religions and constructions and added additional layers of interpretation, often, as in the case of Chartres, combining concepts of various cultures and religions. With each implementation of the labyrinth, a time returns; and the passage of time, of beginning and end, birth and rebirth, is symbolically illustrated. It underlined the ancient concept that time was not linear, but cyclical . . . or labyrinthine?

The most celebrated and intricate—design-wise—labyrinth of all is that of Chartres. Its design has been copied numerous times, perhaps most famously at Grace Cathedral in the heart of San Francisco, where there is an indoor and outdoor labyrinth.

Though the labyrinth is a key feature of the Gothic cathedral that dominates the French town, the Church, which operates the building, treats the structure with almost utter disdain. Normally, except for Fridays from Easter till late September, the labyrinth is covered with chairs. This has resulted in damage to the stones, but, more significantly, it stops people from walking it and using the structure for its intended purpose: meditation. This has caused outrage.

New York Times bestselling author Kathleen McGowan talks about the Chartres labyrinth both in her novel *The Book of Love* and her self-help book *The Source of Miracles*. The latter specifically uses the Chartres labyrinth as a meditative tool—relating personal experiences of how the labyrinth has helped in her spiritual development. Both books powerfully underline what visitors have experienced for decades if not centuries: that the Chartres labyrinth is a powerful prayer tool. McGowan, however, is upset that the Church restricts access to the labyrinth: "The labyrinth at Chartres Cathedral is a priceless piece of medieval art. As a UNESCO heritage site, I believe the labyrinth deserves the same protection as the sculptures and the stained glass in the cathedral. The fact that the Church intentionally damages it by covering it with unnecessary chairs for the sole purpose of denying pilgrims access to it is nothing less than vandalism."

In the 21st century, it seems that we might once again penetrate the true purpose of labyrinths: and yet the most famous labyrinths of all in Crete or Egypt remain undiscovered, while the one at Chartres is in the process of being lost.

This article first appeared in *Atlantis Rising* #81 (May/June 2010).

28

THE COPPER SCROLL CONUNDRUM

It's Certainly a Treasure Map, but Where Does it Lead?

BY PHILIP COPPENS

In 1947, a number of scrolls were discovered in caves along the Dead Sea coast. They have gone down in history as "The Dead Sea Scrolls" and continue to be at the center of worldwide controversy. Why? Because the discovery and especially decipherment of these scrolls opened a radically different point of view on early Christianity and Judaism around the time of Christ. At the time of the discovery, some experts believed that the community that resided nearby, at Qumran, and which some have labeled the Essenes, might have been the religious group out of which John the Baptist and/or Jesus himself emanated. Today, most have abandoned the idea that Jesus was linked to these Essenes, but several are still pondering whether the Baptist might have been—the Qumran community was known, as was the Baptist, to be extremely ascetic.

Scholarly experts have identified the remains of about 825 to 870 separate scrolls from several caves near Qumran. Many of the texts have provided new insights. For example, before 1947, the oldest Hebrew texts from the Bible dated to the 9th century AD; the Dead Sea Scrolls pushed this date radically back, as the community that lived at Qumran compiled these texts from a few centuries BC to about AD 68. The discovery was on par with finding a dinosaur's actual carcass rather than having to rely on analysis of its bones.

Originally, the Dead Sea Scrolls were found by local shepherds who took one document from the collection to Bethlehem, in the hope of selling it. At first, they met with no success, but then an interested party was willing to buy it for seven pounds (around $30 today). When the scrolls hit the antiquities market, academics soon learned of them and set out to uncover where the material had originated.

By 1952, the caves in which the Dead Sea Scrolls had been found were under intense excavation from a collective of universities and academic institutions. Then, on March 14, 1952, inside the so-called "Cave 3," another enigmatic scroll was found made entirely from copper.

Heavily corroded, the ancient metal could not be unrolled, clearly posing a significant challenge for those intent on knowing what was actually written on this curious find—unique among the Dead Sea Scrolls. It fell to John Allegro of Oxford University to convince the leaders of the archaeological team to permit him to take the scroll to England. There, it was most carefully sliced into 23 strips by H. Wright Baker of Manchester University. But when Allegro began, in fact, to read the scroll a new mystery was born.

Cave at Qumran

The scroll was one foot wide and eight feet long. Allegro transcribed it immediately and made a quick English translation. It contained a list of 64 locations written down in twelve columns. Each entry pertained to a treasure site and there were indications specifying where a large quantity of gold and silver and other precious objects, like jewelry, perfumes, and oils, had been hidden. The nature of the scroll—unlike the other material hidden in the Dead Sea caves—it was realized, was not religious. The Copper Scroll appeared to be a treasure map! The Dead Sea Scrolls—already controversial—had become an even hotter potato!

Ever since its discovery, a number of researchers—from both within and without the academic community—have attempted to use the scroll in support of their own particular theories. Some, like maverick American Bible scholar and archaeologist, Vendyl Jones, believe the treasure includes the lost Ark of the Covenant as well as the lost wealth of the Temple of Solomon. Even though the scroll, itself, does not refer to other scrolls but rather to hidden precious metals, Christopher Knight and Robert Lomas, in their book *Second Messiah*, which focuses on the Copper Scroll, argue that "at least twenty-four such scrolls were secreted below the Temple." At no point does the Copper Scroll claim that the treasures are below the Temple, but the possibility cannot be ruled out.

Being a treasure map, the scroll was bound to attract treasure hunters, and it was clear that it would not remain the exclusive bailiwick of academics. Most academics, in fact, have stayed well clear of the Copper Scroll.

The official translation of the text was assigned to Father Józef Milik, the Jordanian Director of Antiquities. But Allegro grew dissatisfied with the slow pace in which the translation was carried out; there were, after all, only 64 short entries. For a number of years, Allegro wanted to publish his own translation ahead of the official publication, but his superiors in Israel would not allow it. The argument was that such publication would bring a flood of treasure hunters to the Qumran area, thus interfering with

The Copper Scroll

ongoing excavations. Their fears were not totally misplaced. In December, 1959, and March, 1960, Allegro himself organized two expeditions to Jordan in the hope of finding some of the treasure mentioned in the Copper Scroll. He found nothing.

In 1960, Allegro finally broke with protocol and published *The Treasure of the Copper Scroll* anyway. His superiors, Roland de Vaux and Józef Milik, both denounced the translation as defective. Furthermore, both claimed initially that the inventory was fiction and did not refer to genuine caches of gold and silver. In the years since, that view has been abandoned by most scholars as simply untenable.

In 1962, the official translation was finally released. Along with the translation came a number of other observations: the scroll was probably dated to around AD 50–100. The script was identified as being similar to the Mishnaic Hebrew dialect but also to contain some Greek. As this was a scroll made from copper, the writing was done with hammer and chisel and it is clear from the effort that went into creating it, that it was a very important document—most unlikely to be a work of fiction. Even the choice of copper is considered evidence that its creator(s) wanted a certain longevity for it, which would be impossible with most other available materials.

Clearly intended as a treasure map, it still has the complexities and problems intrinsic to such maps. While no one disputes that there are 64 locations where precious metals and objects are said to be hidden, there is disagreement over how much gold and silver is actually involved. The amount is usually considered to be about of 43 tons of gold and 23 tons of silver. At today's rate—using only the quantified parts of the treasure (some entries on the list mention no weights at all)—that is more than a billion dollars. No wonder several treasure hunters have become obsessed with the Copper Scroll!

How, though, could a small, ascetic community on the Dead Sea have come to possess a treasure that could only have belonged to kings or high priests?

Identifying the source of the treasure has been the principal challenge for most scholars. Some believe it came from the Second Temple of Jerusalem, which was destroyed by the Romans in AD 70. It is in this time frame that the Qumran community seems to have disappeared. Proximity in time is one method used to draw two apparently unrelated items together.

John Allegro wrote, "The Copper Scroll and its copy (or copies) were intended to tell the Jewish survivors of the war then raging where this sacred material lay buried, so that if any should be found, it would never be desecrated by profane use. It would also act as a guide to the recovery of the treasure, should it be needed, to carry on the war."

These scholars therefore argue that the Qumran community hid the treasure just before the temple's destruction. They note that the Triumphal Arch of Titus in Rome, which celebrates his sacking of Jerusalem, depicts some of the Temple treasure being removed from the Temple; but none of those items are listed on the scroll. The argument therefore is that some of the Temple treasure was left inside the Temple for the Romans to find, but that a large part was hidden; and its locations were entered on this scroll, which was then secreted away in a cave on the Dead Sea so that future generations could recover it—and recover the treasure.

There are a number of variations on this theory, including that by Dr.

One of the jars in which the ancients scrolls were found.

Norman Golb, who argues that the treasures were hidden by Second Temple personnel and that the Qumran community had nothing to do with it; the scroll merely ended up with this community.

A number of expeditions have been mounted to recover the treasures listed in the scroll. But, as with most treasure maps, its entries have been anything but easy to read. What to make of "In the cave that is next to the fountain belonging to the House of Hakkoz, dig six cubits. (There are) six bars of gold"? We need to know where the House of Hakkoz is, and we don't. Some instructions, though, look easier to follow: "In the ruin which is in the valley of Acor, under the steps leading to the East, forty long cubits: a chest of silver and its vessels with a weight of seventeen talents." Acor is believed to be Achor, a valley near Jericho. Alas, ancient sources are unclear as to the precise location of this valley, whether it is north or south of Jericho. Multiply the above two problems by 32, and any treasure hunter— or academic—is confronted with at least 64 problems to solve.

The conclusion drawn by most of those who have studied the texts is that whomever the intended recipient of this document was, he must have been intimately familiar with the places described, which begs the question as to why the entries were intended to be preserved for a long time. Why did those transcribing the treasure locations not provide readers in a distant future with more complete directions to the sites mentioned?

If the treasure was indeed that of the Jewish Temple, maybe it was meant to be handed down within one or a few families—maybe those of the Temple priests? Supporting evidence for this claim is the fact that the Hakkoz family had been involved in the rebuilding of the Temple, and the inclusion of their name on this list definitely pointed toward a Temple connection. But that is far from telling the entire story which should, it seems, include how the scroll finally ended up in a cave near the Dead Sea!

The actual contents listed in the Copper Scroll present other serious problems as well. Indeed, if taken literally, the amounts of gold and silver listed in the scroll becomes truly incredible when compared with the total amounts believed smelted up to that time. Only 160 tons of gold were mined across the Old World prior to AD 1, meaning that the Copper Scroll accounted for a fourth of the total refined gold in existence. Sixty-five tons of silver is believed to be the total amount mined by the entire world. The Copper Scroll therefore lists almost a third of the world's stock. It seems impossible that an obscure ascetic sect could have accumulated all of this on their own.

In one attempt to address this issue, British metallurgist Robert Feather proposed that the units of measurement were Egyptian. The unit of weight given as K is generally assumed to refer to the Biblical Talent, which is approximately 76 pounds (or 35 kilograms). But the ancient Egyptians developed a system of weights specifically for precious metals, specifically copper, gold, and silver, based on the "kite," or *qedet*, with a weight of 9 to 10 grams. This would mean that the scrolls' inventory would add up to 57 pounds (26 kilograms) of gold and 30 pounds (14 kilograms of silver)—a far more reasonable, yet still substantial amount of money, about one million dollars of gold and 10,000 dollars of silver.

Why a community at the Dead Sea would use this Egyptian unit, which had been discontinued around 500 BC, poses an initial problem. Feather, however, found references to suggest that the Copper Scroll, though dated between to 150 BC and AD 70, might instead have been a copy of an older document. John Elwolde has noted there are passages in the scroll that correspond to early Biblical Hebrew (800–700 BC), therefore within the time frame of the Egyptian kite.

Feather further notes that the use of copper for writing was unknown in Judaea at the time of, or before, the Qumran community. Copper scrolls were, however, used for writing by the ancient Egyptians (even though the practice was far from common). One Egyptian copper scroll was found at Medinet Habu dating from the Roman period; another exists from the lifetime of Ramses III (circa 1156 BC). Indeed, Egypt was the only known place where copper was used for writing!

Furthermore, the Copper Scroll is made from very pure copper (99.9 percent), with traces of tin, iron, and arsenic—almost identical to the chemical composition of copper as used in Egypt during the 18th Dynasty. Feather is convinced that the copper from the Copper Scroll came from a piece of Egyptian copper, similar to those once in the possession of Ramses III. Somehow—and so far inexplicably—centuries after the ancient Egyptians had abandoned both the measuring system and the use of copper for writing, someone between 150 BC and 70 AD found or recreated a piece of copper, fashioned it into the right format, and began to hammer a listing of treasure locations. Obviously, whoever did so went to great trouble to accomplish this task, which once again underscores the importance of the list in the scroll. Indeed, I would argue that the effort that went into its creation suggests that the treasure could have had a more than material value.

The central question for Copper Scroll scholarship remains: Where to dig? What is the area or region where the treasure was hidden? For John Allegro, there were four likely locations: The Dead Sea itself, of course, because that is where the scrolls were found; Jerusalem, at that time the capital of the Jewish nation and the site of the Temple and, in fact, many of the locations appear to be in and around Jerusalem; third, Jericho, an ancient and important city for the Jews; finally, Mount Gerizim, which is a sacred mountain to the Samaritans who regard it, rather than Jerusalem's Temple Mount, as the location chosen by Yahweh for his people. However, in none of these four locations has any such treasure ever been found and it is unlikely that excavation will ever be permitted in most of them. So is the treasure identified in the Copper Scroll one of unknown location, forever lost? Maybe not.

Robert Feather has not only placed the metallurgy of the Copper Scroll within an Egyptian context, but he also believes that the sites mentioned in the Scroll are to be found in Egypt.

Egypt, alas, is an even bigger nation than Israel, meaning that the recovery there could be even more unlikely. Still, Feather has developed a historical scenario in which he has placed the contents of the Copper Scroll— and in which the treasure of the Copper Scroll has already been found!

He looks toward the brief and volatile reign of Pharaoh Akhenaten, who ruled for 17 years in the second half of the 14th century BC. He is principally associated with abandoning the worship of the old gods and substituting belief in a new deity, the Aten, thus creating a monotheistic religion. Various scholars, including the father of psychiatry Sigmund Freud, have focused on Akhenaten; many have seen parallels between Akhenaten's monotheistic drive and the origins of the Jewish religion and the request of Moses for "his people," who indeed worshipped one God, Yahweh, to leave Egypt.

Relief of a man, at Tell el-Amarna.

Akhenaten also built a new capital, Akhetaten, or "the Horizon of the Aten." Today, the ancient capital is buried beneath the sand of several villages, principally Tel el-Amarna, el-Till, and el-Hagg Qandil. Since it did not possess the power of the pyramids or the elegance of the other temple complexes, Amarna's exploration occurred relatively late. The Deutsche Orientgesellschaft expedition, led by Ludwig Borchardt, excavated between 1907 and 1914, discovering the famous bust of Nefertiti, which is now on display in the Berlin Museum. But it was after the First World War, in excavations from 1921 to 1936 by the Egypt Exploration Society, that a series of discoveries were made, which in retrospect might have been the treasure of which the Copper Scroll speaks.

In 1926, under the leadership of Dr. Henri Frankfort, a jug was found which contained 23 gold bars with nearby silver ingots, rings, and more precious objects. The area where it was found is now known as the "Crock of the Gold Square." Frankfort found 9 pounds (four kilograms) of gold in total, which was apparently all ready for smelting. Feather is convinced that what was found, were the ingots indexed on the Copper Scroll.

As to why Feather was the first to highlight this: No one else seems to have drawn the conclusion, since this treasure was found before the Copper Scroll itself was found. He adds that villagers of el-Hagg Qandil have found total quantities of gold roughly equivalent to that specified in the Copper Scroll. He argues that, when faced with an Egyptian measurement system and the known use of copper during the 18th Dynasty, this cannot be a coincidence.

Martha Bell has summarized the discovery of the "Crock of Gold" as a hoard of "gold and silver ingots and silver scrap, jewelry, and vessels, all of which can reasonably be interpreted as the possessions of a metal smith. Since, however, the house in which the hoard was found seems to have been in a "slum," and it contained no evidence for industrial activity, the material could have been a robber's loot."

In short, this description fits perfectly with what we know of the Copper Scroll. What the hoard contains conforms to what is listed in the Scroll. The bizarre circumstances of its location equally map onto what is known and believed about the scroll.

In other words, the mystery of the Copper Scroll may never have been—or was, at least, resolved before it came about. Today, the hoard is on display in the Egyptian Museum in Cairo. But no treasure hunter is required to go and look at it.

This article first appeared in *Atlantis Rising* #82 (July/August 2010).

29

THE WILL TO DISBELIEVE

What Makes Some People Deny Evidence for the Invisible World?

BY MICHAEL TYMN

In his 1989 presidential address to the Society for Psychical Research (SPR), the late Professor Ian Stevenson pointed out that between 1910 and 1980 at least six presidents of the SPR asserted that telepathy had been proved, or nearly so. He wondered why, if telepathy had been proved by 1910, later presidents found it necessary to reiterate the claim.

Dr. Stevenson speculated that each generation of researchers tends to believe its methods superior to those of its predecessors and therefore they may have seen the earlier evidence as not so strong. He also theorized that mainstream science and the world at large did not hear the earlier assertions and therefore it was necessary to repeat them again and again.

Now, more than three decades after the 1980 assertion, two years short of a century since it was first announced that telepathy had been proved, it does not appear that mainstream science is any closer to accepting it now than it was then. In the foreword to *Parapsychology and the Skeptics*, Dr. Rupert Sheldrake quotes Professor Peter Atkins, an Oxford chemist, as saying that "there is no reason to suppose that telepathy is anything more than a charlatan's fantasy." In a BBC debate, Sheldrake asked Carter if he had actually looked at the evidence. Atkins' reply, "No, but I would be very suspicious of it."

At his website, Sheldrake, one of the few present-day scientists speaking out in favor of paranormal phenomena, mentions an August, 2007, television debate with Richard Dawkins, geneticist and author of the book *The God Delusion.* Sheldrake reported that Dawkins said he would like to believe in telepathy, but there just isn't any evidence for it. Dawkins added that if telepathy really occurred it would "turn the laws of physics upside down" and that "extraordinary claims require extraordinary evidence."

In effect, Dawkins was restating the precept of early 19th century astronomer and mathematician Pierre-Simon Laplace, which is that "the rigor of proof must be proportionate to the gravity of the conclusion." Apparently, the ganzfeld experiments, considered the best in the area of telepathy, didn't impress Dawkins, if he bothered to study them.

And so it is also with the evidence for the survival of consciousness at death, which goes beyond telepathy in defying the mechanistic laws of the universe accepted by mainstream science. Nearly all of the early psychical researchers concluded that the evidence for survival was conclusive. Consider these statements:

Dr. Alfred Russel Wallace (1823–1913), co-originator with Charles Darwin of the natural selection theory: "My position is that the phenomena of Spiritualism in their entirety do not require further confirmation. They are proved quite as well as facts are proved in other sciences."

Sir William Barrett (1844–1925), professor of physics at the Royal College in Dublin for 37 years, knighted for his contributions to mainstream science: "I am personally convinced that the evidence we have published decidedly demonstrates (1) the existence of a spiritual world, (2) survival after death, and (3) of occasional communication from those who have passed over."

Sir Oliver Lodge (1851–1940), professor of physics and pioneer in electricity and radio: "I tell you with all my strength of the conviction which I can muster that we do persist, that people still continue to take an interest in what is going on, that they know far more about things on this earth than we do, and are able from time to time to communicate with us."

Dr. James H. Hyslop (1854–1920), professor of ethics and logic at Columbia University before becoming a full-time psychical researcher: "Personally, I regard the fact of survival after death as scientifically proved. I agree that this opinion is not upheld in scientific quarters. But this is neither our fault nor the fault of the facts. Evolution was not believed until long after it was proved. The fault lay with those who were too ignorant or too stubborn to accept the facts. History shows that every intelligent man who has gone into this investigation, if he gave it adequate examination at all, has come out believing in spirits; this circumstance places the burden or proof on the shoulders of the skeptic."

Dr. Robert Crookall (1890–1969), a geologist who became a full-time psychical researcher in 1952: "The whole of the available evidence is explicable on the hypothesis of the survival of the human soul in a Soul Body. There is no longer a 'deadlock' or 'stalemate' on the question of survival. On the contrary, survival is as well established as the theory of evolution."

Based on the conclusions of those early researchers and several dozen other very credible scientists and scholars, there should be no further need for survival research. We should be able to invoke the legal doctrine of *Res Judicata*—"It has been decided." We live on! Case closed!

Yet, the research of those early pioneers has been filed away in dust-covered file cabinets and all but forgotten. It has been repudiated, rejected, refuted, resisted, and ridiculed. Mainstream science has smirked, snickered, scoffed, and sneered at it, calling it outdated and pseudoscience. In an article titled "The Mystery of Consciousness" (*Time* magazine, January 29, 2007), Steven Pinker, a professor of psychology at Harvard University, states that "attempts to contact the souls of the dead (a pursuit of serious scientists a century ago) turned up only cheap magic tricks."

In the December 27, 2007 issue of the *Arizona Daily Star*, David Sbarra, an assistant professor of psychology at the University of Arizona, is quoted as stating, "I can say with 100 percent certainty that there is no scientific evidence that individuals are capable of channeling with dead relatives…"

Recent authors waving the banner of science, including Dawkins, Christopher Hitchens (*God is Not Great*), Sam Harris (*The End of Faith: Religion, Terror and the Future of Reason*), Victor J. Stenger (*God: The Failed Hypothesis*) and Michel Onfray (*Atheist Manifesto*) indirectly dismiss the evidence for survival by dismissing God. They all seem to take a deductive approach, that is, assuming that God must be identified or discovered before afterlife survival can be considered—or, no God, no survival. None seems to have seriously considered taking the inductive approach of finding God by looking at all the evidence in favor of survival.

Contrary to the claims by pseudoskeptics that all of that old research is outdated or has been overturned, the fact is that it is as solid now as it ever was, as modern theories of quantum mechanics have given more meaning to it. It is simply not understood by the pseudoskeptics because they are unwilling to take the time to really examine it. They have a will to disbelieve.

While the case for spirit communication and, concomitantly, survival, was seemingly made a century ago, we have more recent evidence for survival coming to us through research in the areas of reincarnation, near-death experiences, clairvoyance, and induced after-death communication. However, scientific fundamentalists have also found ways to dismiss that evidence. Indeed, it seems that those involved in paranormal research that ultimately leads to the question of whether consciousness survives physical death must continually reinvent the wheel. In the engineering profession, they speak of reinventing the square wheel, which, in effect, means ending up with a result worse than the standard already achieved. It often seems that survival research is doing just this.

One would assume that the evidence for survival would be welcomed as good news, since total extinction or obliteration of the personality is not a particularly inviting thought for most people. "The decisive question for man is: Is he related to something infinite or not? That is the telling question of his life," wrote Carl Jung, the pioneering Swiss psychiatrist. "Only if we know that the thing which truly matters is the infinite can we avoid fixing our interest upon futilities, and upon all kinds of goals which are not of real importance."

And yet, the subject is still met with scorn and contempt by mainstream science and orthodox religion, while the media makes light of it, taking serious reports about paranormal phenomena and translating them to tongue-in-cheek "spook" stories.

Why are mainstream science, orthodox religion, and the media so reluctant to accept the evidence for spiritual phenomena and survival? Why hasn't the evidence stood the test of time?

It is clear why orthodox religion rejects it. While most of the communication coming through post-biblical mediums and near-death experiencers is consistent with their dogma and doctrine, a small portion of it is in conflict with that dogma and doctrine. Thus, it threatens the authority of the religious leaders and they find it necessary to say that the Book of Revelation is closed. They cite various passages of the Old Testament which seem to suggest that it is all demonic, while ignoring or giving self-serving interpretations to passages in the Bible which appear to be in opposition to those Old Testament passages. Canon (Dr.) Michael Perry of the Church of England states that many Old Testament prohibitions no longer have any force for Christians, pointing out that in the 19th chapter of Leviticus, where we are told not to listen to mediums, we are also told not to wear a garment woven of two kinds of cloth or to shave the edges of our beards. He believes such prohibitions were part of an attempt to maintain the purity of Israelite religion at a time when the beliefs of other surrounding nations were filtering in. Yet, religious fundamentalists cling to the old teachings out of fear.

Scientific fundamentalists, most media representatives included, claim to reject the evidence because it does not meet strict scientific methodology or standards, including being subject to replication. And, yet, they accept many other things in this category, including biological evolution. Very few things in science have been proved with absolute certainty.

In an article appearing in the winter 2002 issue of the Journal of Near-Death Studies, Dr. Arthur Hastings, professor and director of the William James Center for Consciousness Studies at the Institute for Transpersonal Psychology, addressed this resistance to belief. "The fear of being irrational is powerful," he wrote. "In this Western culture, which is strongly rationalistic, the charge of being irrational is a damning one."

Hastings further suggested that many scientists, acting out of fear, arrive at a determination not to believe. This, he concluded, is often a product of ego defense mechanisms, such as rationalization, projection, and dissociation. He discussed the Pam Reynolds' NDE, considered one of the most evidential, commenting that if the case were taken seriously it would challenge accepted beliefs, self-identity, emotions, commitments, and scientific personas as well as raise fears and result in conclusions that would require deep shifts in belief systems.

Dr. John O'M Bockris, a retired professor of physics, sees it much the same way. "It is simply hubris—that exaggerated pride in one's own achievements which means that—and this applies in particular to professors at universities—those whose careers have been built upon certain theories—existing viewpoints—and who have taught a science based on these, are horrified to learn that they may not have been speaking the truth," which explains the resistance to ideas outside of the existing scientific paradigm. He blames these closed-minded scientists for leading many in the West to approach death without hope, thereby giving rise to a more materialistic and hedonistic world.

"The antagonism which it excites seems to be mainly due to the fact that [a spirit world] is, and has long been in some form or other, the belief of the religious world and of the ignorant and superstitious of all ages, while a total disbelief in spiritual existence has been the distinctive badge of modern scientific skepticism," Alfred Russel Wallace opined.

I recently discussed the resistance of academia to survival evidence with Dr. Stafford Betty, professor of religious studies at California State University, Bakersfield. His observations have been much the same as Wallace's. "My atheistic friends resist even the slightest whiff of an argument for an afterlife," Professor Betty told me. "I have not seen more closed minds. Why is this? Why would anyone resist such good news—the kind of news strongly supported by serious, in-depth research on the NDE, for example? I think I know. It is not so much that my hard-bitten friends hate the thought of living beyond death; what they hate is religion. And they associate religion with the afterlife. It doesn't matter how hard you try to convince them that the contemporary case for afterlife is not based on sacred texts, but on empirical studies conducted by well-credentialed social scientists or doctors. It doesn't matter. Their minds are set. Also, the older generation (in their seventies and eighties) grew up hearing that the only things that were real were material. Changing their minds on that score would threaten their very identity. So they bravely move toward death, trying not to think about it, and gritting their teeth when they have to. I think the young are less invested in metaphysical materialism than the elderly. Their minds are slightly more open, if only because of the barrage of Hollywood films set in an afterlife."

It may very well be that we are not supposed to know for certain. During the 1850s, Victor Hugo, the distinguished French author, was sitting with a medium and communicating with a spirit that claimed to have been Martin Luther, when alive. Hugo asked why God does not better reveal himself. To which the spirit of Luther replied, "Because doubt is the instrument which forges the human spirit. If the day were to come when the human spirit no longer doubted, the human soul would fly off and leave the plough behind, for it would have acquired wings. The earth would lie fallow. Now, God is the sower and man is the harvester. The celestial seed demands that the human ploughshare remain in the furrow of life."

If absolute proof is neither desirable nor possible and the blind faith of religion falls well short of meeting the needs of the rational mind, it would seem that the best we can hope for is the conviction, or true faith, that has been given to those who have been able to properly test, discern, and accept the phenomena.

This article first appeared in *Atlantis Rising* #72 (November/December 2008).

30

GRASPING THE FUTURE

Can We Change It or Is Free Will an Illusion?

BY ROBERT M. SCHOCH, PH.D.

B ased on the evidence, some of which I summarized in a previous issue of *Atlantis Rising* (issue #71), I am convinced that at least some "signals" (for lack of a better term) can pass from the future to the present and leave their influence. But how is this possible? Doesn't it go against the fundamental principles of physics upon which our modern technological and scientific society is built? Doesn't it defy plain logic and commonsense? The very notion of the future affecting the present or past suggests that the future is already set or determined, so does that imply that free will is simply a delusion? Are our actions already as firmly set in the future as they are in the past? Or conversely, is it strangely possible that the past as well as the future is malleable?

A common misconception is that we know definitively, based on modern physics, that the future cannot influence the present. Time's arrow is one way, irreversible, and cause must precede effect, or so many people assume. (Notice that the term "precede" is a temporal term.) However, when one looks carefully at the equations, which summarize so much of our contemporary understanding of physics, in many cases there is a symmetry in the solutions that allows for time to flow either "forward" or "backward." The mathematics does not distinguish between time flow in the direction we are accustomed to, or the reverse. Classically the solutions that correspond to time flowing backward have been discarded as meaningless, but is this really justifiable? Take for example the research of the Nobel Prize winning physicist Paul Dirac in the late 1920s. Equations he was working on related to the electron (a negatively charged particle with a certain mass) also gave as an alternative solution a positively charged particle with the same mass as the electron, yet no such particle was then known. This particle, which has since been discovered to indeed exist, is now referred to as the positron, the anti-particle of the electron. Physicist

Richard Feynman, also a Nobel laureate, suggested that a positron is an electron that is moving backward in time (from the future to the present to the past).

In classical electromagnetic theory, the equations describing the field generated by a moving charge can also be solved in two different ways. In one the field is observed after being generated by the source, but in the second solution the field exists and presumably can be observed before it is generated by the source (known as advanced-time or advanced-potential; see the chapters by H. E. Puthoff and R. Targ, and E. Douglas Dean, in *Psychic Exploration*, 1974).

Building on such ideas, various models have been proposed that might account for the present perception of future events. When an event occurs, it generates various fields and gives off various waves (the exact nature of the field or fields and wave or waves is not clear). These waves, carrying information, travel away from the event temporally, both forward in time (as we expect, based on everyday commonsense) and backward in time. Furthermore, different types of waves emanating from a single event may move "faster" or "slower" relative to each other. As we travel forward through time, we may encounter the waves emanating from an event that, from our perspective, has yet to happen (that is, it is in the future). As we move closer to the event, the waves from it are stronger and more numerous (including different sets of waves), and when we are further from the event the waves are weaker and less numerous.

According to such a model, the possibility of precognitive knowledge of a future event will increase with temporal proximity to the future event. In fact, as I discussed in my previous *Atlantis Rising* article (issue #71), based on both experimental laboratory work and careful analysis of cases of spontaneous precognition, this is just the pattern observed. The most common and strongest precognitions occur within seconds of the events that trigger the precognitions. Precognition of events months or years into the future seems to be very rare.

Another aspect of such models may be that not all events give off signals of equal magnitude. A very strong, emotionally-charged, event might give off a very strong set of signals that can penetrate back in time much further than a weaker event. What constitutes a strong versus a weak event may be relative to the person receiving the signal. It can be suggested that any particular perceiver of future events will be most acutely tuned into his/her own signals (those generated by himself/herself in the future), and secondarily strongly tuned into the signals of persons who are emotionally close to the perceiver. Thus a mother would be predicted to respond, perhaps in terms of a strong precognition, to the future death of her child (or, perhaps more alternatively, to her own future grief over the death of her child) than a stranger will respond to simply reading the obituary of the death of the child in the local newspaper.

A third prediction of this class of models is that if an event gives off various types of waves traversing time (moving backward and forward) at various "speeds," then an event at some level may be precognized yet not be fully determined. That is, such a model may allow for both precognition of the future to a certain extent as well as a certain ability to change the future (thus, perhaps, saving the concept of free will). So, for instance, in the incident of a mother having a precognition that a storm will cause a chandelier to come crashing down on her baby's crib, killing the child, she may receive this precognition based on an advanced signal carried by one type of wave emanating from the future event. But, she may have time to alter the situation such that the event does not happen exactly as her precognition suggests, and thus the future is modified to a certain extent. The later waves emanating from the event carry this modified information corresponding to the modified event, namely in our example that the chandelier comes crashing down and falls on the crib, but the baby is

Patterns from a Random Event Generator (Princeton Univ.)

no longer there and thus is not killed. Of course this is all very difficult to conceive, and admittedly very hypothetical, and our logical analysis attempting to describe this model is bound by temporal-laden language.

Few people, from a common-sense perspective, doubt that we can change the future by our actions—an extreme alternative view being that the future is already entirely determined and we must simply resign ourselves to fate— thus we have the "problem of precognition," since precognition seems to imply that at least part of the future is predetermined. Perhaps even fewer people would doubt that once the past is in the past it cannot be changed. If the future is still malleable, the past is set in stone, immutable and unalterable. Oddly, there is experimental evidence that can be interpreted as indicating that maybe the past is not quite so unalterable after all.

As I discussed previously in the pages of *Atlantis Rising* (issue #67, January/February 2008; see also R. Schoch and L. Yonavjak, *The Parapsychology Revolution*, 2008), repeatable laboratory experiments have shown that human intention can influence the output of various types of random event generators. This is a form of micro-psychokinesis. Mind-over-matter, even if at a microscopic or submicroscopic scale is astounding enough, but that is not all. Experiments indicate that the operators focusing on the machines can produce an effect not only in real time, but also retroactively and proactively. Sending a signal to the machine before it is operating, that is, sending an intention into the future, gives statistically significant results. This may be strange and perhaps unbelievable to many, but at least it does not compromise our concept of cause, effect, and the one-way linearity of time. But what about retroactive causality? Can we reach back in time and change the past? In various tests the machines were allowed to run without anyone focusing on them, and then after the fact an operator attempted to influence the machine. It turns out that this, too, gave statistically significant results. However, it appears that it is important that even though the machine has generated the data before the experiment is carried out, and the data is recorded in some form (such as on a computer print-out), no person can view the data until after the operator has attempted to influence the machine. Somehow the data, or the past, is only malleable before it is viewed or studied by somebody. So, here the linearity of time comes into play again at some level. Admittedly this is all very confusing and even mind-boggling, but it does suggest that our concept of time and causality is not as straightforward as it might appear.

Oddly, and interestingly, some cases of retro-cognition (apparently receiving information directly from the past by other than normal means) may actually be examples of precognition. A long respected method of divination is crystal-gazing or scrying (think of the popular image of a fortune-teller looking into her crystal ball). Note that as used in various contexts, divination can refer to looking into the past, present, or future. The late 19th-century psychical researcher F. W. H. Myers recounted the story of a certain "Miss A" who was adept at genuine crystal-gazing. While at Longford Castle, Wiltshire, UK, Miss A did some crystal-gazing and, among other visions, saw above a fireplace, as stated in Miss A's own words, "a coat of arms in the middle and curious serpents entwined" as well as "[t]he name 'Edwye de Bovery' was then spelt out in the crystal." Miss A was told by the Lady Radnor, of the Castle, that the crystal vision must be wrong as though she knew of the person whose name appeared in the crystal (Sir Edward des Bouverie, Kt.); it was never spelled the way Miss A saw it. Miss A, however, continues her narrative: "A few days afterward, when I was looking at some books in the library, I saw a curious old book with crests and coasts of arms, drawn by hand, not printed; and in this book, I found one of the coats of arms which I had seen in the crystal [apparently the one described above]. . . . A little while afterward, in an old church register or account-book or something, the name of Sir Edwye de Bovery was found [spelled as Miss A had seen it in her crystal vision]." (Cited by Archie Roy, in *A Sense of Something Strange*, 1990, p. 168.)

What do we make of Miss A's crystal-vision? Assuming that it is faithfully reported and true (and F. W. H. Myers was known for his careful checking and double-checking of any ostensible stories of the paranormal, weeding out fraud, deception, and self-delusion), did Miss A really "see" into the past, or did she actually have precognition of the coat of arms and oddly spelled name that she would encounter just a few days after her crystal-gazing session? Based not solely on this case, but also on my familiarity with other so-called time travelers, "psychic archaeologists," and the like, in many instances I believe it is equally tenable that the person is not "traveling back into the past" but rather precognizing their immediate future. For instance, if a "psychic archaeologist" sees a vision of an ancient building in an empty, unexcavated field, and over the next week excavations reveal that indeed there is the foundation of an ancient building there, did the "psychic archaeologist" simply precognize the finding of the building a week in advance? Of course, in such a case there is the curious interplay of the possible precognition of the building being found serving as the incentive to excavate the site to find the building. Cause and effect—past, present, and future— may not be so clear and discrete as we commonly believe.

It seems that both on an experimental level, and based on well-documented spontaneous experiences, psychical phenomena do not respect temporal boundaries. The future appears to be able to influence the present as well as vice versa. Some such future-influencing-present effects (FIPs, a phrase coined by the writer J. B. Priestly) may be very subtle and only recognized in hindsight. For instance (a fictional account for illustrative purposes, but based on genuine stories of a similar nature), a man passes by a certain house everyday on his way to work, and he often gets a strange unexplained tingling sensation as he sees that particular house. After a few years go by, he happens to meet a wonderful woman at a party; they date (meeting at restaurants and other public places) and eventually fall in love. At that point, she invites him to her home—which turns out to be the exact house that had engendered in him the strange tingling sensations. Did he, at some unconscious level, have a vague precognition that that house or someone in it would be important to him in the future?

J. B. Priestly

Consider the statistical study by psychical researcher W. F. Cox who examined the number of passengers on trains when the particular trains had accidents compared to the number of passengers the same trains typically carried on days they did not have an accident. Cox found that in many cases, on the days when accidents occurred, the number of passengers on the particular train tended to be less than otherwise. Cox suggested that perhaps this was due, at least in part, to unconscious premonitions on the part of the potential passengers. Without consciously thinking about it, potential passengers may have changed their plans or even simply run late and missed the ill-fated train. This makes me recall a personal experience I had not too long ago (late 2007, I believe). I was driving on a crowded highway in a torrential downpour, doing my best to focus and not lose my way. Low and behold, I took a wrong branch where the highway split and found myself on an exit where I did not want to be. I circled around and got back on the highway again, only to encounter the cars just beginning to back up. I saw that a multi-car accident had just occurred, and I suddenly realized that if I had not taken that wrong turn, there is a very high likelihood that I would have been involved in the accident. Is it possible that at an unconscious level I had a premonition of the accident about to happen and took the wrong turn to get off the highway briefly so as to avoid it? I just do not know, but it makes me wonder.

At the most fundamental level, precognition seems to work on an emotional level. In the case of my possible precognition of the traffic accident, the unconscious message may have been "quick, get off the highway, potential danger ahead." This same type of precognition is exemplified in a fictional form in the movie *Star Wars, Episode V, The Empire Strikes Back*. Luke Skywalker, while developing control of the Force under the tutelage of the Jedi Master Yoda, gets the strong and inescapable feeling that his friends and comrades are in trouble (in particular Hans Solo and Princess Leia). As Yoda explicitly points out, Skywalker is receiving a telepathic message from the future. Later in the movie, Darth Vader and his cohorts torture Hans Solo. Solo, a bit perplexed, comments afterward that though he was tortured, he was not even asked any questions. As Darth Vader fully understood, Solo was being tortured simply to send a telepathic message *back* to Luke Skywalker and lure Skywalker into a potential trap. It strikes me that in this fictional account the creators of Star Wars demonstrate a clear understanding of precognitive telepathy.

This article first appeared in *Atlantis Rising* #73 (January/February 2009).

Contributing authors

ANDREW COLLINS is a cutting-edge science and history writer. He is author of many books that challenge the way we perceive the past. They include *From the Ashes of Angels*; *Gateway to Atlantis*, and *The Cygnus Mystery*. His latest book, *Beneath the Pyramids*, uncovers Egypt's cave underworld for the first time and has received considerable international news attention. He lives in England. (*andrewcollins.com*)

PHILIP COPPENS, deceased in 2012, was an author and investigative journalist, reporting on subjects from the world of politics to ancient history and mystery. He lectured extensively and appeared on numerous television and DVD documentaries, including *Ancient Aliens: The Series* (The History Channel). He is the author of several books, including *The Stone Puzzle of Rosslyn Chapel*, *The Canopus Revelation*, *Land of the Gods*. (*philipcoppens.com*)

GARY DAVID is an independent researcher and writer living in rural Arizona. His book, *The Orion Zone: Ancient Star Cities of the American Southwest*, published in late 2005, discusses an Orion correlation of Hopi villages and ancient pueblo ruins in the Four Corners region of the U.S.

WILLIAM HENRY is an author, investigative mythologist, regular guest presenter on *Ancient Aliens*, and star of Arcanum TV. He is the author of *The Secret of Sion*, *Mary Magdalene the Illuminator: The Woman Who Enlightened Christ*, *Cloak of the Illuminati*, among many others.(*williamhenry.net*)

FRANK JOSEPH is a leading scholar on ancient mysteries, and the editor-in-chief of *Ancient American* magazine. He is the author of many books, including *Atlantis and 2012*, *The Destruction of Atlantis*, *The Lost Civilization* *of Lemuria, Survivors of Atlantis*, and *The Lost Treasure of King Juba*. He lives in Minnesota. (*ancientamerican.com*)

LEN KASTEN has written numerous articles for Atlantis Rising. While in the Air Force, Kasten experienced a UFO encounter that transformed his life. Since then, he has been deeply involved in UFO research, life after death, sacred geometry, Atlantis, and related subjects. He brings his extensive metaphysical background to he writing of *The Secret History of Extraterrestrials*, which provides the reader with a depth of understanding of UFO phenomena not otherwise readily available. (*et-secrethistory.com*)

JOHN KETTLER is a former military aerospace intelligence analyst with a life-long interest in the "black world" of covert and special ops, government secrets and coverups, world-wide conspiracies, UFOs, ETs, secret technology and much more. He spent years working on defense projects for Hughes Aircraft and Rockwell. Kettler was a frequent contributor to *Atlantis Rising* magazine for more than a decade. (*johnkettler.com*)

STEPHEN O'ROURKE is an American writer based in Singapore. He can be contacted at stephenvincent@myway.com.

MARK AMARU PINKHAM is the author of *Guardians of the Holy Grail: The Knights Templar, John the Baptist and The Water of Life*. Mark currently serves as the North American Grand Prior of the International Order of Gnostic Templars, a division of the Scottish Knight Templars dedicated to reviving the Goddess and Gnostic rites and wisdom of the original Knights Templar. (*gnostictemplars.org*)

ROBERT M. SCHOCH, a full-time faculty member at Boston University, earned his Ph.D. in geology and geophysics at Yale University. He is best known for his re-dating of the Great Sphinx of Egypt featured in the Emmy-winning NBC production *The Mystery of the Sphinx*. He is a frequent guest on many top-rated talk shows. His latest book is *The Parapsychology Revolution*. (*robertschoch.com*)

STEVEN SORA lives on Long Island. In 1999 he published the widely read and frequently quoted *Lost Treasure of the Knights Templar*. He is the author of many books dealing with esoteric history and over 100 articles. He is a frequent guest in documentaries dealing with ancient mysteries and lost history.

MARK STAVISH is the Director of Studies for the Institute for Hermetic Studies, and a life-long student of esotericism with over 25 years experience in comparative religion, philosophy, psychology, and mysticism with emphasis on Traditional Western Esotericism. His articles have appeared in academic, specialty, and mass market publications specializing in spiritual studies. Mark is considered one of the leading authorities in Hermeticism today.

MICHAEL E. TYMN, a resident of Hawaii, is vice-president of the Academy of Spirituality and Paranormal Studies, Inc., and is editor of the Academy's quarterly magazine, *The Searchlight*. His articles on paranormal subjects have appeared in many publications and he is widely read and referenced on these topics. He is the author of *The Afterlife Revealed*, *The Articulate Dead*, and *Running on Third Wind*. (*whitecrowbooks.com/michaeltymn*)

JOHN WHITE is an internationally known writer and educator in the fields of consciousness research and higher human development. He was formerly Director of Education for The Institute of Noetic Sciences founded by Apollo 14 astronaut Edgar Mitchell. His fifteen books include *The Meeting of Science and Spirit*, *Pole Shift*, *What Is Enlightenment?*, *Kundalini, Evolution and Enlightenment*, and *A Practical Guide to Death and Dying*. His writing has appeared in *The New York Times*, *Reader's Digest*, *Omni*, *Esquire* ,and *Woman's Day*. His books have been translated into several languages.

JAN WICHERINK is the author of *Souls of Distortion Awakening: A Convergence of Science and Spirituality* (2005), currently available in English, Dutch, and Croatian. Jan's special interests include research of the astrological aspects of the 2012 prophecies, known as the Great Celestial Conjunction. He is the founder of Piramidions, a platform for writers of esoteric and spiritual literature. (*www.soulsofdistortion.nl*)

About the Editor

J. DOUGLAS KENYON is the editor and publisher of *Atlantis Rising* magazine. He is also the editor of *Paradigm Busters, Missing Connections, Unseen Forces, Forgotten Origins, Forbidden History, Forbidden Science,* and *Forbidden Religion. (atlantisrising.com)*